Muhammad Ali
& Company

Books by Thomas Hauser

Non-Fiction

- *Missing*
- *The Trial of Patrolman Thomas Shea*
- *For Our Children (with Frank Macchiarola)*
- *The Family Legal Companion*
- *The Black Lights: Inside the World of Professional Boxing*
- *Final Warning: The Legacy of Chernobyl (with Dr. Robert Gale)*
- *Muhammad Ali: His Life and Times*
- *Muhammad Ali: Memories*
- *Arnold Palmer: A Personal Journey*
- *Confronting America's Moral Crisis (with Frank Macchiarola)*
- *Muhammad Ali: In Perspective*
- *Healing: A Journal of Tolerance and Understanding*
- *Muhammad Ali & Company*

Fiction

- *Ashworth & Palmer*
- *Agatha's Friends*
- *The Beethoven Conspiracy*
- *Hanneman's War*
- *The Fantasy*
- *Dear Hannah*
- *The Hawthorne Group*

For Children

- *Martin Bear & Friends*

Theatre

- *The Four Chords*

Muhammad Ali & Company

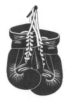

THOMAS HAUSER

HASTINGS HOUSE

A Division of United Publishers Group

Hastings House A Division of United Publishers Group Inc.
50 Washington Street
Norwalk, Ct. 06854

Library of Congress Cataloging-in-Publication Data

Hauser, Thomas.
    Muhammad Ali & company / by Thomas Hauser.
      P. cm.
    Includes index.
    ISBN 0-8038-9411-2
    1. Boxing—United States. 2. Ali, Muhammad, 1942– . 3. Boxers
    (Sports)—United States—Biography. I. Title.
GV1125.H29 1997
796. 83' 092—d c2 1
    [B]   97-33174
                                                          CIP

Distributed by Publishers Group West

Printed in the United States of America

10 9 8 7 6 5 4 3 2 1

Dedication

I've often said that some of the best people I've ever
met are in boxing, and some of the worst people
I've ever met are in boxing.

■

This book is dedicated to the best.

Contents

Round 3: The Fights

Round 4: Non-Combatants

Round 5: Issues and Answers

Round 6: Curiosities

Round 7: Afterthought

Author's Note

"Boxing gets in your blood."

I was told that many times in 1983, when I began researching a book about professional boxing. And it turned out, the message was right. When I finished writing *The Black Lights*, I kept my finger on the pulse of the sweet science by writing occasional articles about boxing. Then, in 1988, I joined forces with Muhammad Ali to author *Muhammad Ali: His Life And Times*. Three more Ali books followed—*Muhammad Ali: Memories*, *Muhammad Ali: In Perspective*, and *HEALING: A Journal of Tolerance And Understanding*. Meanwhile, I kept writing articles, all of which are gathered here in book form for the first time.

Special thanks are due to the following publications in which the articles first appeared: *The New York Times*, *Sports Illustrated*, *Boxing Illustrated*, *International Boxing Digest*, *The Ring*, *The National*, *Sports Inc.*, *The London Sunday Express*, *Penthouse*, *Gallery*, *Emerge*, *The Nation*, *Boxing Beat*, *Boxing Writers Association of America Newsletter*, and various fight programs, particularly those of Madison Square Garden.

Introduction by Muhammad Ali

I met Tom Hauser when he began writing a book about my life. Although he came highly recommended to me, as far as I was concerned, Tom was just another writer. Soon, I began to realize he was a very good writer. That was nine years ago. Today, Tom is not just another writer. He is my friend.

Tom's books about boxing are well-known. *The Black Lights* is a wonderful book about the sport and business. *Muhammad Ali: His Life And Times, Muhammad Ali: Memories, and Muhammad Ali: In Perspective* cover my life better than anything that has been written about me. And I'm proud to have worked with Tom on *HEALING: A Journal of Tolerance and Understanding*—a book that expresses our collective feelings about the need to combat bigotry and prejudice.

Now Tom has gathered together his articles about boxing—every one of them—and put them in *Muhammad Ali & Company*. It's a good book. I hope you like it as much as I do.

Muhammad Ali
Berrien Springs, Michigan

Round I

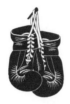

Muhammad Ali

In October 1988, I was scheduled to meet with Muhammad Ali and his wife Lonnie to discuss writing the book that would eventually become *Muhammad Ali: His Life And Times*. Writing a book is an extremely personal endeavor, and I wanted to make sure that if the project went ahead, Muhammad and I would get along. I also wanted to make sure that I could capture Muhammad's voice both the way he was when he was young, and the way he is now.

In 1988 Mike Tyson was the undefeated, undisputed heavyweight champion of the world. Some experts were even proclaiming that Tyson was better than Ali in his prime. Before I met with Muhammad, I spent an afternoon writing "I'm Coming Back To Whup Mike Tyson's Butt." Then, when Ali and I met, I read the piece aloud and presented it to him. His response was to take a pen from his pocket and write across the front page, "To Tom Hauser from Muhammad Ali—This is what I can still do to Tyson right now."

Later, Muhammad and I made a few changes in the article and it was published in *Boxing Illustrated*, the first of many collaborations between us.

"I'm Coming Back To Whup Mike Tyson's Butt"

People are weeping and crying all the time these days, because Mike Tyson is heavyweight champion of the world. He's a bully, and no one can beat him. But that don't mean nuthin'. They said Sonny Liston was unbeatable, and I beat him. They said George

Foreman was unbeatable, and I beat him. They say Tyson is unbeatable, but I'm coming back. I got a time machine, and I'm coming back to whup Mike Tyson.

Mike Tyson is too ugly to be champion. He's got gold teeth. He's got bald spots all over his head. I used to call Joe Frazier "The Gorilla," but next to Tyson, Joe Frazier was like a beautiful woman. Everyone I fought I had names for. Sonny Liston was "The Bear." George Chuvalo was "The Washer Woman." Floyd Patterson was "The Rabbit." George Foreman was "The Mummy." Mike Tyson is ugly; he's ugly like King Kong, so I'm calling him "Kong."

And Tyson is nuthin'. He never fought no one. He fought Larry Holmes when Holmes was an old man. He fought Trevor Berbick, and Berbick was a crazy old man. He fought Tyrell Biggs, and Biggs was an amateur. Michael Spinks was a light-heavyweight. Tony Tubbs was an embarrassment. Bonecrusher Smith; he lost the first nine rounds against Frank Bruno. Tyson never fought Sonny Liston, Joe Frazier or George Foreman like I did, when all of them were in their prime.

So I'm coming back to whup Mike Tyson. It's the biggest fight in the history of time. Bigger than David against Goliath; bigger than Napoleon against England and Russia. Too big for home television. Too big for closed circuit. They're putting this fight on special 3-D closed-circuit with cameras and lenses like you ain't never seen before.

And the whole world is holding its breath. Everyone's rooting for me, but they're saying, Muhammad Ali, he's just a man and now he's fighting Kong. They're saying Mike Tyson is too strong, too mean. He hits too hard.

Here's how it goes.

Round One: It'll be all over in one; that's what they're saying. And

Tyson comes out for the kill. Ali's dancing, jabbing. Pop-pop-pop-pop. Tyson swings—WHOOSH—hits nuthin' but air.

Pop-pop-pop-pop.

WHOOSH. Tyson hits nuthin' but air again.

Pop-pop-pop-pop. At the end of the round, the television people are adding up their punch-stats and they can't believe it. Muhammad Ali; 107 jabs, 92 landed. Mike Tyson; 40 punches, and he didn't land one.

Round Two: It's just like round one.

Pop-pop-pop-pop.

WHOOSH.

Pop-pop-pop-pop.

WHOOSH.

Ali is pretty. The crowd's going wild. *Ali! Ali!*

Tyson lands a punch, but it don't do no harm.

Round Three: Ali's landing right hands. It's early in the fight, and already Tyson's left eye is starting to close. Women and children are holding their breath. Ali looks good. He's better than good. Muhammad Ali is the greatest, but there's nine more rounds to go and Tyson is getting dirty now. He's butting and thumbing, throwing elbows, and hitting low.

Round Four: Pop-pop-pop-pop. Ali is still dancing. Floats like a butterfly, but he stings like a bee. Pop-pop-pop-pop. Tyson is bleeding; the left eye. He's cut and the blood is flowing. The experts are shaking their heads. Muhammad Ali is making Tyson look like a child.

Round Five: Tyson is taking a bad whuppin'. The crowd's going wild. Ali! Ali! Tyson's getting tired. Ali's talking to him, asking, "Who's the greatest?" Tyson won't answer, so Ali hits him four-five-six right hands.

Round Six: It's the Ali Shuffle. Two billion people 'round the world, they're jumping up and down, hugging each other, weeping with joy. It's the real Ali. Not the Ali who lost to Larry Holmes; not the Ali you thought was old. This is Muhammad Ali who destroyed Zora Folley; Muhammad Ali who done in Cleveland Williams. Ali! Ali!

Round Seven: Tyson's gold teeth get knocked out into the crowd, and you can see his mother-in-law running after them. The crowd's in a state of histomania. Ali's punching so fast now no one can hear the pops. It's p-p-p-p-p-p-p-p. Ali winds up for a bolo punch. The crowd is praying. They're pleading, don't take no chances, don't get careless with Tyson. But Ali's still winding up for the bolo, and Tyson's moving closer. Tyson is getting ready. He's gonna kill Ali. The crowd holds its breath. Tyson leaps with a left hook. But Muhammad Ali throws a right hand. It's faster than a speeding bullet. Faster than the punch that knocked down Sonny Liston. The eye can't see it, except with a super slo-mo replay camera.
    TYSON IS DOWN!!!
    Tyson gets up at seven.
    Ding! There's the bell.
    And now Tyson is mad. He's embarrassed. He's been humiliated. He's coming out for the next round, determined to put Muhammad Ali down.

Round Eight: Tyson charges out of his corner, throwing punches like wild. He's spitting blood. There's fire in his eyes. He's doing everything he can. And. . . . OH NO! Ali is tired. Ali has stopped dancing. After seven rounds with Kong, Ali's legs are gone. Ali's moving back. Tyson comes in for the kill. Ali's in a corner; he's in trouble. Tyson is ugly. He's a monster that has to be fed, and

Muhammad Ali is the monster's meal.

Tyson with a left. Tyson with a right. The whole world is covering its eyes.

Wait a minute!!!

IT'S THE ROPE-A-DOPE!!!

Muhammad Ali tricked the monster, and now Ali is coming back strong.

Ali with a left. Ali with a right. It's Muhammad Ali, the greatest fighter of all time.

AND TYSON IS DOWN!!!

The count is one, two. . . .

Tyson's eyes are closed!

Three, four. . . .

He's not moving!

Five, six. . . .

We have a brand new champion!

Seven, eight. . . .

This is the greatest moment of all time!

Nine, ten. . . .

It's all over! It's all over! The tyrant is dead! Long live the true King!

In November 1990, on the eve of the Gulf War, Muhammad Ali traveled to Iraq and met with Saddam Hussein in the hope that his presence would promote dialogue and forestall a wider conflict. Although his broader goal was not met, Muhammad did return to the United States with fifteen American hostages who had been held captive by the Iraqi government. At the request of *The New York Times*, I elaborated upon Ali's motives.

Why Muhammad Ali Went To Iraq

Last month in Baghdad, Muhammad Ali embraced Saddam Hussein and kissed him on the cheek. The moment was televised throughout the world and troubled many people. Ali isn't a diplomat. His actions aren't always wise. There was danger in the possibility that a visit from history's best-known fistic gladiator would feed Hussein's ego and stiffen his resolve. Regardless of what else happened, the meeting would be used for propaganda in the Third World, where Ali is particularly loved.

Some of Ali's closest friends were also concerned that, in going to Iraq, he was being used for personal gain by one or more members of his entourage. Several of his associates, past and present, are the subject of a federal inquiry into alleged financial irregularities. While Ali was in Iraq, one of his attorneys was indicted on charges of conspiracy and tax fraud. And among those who accompanied Ali to Baghdad was Arthur Morrison, a self-described businessman who has traversed the United States leaving a trail of arrest warrants behind.

As Ali's trip progressed, it became increasingly difficult for the world outside to distinguish between what he really said and what was reported by the Iraqi News Agency. There were self-appointed spokesmen purporting to act on "hand signals" from the former champion. Others said, falsely, that Ali was unable to speak. But none of this is new to Ali. He has often dealt with con men and crazies. And the sideshow that accompanied him on his recent journey shouldn't be allowed to overshadow why Ali went to Iraq. It was an act of love in quest of peace; he hoped that his presence would promote dialogue and forestall war.

I've spent the past two years researching and writing about Muhammad Ali. For much of that time, I've lived with him, traveled with him, and interviewed hundreds of his family members, associates and friends. I know him well. At least, I think I do. And one thing is certain: even though Muhammad's voice is not as clear as it used to be, his mind is alert and his heart is pure.

I've seen Ali get on a plane and fly to India because the children in an orphanage wanted to meet him. I've sat in his living room as he talked with sadness of hatred and racism in all of their virulent forms. He's a gentle man who will do almost anything to avoid hurting another person.

Ali was in Louisville visiting his mother who had suffered a stroke, when he was asked to go to Iraq. He is on medication for Parkinson's disease. When he left that afternoon he had enough medication with him to last for five days; yet he stayed in Iraq for two weeks. He quite literally endangered his health because he believed that what he was doing was right.

That of course, has been a constant theme throughout Ali's life. He has always taken risks to uphold his principles. During the 1960's, he was stripped of his title and precluded from fighting for three-and-a-half years because he acted upon his beliefs and refused induction into the United States Army during the height of the war in Vietnam. He now believes that all war is wrong. Ali is, and since Vietnam, has been, a true conscientious objector.

Ali knows what many of us sometimes seem to forget—that people are killed in wars. Every life is precious to him. He understands that each of us has only one life to live. Many Americans now favor war with Iraq, although I'm not sure how many would feel that way if they personally had to fight. Ali, plainly and simply, values every other person's life as dearly as his own, regardless of nationality, religion, or race. He is a man who finds it impossible to go hunting, let alone tolerate the horrors of war.

It may be that war with Iraq will become inevitable. If so, it will be fought. But that shouldn't cause us to lose sight of what Muhammad Ali tried to accomplish last month. Any war is a human tragedy, and we should always be thankful for the peacemakers among us. After all, it's not how loudly Ali speaks but what he says and does that counts.

On July 19, 1996, more than three billion people around the world watched as Muhammad Ali stepped from the shadows to light the cauldron signaling the start of the 1996 Olympics. It was a spectacular moment. And afterward, quite a few people from NBC and the Atlanta Olympic Organizing Committee took credit for having originated the idea, with statements like, "I thought it up a month before the Olympics. . . . No, it was my idea six weeks before the games." Sorry, guys. I went on record in 1993.

The Olympic Flame

The Atlanta Olympics are three years in the future, but elaborate groundwork has already been laid. Budweiser has agreed to become a national sponsor for a sum that might otherwise be used to retire the national debt. On-site construction has begun, and television planning is underway. Eventually, the Olympic torch will be transported to the United States. And the triumphal procession that follows will lead to the highlight of the games' opening ceremonies—lighting the Olympic flame.

Traditionally, someone from the host country ignites the flame. At the 1984 Olympics in Los Angeles, Rafer Johnson received the torch and carried it up the Coliseum steps to rekindle the world's most celebrated fire. Last year in Barcelona, a Spanish archer shot an arrow into a cauldron, thereby reawakening the flame. The eyes of the world are always on this moment. And one wonders who will be chosen to fulfill the honor in Atlanta.

The view here is that the choice is obvious. One man embodies the Olympic spirit to perfection. He's a true American in every sense of the word and the foremost citizen of the world. At age eighteen he won a gold medal in Rome fighting under the name "Cassius Clay." Since then, he has traversed the globe, spreading joy wherever he goes. Atlanta has special meaning for him. It was there, after three years of exile from boxing, that he returned to face Jerry Quarry in the ring. He loves the spotlight, and the spotlight loves him. Indeed, one can almost hear him saying, "When I carry that Olympic torch, every person in the world will be watching. Babies in their mother's tummies will be kicking and hollering for the TV to be turned on. It will be bigger than Michael Jackson. Bigger than Elvis. Bigger than the pyramids. Bigger than me fighting Sonny Liston, George Foreman, and Joe Frazier all at the same time. Bigger than the Olympics—"

Wait a minute, Muhammad. This *is* the Olympics.

Anyway, you get the point. So I have a simple proposal to make. I'd like the International Olympic Committee to announce that, as its gift to the world, Muhammad Ali has been chosen to light the Olympic flame in Atlanta. Muhammad has already given us one memorable Olympic moment as Cassius Clay. Now let him share another with the world as Muhammad Ali. That way, the 26th Olympiad will truly be "the greatest."

In 1991, Magic Johnson announced to the world that he was HIV-positive. That prompted some reflections on the parallels between Magic and Muhammad Ali.

Magic Johnson and Muhammad Ali

The world became a different place on November 7, 1991. That was the day we learned Earvin "Magic" Johnson had tested positive for the virus that causes AIDS.

Johnson's on-court achievements are the stuff of legend. Perhaps his most memorable performance came in the last game of the 1980 NBA finals. Kareem Abdul-Jabbar was injured and unable to play. The Philadelphia 76ers were heavily favored over the Lakers. Johnson was a guard in his rookie season, only three years out of high school. He started at center, played all five positions, scored 42 points, and grabbed 15 rebounds, leading Los Angeles to the first of five championships that would make them basketball's "Team of the 1980's." During the next twelve years, he would win both the league's regular-season and playoff MVP awards three times.

My own most vivid memory of Johnson dates to December 1988. I was in Los Angeles, when Howard Bingham (Muhammad Ali's longtime friend and personal photographer) invited me to the Forum to watch the Lakers play. Like all fans, I'd marveled at Magic on television. But watching sports on TV, you see only what the men in the truck want you to see. So I went to the Forum with a special intent. I would ignore the ball and forget about rebounding and scoring. Whenever Magic was in the game, I would watch him for every second of play.

It was an extraordinary night. The Lakers were playing the Washington Bullets. The Bullets were hot; Los Angeles wasn't. But Magic never stopped trying. With the ball, without the ball, on offense and defense, he was always moving, hustling, exhorting. Finally, with one second left in regulation time, the Bullets led by three points. Los Angeles had the ball at midcourt after a time-out. The inbounds pass went to Johnson who, in a single motion, caught it, threw up a hook shot, and—*swish!*—three points. In overtime, the Lakers blew Washington away.

I think I know something about greatness. For two years, while writing a book, I hung out with a fellow named Muhammad Ali. But in reflecting on Magic Johnson's life, what strikes me most are the parallels between him and Ali.

Both men revolutionized their sport. Boxing had never seen a fighter, let alone a heavyweight, who moved with the speed and grace of Muhammad. And before Magic, no one could imagine a 6-foot-9-inch point guard dominating play with no-look passes, fast breaks, and baseline-to-baseline rushes. Each man had a sense of his sport that was intuitive, cerebral, and spectacular at the same time. Indeed, there were moments when it seemed as though Ali and Magic were movie directors starring in their own fantasy films with opponents reduced to screen extras. If Magic were a fighter he'd have fought the way Ali fought. And watching Magic on television one afternoon, Ali told me, "If I was a basketball player that's the way I'd want to play." Each man led his sport to unprecedented heights in the United States and overseas. And now, each has been struck with a physical disability that saddens admirers everywhere.

Ali's condition, known as Parkinson's syndrome, resulted from too many blows to the head. It affects his speech. There are no intellectual deficits. It's not life-threatening in any way. Johnson's is more serious. As a consequence of one or more sexual encounters, he has tested HIV-positive. Barring a medical breakthrough or a miracle, statistics tell us that he will be dead in three to twelve years.

Thirty-two is young for a superstar to retire. If Ali had quit at age 32, he wouldn't have beaten George Foreman in Zaire. Nor would there have been a "Thrilla in Manila" against Joe Frazier. But the tragedy of Magic Johnson's life isn't that he won't be playing basketball anymore. It's that, in all likelihood, his life will end at an age when most of us are just beginning to discover our full potential.

Like Ali, Magic is facing his difficulties with courage, dignity, and grace. His illness has led him to educate the public regarding the dangers of AIDS. Just as Ali has his religion to sustain him, Johnson has found a larger cause. Boxing, unfortunately, has failed to learn from the tragedy of Muhammad Ali. Too many old and damaged men fight on in the ring today. But if people pay attention to Magic's message, it will save lives.

"When I see Ali today," Kareem Abdul-Jabbar once told me, "part of me feels sad, but I know what it's all about. It's the result of his having had every bit of fun that he wanted to have." Now, several years later, Kareem's words are equally appropriate to his friend and teammate, Earvin "Magic" Johnson, particularly the parting thought that Kareem expressed about Ali: "Unfortunately, some of the lessons we learned from him were negative—what *not* to do. But that will never stop people from loving him. He has won our hearts."

Magic Johnson and Muhammad Ali. They still have the two best smiles I've ever seen.

When someone is trying to hype a heavyweight, the boldest, the most advantageous, and sometimes the most frivolous way to do it is to compare the fighter with Muhammad Ali. In 1995, supporters of Mike Tyson and George Foreman were trying to do just that.

There's Only One Ali

The past few months have seen quite a few columns comparing Mike Tyson and George Foreman with Muhammad Ali. Tyson expects to be released from prison in May, which has led commentators to draw parallels between his layoff from boxing and the exile imposed upon Ali. And Foreman, to use one of "The Greatest's" favorite phrases, "upset the world" when he knocked out Michael Moorer this past November. So let me offer a word to the wise. Don't believe the hype.

First, the Ali–Tyson comparisons. Each man was a great fighter, deprived of the right to fight during the middle of his career. But Ali's career was interrupted by an act of principle—his refusal to accept induction into the United States Army during the war in Vietnam. That stand was taken in sunlight in full view of the world; not in an Indianapolis hotel room at two o'clock in the morning. Moreover, as the United States Supreme Court later unanimously ruled, Ali never committed a crime; whereas twelve jurors found Mike Tyson guilty of rape. At the time Ali was exiled from boxing, he was heavyweight champion, whereas Tyson was a contender. Ali's ring skills were peaking, whereas Tyson's were at least temporarily in decline. And Tyson seems to be blaming everybody but himself for his plight, expressing bitterness toward white people, the American criminal justice system, and the entire state of

Indiana. Ali, by contrast, said of his exile, "There were people who tried to put me in jail. Some of them did what they thought was proper, and I can't condemn them for following their conscience."

As for Ali and George Foreman; both are deeply religious men, who charm with their wit. Both have been blessed, or cursed, with the ability to take endless punishment to the head without going down. Each came back after a long lay-off to regain the heavyweight crown. But Foreman beating Michael Moorer was a good story; whereas Muhammad Ali beating George Foreman was the ultimate sports fantasy of all time. Ali conquered an "unbeatable" foe in Zaire, and afterward, was presumed to be the best fighter in the world. By contrast, there are a dozen fighters who would enter the ring today as a favorite over "Big George." Foreman topping Michael Moorer brought a smile, whereas Ali vanquishing Foreman engendered worldwide joy. Indeed, Buster Douglas's triumph over Mike Tyson was far more reminiscent of Ali's greatest upsets than anything George has done so far. So if Foreman is to be likened to "The Greatest," it shouldn't be to the man who beat him in Zaire, but to Cassius Clay circa 1962. Clay, like Foreman, entertained but didn't threaten. Clay like Foreman, was liked but not loved.

So don't fall victim to false analogies. There was only one Joe Louis. There was only one Sugar Ray Robinson. And although Mike Tyson and George Foreman might be legends in their own right, there's only one Muhammad Ali.

I met Muhammad Ali's mother in 1989, and had the pleasure of her company on several occasions. Muhammad has said that her long illness and death were the saddest chapter of his life.

Odessa Clay

February 12, 1917–August 20, 1994

On August 20, 1994, Odessa Clay died after a long illness. It's customary in the boxing community to acknowledge the passing of great fighters. The death of their parents is seldom observed. But Odessa Clay was no ordinary parent. One of her sons changed the world.

Mrs. Clay had a hard life when she was young. Her parents separated when she was a child. She rarely saw her father or knew much about where he'd come from. Her mother had difficulty raising three children, so for much of her childhood, Odessa Clay lived with an aunt. At age sixteen she met Cassius Marcellus Clay and married him soon after. Their first son, Cassius Marcellus Clay, Jr., was born on January 17, 1942.

"My mother is a Baptist," Muhammad Ali once said. "And when I was growing up, she taught me all she knew about God. Every Sunday, she dressed me up, took me and my brother to church, and taught us the way she thought was right. She taught us to love people and treat everybody with kindness. She taught us it was wrong to be prejudiced or hate. I've changed my religion and some of my beliefs since then, but her God is still God; I just call him by a different name."

Odessa Clay's sweetness and generosity will live on in her children and grandchildren, just as Muhammad's good qualities will live on in all the people of this planet long after he has gone. No mother ever gave more of herself to her children. And no son ever did more to make a mother happy and proud.

"I always felt like God made Muhammad special," Odessa Clay once told me; "but I don't know why God chose me to carry this child."

None of us do. But Odessa Clay carried him safely and raised him well. And for that, all of us should be grateful.

> It's remarkable how many roads in boxing begin and end with Muhammad Ali.

What's In A Name?

The everyday sounds of boxing are a jangling bell, the drumbeat of punches, and the crescendo of a roaring crowd. But every once in a while, the ring is graced by a great fighter with a great name that's particularly appropriate to his craft. When that happens, the name itself is a wonderful sound.

At the moment, the leading heavyweights in the world are Riddick, Lennox, and Evander. The best fighter "pound-for-pound" is either Julio or Pernell. These are very nice names, but they don't sound like music. So herewith, my list of great fighters who also had very special names:

1. **Muhammad Ali**—He forced us to accept the name. At first, it sounded all wrong. But twenty-nine years later, it's synonymous with everything good about professional boxing. And Ali himself says, "Changing my name was one of the most important things that ever happened to me. It freed me from the identity given to my family by slavemasters. It let me be me."

2. **Sugar Ray Robinson**—The man once known as Walker Smith, Jr. isn't just the original Sugar Ray. He's *the* Sugar Ray. He owns the name; the same way the title "pound-for-pound" will always be his, no matter who else comes along. And what a sweet sound it is; "Sugar Ray Robinson."

3. **John L. Sullivan**—The middle initial is important. It bestowed a classic elegance upon the man who founded a line of heavyweight kings.

4. **Jack Johnson, Jack Dempsey, Joe Louis**—Put these three together, because these are the names fans came to expect for the heavyweight champion of the world. Not wishy-washy sounds like John Arthur Johnson, William Harrison Dempsey, and Joseph Louis Barrow. These guys had short, brutal, "impact" names.

5. **Henry Armstrong**—"Armstrong" conjures up images of strength; and it has a noble sound. Much better than "Henry Jackson," which is the way Hammering Hank began.

6. **Willie Pep**—Guglielmo Papaleo? Forget it. But Willie Pep was always on the move. In and out; lightning speed. No one could catch him until he grew old, and opponents were wasting their time if they tried.

7. **Rocky Marciano**—There's only one Rocky, and it ain't Stallone. Rocco Francis Marchegiano simplified his name to a sound that said it all.

8. **Sonny Liston**—There's some irony here. Charles Liston was anything but "sunny." And even though he was Sonny, no one ever called him "boy." But the name had character.

9. **Yama Bahama from Bimini**—Unlike the others on this list, Yama Bahama wasn't a great fighter. But he compiled a record of 76–14–3 in the 1950's and 60's. And Angelo Dundee recalls, "Yama was a steady boxer. Good chin; beat a lot of quality fighters; lost to some great ones." And what a name! Woe to the ring announcer who forgot to add "all the way from Bimini, my good friends." Say it out loud—"Yama Bahama from Bimini." There's a definite lyrical sound.

10. **Cassius Marcellus Clay, Jr.**—This is the only guy I know of who became internationally famous under two different names (unless you count Clark Kent and Superman). And both names were wonderful. Cassius Marcellus Clay, Jr. might have been a "slave name," but we never thought of

him as a slave. If Cassius had never changed his name, he'd warrant inclusion on this list. So give the man his due. I can almost hear him saying now, "Everyone else on this list has a great name, but my name is the double-greatest."

I've always been interested in sports collectibles. And over the years, I've amassed a fairly large collection of Muhammad Ali memorabilia. Keep in mind, though; the prices quoted in the following article are from 1995, and Ali memorabilia has risen in value since then.

To Sports memorabilia collectors, he's also . . .

The Greatest

"The rarer a signature is, the more value it has. . . . Dead athletes are worth more than live ones. . . . Boxing memorabilia pales in comparison with collectibles from other sports. . . ."

But as has often been the case during his remarkable career, Muhammad Ali breaks all the rules. His signature is the most common of any athlete ever. He's very much alive. Yet a two-page letter from Cassius Clay to a man seeking to manage him after the Rome Olympics recently sold through a private placement for $6,000. At auction, it would probably have brought $10,000. Trunks and gloves worn by Ali during his career are worth $15,000 to $50,000 depending on verification, and the magnitude of the bout in which they were worn. Fight contracts signed by Ali bring up to $10,000. On-site posters from Ali versus George Foreman in Zaire are worth $3,500. For Cassius Clay fight posters, the going rate is $3,000 to $4,000. Posters from the three Ali-Frazier fights are worth $1,500, $500, and $1,000 respectively.

Often, when a piece of sports memorabilia is signed, the signature amounts to mutilation. But when Ali signs a collectible, it adds value. Thus, Ali fight tickets are worth $50 to $150; doubled when autographed by "The Greatest." Press credentials for Ali fights are in the $100 to $200 range. On-site programs for Ali-Frazier I are worth $225; $325 if signed by one of the fighters, and $425 if signed by both of them. Those early Cassius Clay *Time* and *Life* covers sell for about $25 each.

But all of the items mentioned above are from the past. They're limited in number and, absent an unscrupulous dealer, they can't be duplicated or reproduced. What makes Ali so unique in today's collectibles market is the never-ending demand for new Ali products.

The creation of contemporary Ali memorabilia is largely within the domain of Sports Placement Services—a Malibu, California, company that has been involved with Ali for nine years. SPS also represents Jim Brown, Joe Namath, and Sandy Koufax on the collectibles circuit. SPS Chairman, Harlan Werner, is primarily responsible for the sale of Ali memorabilia, while SPS President, Lee Collegian, spends an increasing amount of time dealing with enforcement. "There are a lot of people out there who ignore the fact that you have to pay an athlete for the commercial use of his name and image," observes Collegian. "And while there has always been a certain amount of phony Ali memorabilia on the market, in recent years we've started to see more of it, including a lot of phony signatures."

Among the many projects that Ali has authorized in conjunction with SPS are:

- A commemorative envelope signed by Ali and postmarked in Rome to coincide with the thirtieth anniversary of his Olympic triumph.
- A limited-edition watch, accompanied by a signed Ali photograph.
- A limited-edition lithograph, signed by Ali and sports artist Steven Holland to commemorate Ali's fiftieth birthday.

- Metal Ali trading cards.
- Statues of Ali in various sizes and poses.

But the most visible of the Ali-SPS ventures are the ten-or-so collectibles shows that Ali appears at each year. Generally, Ali receives $30,000 to $60,000 per show, depending on the number of signatures he's obligated to sign and the number of hours he's expected to be there. The show organizers, in turn, sell Ali "signature tickets" to the public for about $65. Ali's signature on a plain piece of paper is only worth about $25 on the open market. But depending on what he signs, $65 can be a bargain. For example, if Ali signs a twenty-dollar boxing glove, that glove rises in value to $200.

Ali signatures fall into several categories. A vintage Cassius Clay (one signed before Ali changed his name) is worth about $500. Occasionally, Ali will still sign as "Cassius Clay" if asked to by a fan. These modern-day Cassius Clay signatures are worth about $50. Vintage Ali signatures (those signed "Muhammad Ali" when Ali's handwriting was large and clear) are worth about $50.

The most valuable "cut signature" of any heavyweight champion is that of Marvin Hart ($2,500). That's because there are so few of them around. Hart is followed in value by Bob Fitzsimmons ($1,000), John L. Sullivan ($1,000), and Jack Johnson ($600). Except for these four men, Cassius Clay outranks all other heavyweight champions ever, and no living fighter can match even a 1995 Ali signature in value.

What makes it so remarkable, of course, is that Ali gives away an estimated 180,000 signatures a year for free. Every morning, he signs several hundred pamphlets that elaborate upon his Islamic faith, and then he hands them out during the course of his day. He signs photographs, pieces of notebook paper, and virtually everything else that admirers thrust upon him when he's in public. In all likelihood, Ali has signed more than *3,000,000* autographs during his life, and that number will continue to rise in the years ahead.

In other words, there's a lot of Ali memorabilia in existence; it always sells; and there's an infinite demand for more. There are billions of people in the world, and virtually all of them love Muhammad Ali. He'll never be able to give his signature to every person who wants it.

> The bulk of my boxing articles have been written for *International Boxing Digest*. But it's been said that one isn't truly a "boxing writer" until one has written for *The Ring*. Ergo, I penned the following anecdotal recollections and commentary for "The Bible of Boxing."

Some Reflections On Time Spent With Muhammad Ali

Muhammad Ali: His Life And Times was published in 1991. Muhammad helped promote the book and, among other things, attended several book signings in New York. Each signing was enormously successful. Both stores reported that Ali had sold more books in a single session than any previous subject or author.

The final promotional event in New York was Muhammad's attendance at the annual Boxing Writers Association of America dinner. Muhammad spoke briefly, and told the audience about a slave named Omar. It was a parable that preached the message of humility, and was met by sustained applause. Then Ali sat down; the program resumed. And HBO's Jim Lampley was speaking, when suddenly Muhammad returned to the podium and announced, "I forgot to tell you. I had two book signings this week, and I broke the all-time record at both stores."

That left Lampley to wonder aloud, "Muhammad; would Omar the slave brag about his book signings?"

"He would if he sold a thousand books," Muhammad responded.

◆　　◆　　◆

Eventually, *Muhammad Ali: His Life And Times* was published in Great Britain, and we journeyed to England for a book tour. One afternoon, I was sitting next to Muhammad at a book signing in London, when a woman in her forties passed through the line. She looked at Muhammad; then at me. And in a thick Irish accent, she asked, "Excuse me; are you Ali's son?"

"No, ma'am," I replied.

"Oh," she said with obvious disappointment. "You look just like him."

My initial reaction was to dismiss her as daft. After all, I'm white and only four years younger than Muhammad. But then it occurred to me that this was one more example of how, when it comes to Ali, people are colorblind. And of course, it's a compliment of the highest order to be told that you look just like Muhammad Ali.

◆　　◆　　◆

With considerable fanfare, our tour of England continued, until late one afternoon we found ourselves in Nottingham. It had been a long day. That morning we'd been in Leeds, where Muhammad had signed nine hundred books, posed for photographs, kissed babies, and shaken hands with literally thousands of admirers. Now that scene was being repeated with five hundred more people who had waited in line for hours for their hero to arrive.

Ali was tired. He'd been awake since 5:00 A.M., when he'd risen to pray and read from the Qur'an. His voice, already weak from the ravages of Parkinson's syndrome, was flagging. And the facial "mask" which accompanies his medical condition was more pronounced than usual.

Most of the people in line were joyful. But one of them—a

middle-aged woman with a kind face—wasn't. Muhammad's condition grieved her, and as she approached him, she burst into tears.

Ali leaned over, kissed her on the cheek, and told her, "Don't feel bad. God has blessed me. I've had a good life, and it's still good. I'm having fun now."

The woman walked away smiling. For the rest of her life, she would remember meeting Ali. Moments later, she turned to look back at him, but Muhammad's attention was already focused on the next person in line—a tall handsome black man. "You're uglier than Joe Frazier," Ali was saying.

◆   ◆   ◆

And that, of course, brings us to Joe. It's no secret that, of all Muhammad's ring opponents, the one who still holds a grudge against him is Joe Frazier. Joe makes no secret of his dislike for Ali, and sometimes his antipathy extends to Muhammad's friends.

In 1991, I was in Atlantic City for a WBO heavyweight championship bout between Ray Mercer and Tommy Morrison. Frazier was in attendance, and I introduced him to a friend of mine named Neil Ragin.

Joe's response was a resounding, "Grhummpf!"

"It's nothing against you," I explained to Neil. "Joe doesn't talk to me a whole lot."

Which gave Neil a chance to ingratiate himself to Joe and keep the conversation going. "Of course, Joe doesn't talk with you. You're Ali's man. Everybody knows you're Ali's man. Right, Joe?"

Whereupon Joe said simply, "Right! And I ain't talking to you either, 'cause you the friend of Ali's man."

Still, in recent years, Joe and I have gotten along fairly well. He's been a guest in my home. He's cordial when we meet. And in return, I have to say, I've always respected Joe as a fighter, and there's a lot about him that I admire as a person. I also believe that Muhammad went too far in labeling Joe a "gorilla" and casting him as an "Uncle Tom."

Still, none of that justifies the venom that has been pouring recently from Joe Frazier's lips. Throughout his recent "autobiography," Frazier repeatedly referred to Muhammad as "Clay" and "boy." If a white person spoke those words, he'd be branded a racist, and with good reason. Even more troubling is the fact that Joe seems to take pleasure in Muhammad's current physical difficulties, and pride in the thought that he might have contributed to them.

Joe Frazier doesn't get it. For starters, he doesn't understand that, without Muhammad Ali, his own career wouldn't have been as remarkable as it was. Joe was a great fighter. However, fighters are judged, not by bouts that are easy, but by bouts that are hard. Frazier won the heavyweight championship in pieces by beating Buster Mathis and Jimmy Ellis (both of whom also lost to Muhammad). After he beat Ali (which was when Joe truly became champion), his only successful title defenses were against Terry Daniels and Ron Stander. Then he got knocked out by George Foreman, who knocked him out a second time three years later. Take away the three Ali-Frazier fights, two of which were won by Ali, and what have you got?

Like Frazier, George Foreman also fought Muhammad. And Ali was hard on Foreman before their fight, as he was with Joe. By the time they got into the ring in Zaire, Foreman was viewed by the citizens of that nation as a virtual stand-in for the white imperialists who had once ruled the Belgian Congo. But George understands what Joe Frazier does not—the importance of Muhammad Ali. "After the fight, for a while I was bitter," Foreman later said. "But then I realized I'd lost to a great champion; probably the greatest of all time. Now I'm just proud to be part of the Ali legend. If people mention my name with his from time to time, that's enough for me."

People said and did horrible things to Ali during the course of his career, but he forgave each and every one of them. His view of religion and his personal nature both require that he be merciful. Few people are as forgiving as Muhammad. Some might say that he's forgiving to a fault. But Muhammad Ali continues to flower spiritually and grow as a person. Joe Frazier would do well to learn from his example.

Meanwhile, when it comes to Joe Frazier, Muhammad still gives as good as he gets. Several years ago, I was with Ali in New York for a celebration at the United Nations. Muhammad's son, Asaad, who was a year old at the time, was also there, as was Joe. And Joe was looking for trouble. Smiling at Asaad, he told onlookers, "Hmmm; that boy looks just like me."

And Ali didn't miss a beat. "Don't call my boy ugly," he said.

I spent the last week of November 1996 in Los Angeles with Muhammad Ali to promote a book that we co-authored—*HEALING: A Journal of Tolerance and Understanding*. That led to a very special Thanksgiving.

Muhammad Ali— Thanksgiving 1996

As is his custom, Muhammad Ali awoke shortly after 5:00 A.M. on Thanksgiving Day 1996. He was in Los Angeles to pursue his latest mission; teaching people how to love. *HEALING* is a cause that Ali can wrap himself around, and the people close to him feel good about it.

After washing himself with clear running water, Ali put on clean clothes and said the first of his five daily prayers. Then he moved behind his hotel-room desk and began signing bookplates that would be distributed to fans who attended one of several book-signings in the days ahead. Ali's weight has been over 250 pounds for several years, and now he's decided to get down to 220. Accordingly, he skipped breakfast as part of his personalized brand of dieting and announced, "This is my third day of not eating, except for one meal a day," However, as the day progresses, Ali will eat pears, apples, and oranges from a large basket of fruit that has been sent to his room by the hotel management.

"And maybe a muffin," Ali admits.

Correct that. Several muffins. And chocolate chip cookies, cheese, and crackers; all before his "one meal of the day"—a large Thanksgiving dinner.

"I'm losing weight because I'm planning a comeback," Ali says. "On my fifty-fifth birthday, I think I'll fight the top three heavyweights in the world, one round each, at Madison Square Garden."

"You'd better get in shape fast," Muhammad is cautioned. "Your fifty-fifth birthday is in seven weeks."

"Seven weeks? Maybe I'll do it when I'm sixty instead."

At 9:00 A.M. Pacific Coast time, Ali turns on the television to accommodate a guest who wants to watch the Kansas City Chiefs versus the Detroit Lions. "In my whole life," he admits, "I've never watched a football game on television from beginning to end. Sometimes I go to the Super Bowl because the people around me want to go, and because of me, they can get in. But the only sports I'm interested in now are big fights. I like watching big fights to see how I'd do if I was in them."

On the TV screen, Detroit's Barry Sanders is seen making a particularly shifty move, and Muhammad's eyes widen. "How old is he?"

"Twenty-eight."

"When I fought Sonny Liston, that man wasn't even born."

The Detroit Lions score a touchdown, and the obligatory end zone dance follows.

"You started that," Ali is told. "All the dancing and celebrating and showing off started with you."

"I started the big salaries too. Big salaries started when me and Joe Frazier got $2,500,000 each the first time we fought."

The Chiefs vanquish the Lions 28-24, at which point the Dallas Cowboys take the field against the Washington Redskins. Meanwhile, Ali has begun turning the pages of a Bible, pointing out contradictions.

"Look at Exodus 33:11 [And the Lord spake unto Moses face

to face, as a man speaketh unto his friend.] Now look at Exodus 33:20 [And the Lord said, 'Thou canst not see my face, for there shall be no man see me and live.'] Some people think the Bible is the word of God," Ali continues. "But in one part of Exodus, it says Moses saw God's face. And in another part, it says no man can see God and live. How can the word of God be two different things? Here's another contradiction. John 5:31 [Jesus said, 'If I bear witness of myself, my witness is not true.'] Now read John 8:14 [Jesus answered and said unto them, 'Though I bear record of myself, yet my record is true.']. You're educated. You tell me, is Jesus's witness true or not true? Heavy, ain't it?"

Shortly after 2:00 P.M., Ali leaves the hotel to travel to the home of Connye Richardson, a longtime family friend. Richardson lives in Hancock Park; the section of Los Angeles that Ali lived in during his marriage to Veronica Porche. Ali has mixed feelings about his years in Los Angeles. The period encompassed some of his greatest glories, but it was in Hancock Park that his fortunes began to turn. He was living there when he lost to Leon Spinks, Larry Holmes, and Trevor Berbick. It was in Hancock Park that his health began to fail, his family life (now on solid foundation again) began to unravel, and he felt himself growing old.

Connye Richardson's home is spacious and comfortable. During the course of the day, twenty family members and friends will drop by. Ali is wearing tan slacks and a white short-sleeved shirt, his still-powerful forearms visible. Thanks to new medication (a combination of Artane and Medapar) his voice is clearer and his face more animated than they have been for several years.

As he often does when he feels at home in someone else's living room, Muhammad turns on the television. A movie about Vietnam starring Gene Hackman is showing. The last twenty minutes are unremitting violence and gore. "I made a wise decision when I didn't go to Vietnam," Ali tells one of the other guests. "All that killing was wrong." Then he switches to CNN, which has a brief feature on a presidential pardon given by Bill Clinton to a forty-five pound turkey. Instead of winding up on someone's dinner table, the turkey will spend the rest of its years on a petting farm in Virginia. Ali is asked if he thinks it's right for people to kill animals to eat when other types of food are available. He considers the issue and responds, "Everything that God made, he made for a purpose. I don't believe in hunting just to kill an animal. That bothers me. But I think it's all right to eat animals like turkeys and fish and cows."

Connye Richardson has been cooking for days, and it seems as though every one of God's foods is served. If Muhammad is truly planning to fight again in Madison Square Garden, this isn't the place to slim down. But it's a good Thanksgiving. And Ali is both happy and in a reflective mood as the day draws to a close.

"God has been good to me," Muhammad says in the car going back to the hotel. "I'm thankful I've got a good wife and nine healthy children. I'm thankful I was three-time heavyweight champion of the world. I'm thankful I live in a country like America. I'm thankful I've been able to travel and meet people all over the world. I'm thankful that, even though I haven't fought for fifteen years, people still remember me. I have a good life. I've got a lot to be thankful for."

A Special Moment

Since autumn 1996, I've been privileged to travel around the
United States with Muhammad Ali, his wife Lonnie, and Howard
Bingham. The idea for our journey began with a book that
Muhammad and I co-authored. *HEALING: A Journal of Tolerance
and Understanding* is a statement we wanted to make regarding
bigotry and prejudice. With the help of HBO, the Boston Globe
Foundation, Turner Broadcasting, and others, we've visited schools
throughout the nation.

At each stop, Muhammad, Lonnie, and I have addressed students and given them copies of *HEALING*. One person who has
been particularly supportive of our efforts is Roy Jones, Jr. Most
people who are aware of Roy think of him as "pound-for-pound"
the best boxer in the world today. But Roy is also "pound-for-
pound" one of the best people in the world today. Despite a busy
schedule, he has joined us at events from New York to California
and hosted a *HEALING* gathering attended by 7,600 students at
the Pensacola Civic Center.

I have many warm memories of Roy Jones, but one moment, in
particular, stands out in my mind. We were visiting Locke High
School in Los Angeles. When Muhammad was introduced, he
received his usual roar of acclamation. But Roy got something
extra. When his name was mentioned, a substantial number of the
girls screamed. It was the kind of scream reserved over the decades
for Elvis Presley, the Beatles, and other heartthrobs—like
Muhammad Ali. And Muhammad didn't miss a beat. Feigning

jealousy, he stood up from his chair, smacked his fist into the palm of his hand, and challenged Roy to fight. Roy responded. And for thirty seconds, two of the greatest fighters of all time sparred for an adoring crowd.

Muhammad and Roy were having fun. But as fighters, they were also measuring each other. "He's good," Muhammad said afterward. "He has good moves, and he's fast."

"I was surprised at how well Ali moved," Roy acknowledged. "He's got a lot more left than most people realize."

The impromptu sparring session excited the students at Locke High School so much that Muhammad and Roy repeated it for future audiences. And when we visited Pensacola, they climbed into the ring at Roy's gym for a round. No blows were struck, but a lot of strategizing went on. Recently, Roy talked about his "confrontations" with The Greatest:

When I'm fighting, the first thing I do is, I want to see my opponent's jab to find out if there are any flaws in it. The first time my opponent makes a mistake, I pick up on it. And the moment Ali and I started sparring, I could see he was searching for the hole, looking for a flaw in my jab. Right away, he picked up on something I do that I can get away with because of my speed. He thought there was a flaw, and he found it. I've never seen anyone who could go out and search for the flaws that quickly. And I said to myself, this guy fights like I do.

Then Ali went on the offensive against me. And I'll tell you something; people talk about Ali's defense, but I think his offense was the key to his success. When Ali was young, you didn't have time to think against him. He was always putting pressure on you because he could strike at any time. It was like, what his opponent did didn't seem to matter. And he has the safest jab I've ever seen—he still has it—because he doesn't over-commit. He uses his jab to keep you away and keep you in range until he hits you.

I run fights against guys like Sugar Ray Robinson and Marvin Hagler through my head from time to time. I have a strategy for beating all of them. The only guy I can't beat is, sometimes I ask myself, if I was fighting myself, what would I do, and I don't know the answer. So after sparring with Ali, I asked myself, if I was fighting the young Muhammad Ali and we were both the same size, what would I do. And I don't know the answer. If I was fighting the young Ali, I'd try to get inside his head, jab with him, go to the body. There'd be no sense in trying to knock him out. But then again, it would be very hard to out-point him. In a lot of ways, it would be a tactical fight; a little like Ali against Jimmy Young. Except Ali would be at his best, and I wouldn't stick my head outside the ring like Young did. But to be honest, against Ali when he was young, I don't see much that anyone could do with him.

And I'll tell you something else. Sparring with Ali has made me feel better about where he's at today. Physically, he's still strong and a lot quicker than I thought he'd be. The man could get in a boxing ring tomorrow and beat the average person walking down the street easily. And mentally, believe me, Ali is all there. His body might not do what it once did, but he still thinks faster in the ring than anyone I've ever been in with.

Shed no tears for Muhammad Ali.

After a visit to the United States Holocaust Memorial
Museum with Ali, I was left with a very simple
thought. If we can harness the energy and love that
emanate from this man, maybe we can change the
world.

A Day of Remembrance

On June 24, 1997, Muhammad Ali awoke in the nation's capitol at
5:00 A.M. He said his prayers, ate a light breakfast, and read quietly from the Qur'an. Then, accompanied by his wife Lonnie and
several friends, he left the Hay-Adams Hotel and drove to a unique
destination—the United States Holocaust Memorial Museum.

The museum was not yet open to the public when Ali arrived at
7:45 A.M. He had come early because he feared his presence during normal visiting hours would cause a commotion unsuited to
the decorum of his surroundings. Several staff members greeted
Muhammad and his party when they arrived. There were intro-
ductions, and the tour began.

The mission of the United States Holocaust Memorial Museum
is to inform, honor, and inspire. More specifically, it is designed to
present the history of the persecution and murder of six million
Jews and millions of other victims of Nazi tyranny; to commemorate those who died; and to encourage visitors to contemplate the
moral implications of their own civic responsibilities.

Ali began by assimilating facts as he walked through the
museum. . . . One-and-a-half million children were exterminated in
the Holocaust. . . . It wasn't just Jews. . . . Gypsies, the physically
disabled, mentally handicapped, and other "undesirables" were also
victims. . . . Books were burned. synagogues destroyed . . . .

As the tour progressed, Muhammad began to draw parallels between the Holocaust and the slavery that his own ancestors endured. Ali has spoken often about how black Americans were robbed of their African names and given slave names instead. Now he learned of people whose Jewish names were replaced by numbers tattooed on their forearms. Standing in a boxcar used to transport Jews to death-camps in Poland, he imagined himself in the cargo hold of a slave ship two centuries earlier.

Midway through the tour, Ali came to a glass wall bearing the names of thousands of communities eradicated during the Holocaust.

"Each of these names is a whole town?" Muhammad asked incredulously.

"Yes."

"I never knew it was that bad."

The tour went on. . . . A pile of shoes taken from the dead at Majdanek. . . . Bales of hair cut from the heads of concentration camp victims. . . . A crude metal table where bodies were placed and gold teeth extracted with pliers. . . . Grainy films of nude bodies piled high being bulldozed into trenches.

Ninety minutes after the tour began, Ali stopped to read a quotation in silver letters on a gray wall:

First they came for the socialists.
And I did not speak out because I was not a socialist.
Then they came for the trade unionists.
And I did not speak out because I was not a trade unionist.
Then they came for the Jews.
And I did not speak out because I was not a Jew.
Then they came for me.
And there was no one left to speak for me.

Finally, Ali entered the Hall of Remembrance and placed a white rose beside the museum's eternal flame.

During the course of his life, Muhammad Ali has taken many courageous stands. But his presence at the United States Holocaust Memorial Museum on June 24, 1997, is among his most important statements of principle.

The victims' faces on this particular morning were Jewish. But they could just as easily have been faces from Cambodia, Bosnia, or Rwanda. By virtue of his presence, Ali demonstrated once again his solidarity with all victims of persecution. And he joined his spirit with millions of Holocaust victims and with the survivors who remember them.

Round 2

Other Fighters

The Black Lights was my first book about professional boxing. But prior to that, I wrote two articles about the sweet science, including this maiden effort in 1979 about then-light-heavyweight champion, Mike Rossman.

My Son, The Champ

Like all good Jewish mothers, Celia Rossman loves to talk about her son. "Before I tell you anything," she says, "you should know that Michael is a good boy. He doesn't hang around bars or after-hours clubs. He's never been in trouble. He's only twenty-two, and already he's gone far."

The words sound familiar, but the object of Celia Rossman's affection is unique. Her son Michael is hardly your typical grind-it-out doctor-lawyer type. On September 15, 1978, just prior to the second Muhammad Ali-Leon Spinks championship bout, he knocked out Victor Galindez of Argentina (who hadn't been beaten in seven years) to capture the world light-heavyweight championship. In an age when most world title holders are foreign born and virtually all serious contenders are Hispanic or black, Rossman is an American, white, Jewish, and he can punch. Recent speculation has centered on a 1979 bout between "The Jewish Bomber" and Muhammad Ali for the world heavyweight title.

"I don't like it," his adoring mother admits. "I'm always afraid he'll get hurt. Besides, Michael's being a fighter causes lots of problems."

Such as?

"One of them, you wouldn't believe. All through his amateur career, when Michael went into the ring, he wore the same robe.

When he turned pro, I said, 'Michael, you need a new robe; the old one looks terrible.' He wouldn't listen. He said, 'Mom, when I become champ, you can buy me a new robe.'" Her head shakes with sorrow. "'Michael,' I told him, 'you need a new robe now. The old one is coming apart. You can't get in the ring looking like that. People will see you.' Then he signed to fight in Madison Square Garden for the first time, and I put my foot down. 'Michael,' I told him, 'I can't stop you from fighting, but you're not going to do it in that robe. The sleeves are too short, and it's torn under both arms. What will people think?' So, thank God, he got a new robe. If it wasn't for me, he'd still be wearing the old one."

Laugh if you will. Mike Rossman's Jewish mother is the best thing he has going for him. So when Rossman fights, he does so under his mother's maiden name, rather than that of his father-manager, Jimmy DiPiano. That's because boxing, more than any other sport, thrives on ethnic confrontations. Promoters are constantly on the lookout for a Jewish star, and will go to great lengths to find one.

One of boxing's finest legends concerns an unsavory manager who brought a Latin American fighter named Marcos to New York in the early 1960's, changed his name to Marcus, and began touting him in ring circles as "The Star of Zion." The Star, it was widely advertised, was of Orthodox Jewish vintage, fought to bring honor to the Jewish people, and would someday be a superb champion. He blew his cover at a B'nai B'rith luncheon when, hungrily eyeing the matzoh, he said politely, "Please pass the tortillas."

Unlike The Star, Mike Rossman's religion is for real, and promoters are hyping it for all its' worth. In the ring he wears powder blue trunks with a white Star of David on the side. The new robe forced upon him by his mother is similarly adorned. "It's no gimmick either," says DiPiano. "Mike's a Jew."

"That's right," Rossman adds. "My mother's a Jew. And in the Jewish religion, whatever your mother is, that's what you is. I wore the star in my first fight, and I've worn it ever since. I'm proud of being Jewish."

"Michael's first fight was awful," his mother remembers. "Boxing spectators aren't always the best people in the world. When Michael won, this big guy jumped in the ring, tackled him, and started shouting, 'Get that Jew.' The next morning I said, 'Michael, for your own safety, take the star off your trunks.' He said, 'Mom, maybe before it didn't mean much to me. Now I'll never take it off.'"

By the time the Galindez fight came around, Michael also had a Jewish star tattooed on the back of his left calf.

"Galindez!" Celia Rossman exclaims. "I can't tell you how worried I was. That man had beaten up a lot of people very badly. Usually, when Michael fights, I stay home in New Jersey. But this time I thought he might need me. The fight was in New Orleans," she continues. "I sat with my daughter-in-law at ringside and kept my eyes shut the whole time. After each round, the spectators would tell me what had happened. Then, all of a sudden in the middle of the twelfth round, my daughter-in-law started shouting. 'Michael's won! Michael's won!' I ran into the ring crying and hugged him. And you know the first thing he said? 'Take it easy, Mom. I'm all right.'"

Because of his ethnic appeal, Rossman was nurtured carefully as a fighter and many of his opponents were soft touches. But his pre-championship record of thirty-four wins against four losses included victories over several top contenders, and his knockout of Galindez places him in a rather exclusive group of athletes.

Jewish stars in American sports have been few and far between.

In baseball, Sandy Koufax and Hank Greenberg stayed home from the ball park on Rosh Hashanah, but they never had much company. Red Auerbach and Dolph Schayes headed a meager basketball contingent, while All-Pro quarterback Sid Luckman stood out on the football gridiron. Mark Spitz won an unprecedented seven gold medals at the 1972 Munich Olympics. After that, the list dwindles.

Great Jewish fighters of the twentieth century have been even fewer in number. Benny Leonard, who reigned as lightweight champion from 1917 to 1925 was one; Barney Ross another. Max Baer, who won the heavyweight crown in 1934, wore a Star of David on his trunks, but its origins were suspect.

Meanwhile, as Rossman moves up in class among the world's top fighters, his celebrity status has grown. "The letters flood in," his proud father says. "Mike is very big with the Jewish people. When he visits the Yeshiva schools, three hundred children line up for his autograph. Israel is dying to have him fight there. He could be their national hero."

All of which makes Rossman a very popular young man. Recently, he was honored at a B'nai B'rith luncheon and presented with an award as Sportsman of the Year. He didn't even mistake the matzoh for tortillas.

After I started writing about boxing, I became a regular at Madison Square Garden's Felt Forum. Glenwood Brown was an up-and-coming prospect in 1988, when I wrote this piece for MSG's "Fight Night" program.

Glenwood Brown: The Real Beast

"Before my first pro fight, I was so afraid that I was crying going to the ring."

The speaker is Glenwood "The Real Beast" Brown; voted "Prospect of the Year" in 1987 by the Boxing Writers Association of America. Brown is the WBA Americas Champion and world-ranked by all three sanctioning bodies. However, he still recalls his June 19, 1986, pro debut against Robert Harris at Madison Square Garden's Felt Forum.

"All the tears were just coming out of my eyes. I didn't want to be there. He was six feet tall, and I'm five-seven. My knees were shaking so bad when the referee gave the instructions that I could of fell down right there. I took a towel and wiped my eyes just so I could see where I was. Then the bell rang, and all the fear inside me disappeared."

Brown knocked Harris out in the fourth round, and has been a consummate professional ever since. Still, the memory of his first pro victory will never fade. "It felt so good," he recalls, "going out there and winning. Later, I watched the tape and smiled through the whole thing, saying that's really me."

Glenwood Brown is a special young man, thoroughly dedicated to his trade. Clearly, he has a bright future in boxing. But perhaps the most refreshing thing about him is the love, respect, and appreciation he has for his parents. They put a foundation under him, and that's something he'll never forget. Here, in his own words, is Glenwood Brown.

♦   ♦   ♦

My mother is thirty-eight now, and my father is forty-one. Actually, he's not my real father. He's my stepfather, but I consider him my real father because of everything he's done for me. His name is Charles Bailey, and he's had me since I was one year old. I never even knew he was my stepfather until my mother told me. And both of them, my mother and father, they've always done everything they can for me.

I was fourteen when I went to a gym and saw boxing for the first time. Afterwards, I talked to my father, and he took me down to get a physical. Then I went back to the gym and met John Davenport, who was my first trainer. I trained for about three weeks before my first amateur fight, and I was scared. I mean, really scared. I won my first three fights, and lost my fourth. Every day when I got out of school I wanted to play around outside like the rest of the kids, but I had to go to the gym. Every day I did a workout, and then, after I got out from the gym, the whole day was over. So there were times when I wanted to quit boxing, but something just told me to keep trying. I said to myself, "You know, there ain't nothing out on the street that's good to do; I might as well stay."

I know that my mother, when she first found out I wanted to box, she didn't want me to do it, because she'd seen it on TV, how people can get hurt. Then she'd see me come home from the gym with black eyes and stuff like that. And, you know, she's into church; she ain't like that. But after a while, she got used to it and supported me in boxing too.

My father supported me all the way. I could see how much he cared about me, that he really loved me. He did everything he could for me. Every time I had to go on a trip, he paid for it. He never treated my two brothers different from me. He treated everybody the same. Me and my sister Lola, we're his stepkids, but he treated us just like his regular kids. He helps me out all the time. He talks to me. When I graduated from high school, he talked to me about going back to school to take courses in public speaking. Talking and stuff like that; I can't do it. When I go around somebody to talk to them, I start sweating and perspiring. My mother doesn't talk much around people. She likes to keep to herself, and I inherited that from her. But because of my father, my speaking is improving.

The kids that I went to school with, a lot of them are selling drugs today. Some of them are locked up. And you know, it was those kids that I used to walk to school with and play ball with. You know how people are, what it's like on the streets. But I was never into drugs or drinking, nothing like that. My mother and father never did it, and I felt that, if they didn't want me to do it, and they didn't do it, then it was something I shouldn't do. So I never smoked. I never tried drugs. I never went out partying. I'm not a partying person. I always stayed in the house; staying out of trouble. I'd see my friends; they'd be out looking for trouble; and I'd say to myself, "If you all gonna go out there and do that, I ain't gonna be with you."

Plenty of people offered drugs and all that stuff to me, but I always told them no. Now I try to talk to my younger brothers and sisters about staying off the streets and not taking drugs. I say, "If I could say no, you can say the same thing." I'm trying to teach them to have responsibility for themselves like I learned from my mother and father.

And now that I'm older, I have to carry even more responsibility. I'm out on my own. I gotta take care of myself. When I first was getting ready to move to my own apartment, I talked to my mother, and she told me that I got a big responsibility on paying bills for food and rent. I got a car, and I gotta pay the insurance. It's a big responsibility, getting out on your own. And I know my parents, they raised me up to be good and do things right.

They're real heroes, my mother and father. They're a big part of my life. My family comes first to me, even before boxing. I try to please my parents all the time, every day, so people see they brought up a kid that's not a bad kid, that they raised up somebody that they can be proud of. And my mother always says that she's blessed by me, because she sees how I try to do things. And if there's something that I can't do, the first people I would go to is my mother and father, because I know they would help me on whatever I couldn't do. They talk to me all the time. They just help me do.

Howard Davis's career was winding down in 1988, when he made one last serious, and ultimately futile, bid for a world championship.

Howard Davis and His Quest for Fulfillment

Twelve years is a long time. But that's how long Howard Davis has been fighting with one goal in mind—to become a world champion.

Davis burst upon the scene at the 1976 Olympics in Montreal. Prior to that, he'd won four national Golden Gloves titles and an amateur world crown, but outside of boxing circles he was largely unknown. "Winning the gold medal was a moment of mixed emotions," he recalls. "It meant I'd won the greatest prize in amateur sports, but three days before the Olympics, my mother had died. So even now, the Olympics are a memory tinged with sadness. I was never able to complete the feel-good process about them."

Five Americans won Olympic gold medals in boxing that year. Two of them—Sugar Ray Leonard and Michael Spinks—rose to superstardom. Michael's brother, Leon, embarked on a roller-coaster career that included a 1978 upset of Muhammad Ali for the world heavyweight crown. Leo Randolph fought professionally for only two years, but captured the WBA junior featherweight title. Of the five, only Howard Davis—who was voted the outstanding fighter of the 1976 Olympics—has failed to win a world championship.

Twelve years. That's how long Davis has been pursuing his dream. Think about that for a moment; how long that is. Twelve years ago, Pete Rose was two seasons shy of 3,000 hits and Reggie Jackson was a Baltimore Oriole. Gerald Ford was President of the United States, and the Shah of Iran was firmly in power. John Lennon and Elvis Presley were still alive. Mike Tyson was ten years old. For all that time, the time it takes a child to go from kindergarten to twelfth grade, Howard Davis has been laboring toward his goal.

He's come close twice. In 1980, in Glasgow, Davis challenged Scotland's James Watt for the WBC lightweight crown. "In the days leading up to the fight," Davis remembers, "I kept telling myself it was supposed to be the high-point of my career. But the truth is, I was confused. My father and co-managers were fighting about money, opponents, training methods, everything. There was constant bickering, and I was caught in the middle. By the time the fight came, I was asking myself, who am I fighting for, me or them?"

Watt won a hard-fought unanimous decision. Responding to the first loss of his professional career, Davis ran off thirteen consecutive wins. Then, in June 1984, he challenged again for the WBC crown. This time, the opponent was Edwin Rosario, with the bout in Rosario's backyard, San Juan.

Rosario started fast, dominating the first three minutes and flooring Davis in the second round. But in round three, an overhand right caught Rosario flush on the cheekbone and turned the tide. After eleven rounds, one judge had Rosario ahead by two points, and a second favored Davis by three. The third judge, Sid Nathan of Great Britain, had the bout dead-even. The twelfth round would decide. For two minutes and fifty seconds of the last round, Howard Davis dominated. Then, with ten seconds left, a flash knockdown sent him to the canvas again. That was the difference. By a margin of one point, Edwin Rosario retained his crown.

Three hard years followed; years during which Davis won

twice, lost twice, and fought a ten-round draw. "It was a bad time," he remembers. "People were criticizing me, and I wasn't prepared for that. It got me down. I was full of internal conflict and self-doubt. I didn't know whether to keep fighting or not. I kept asking myself, why am I doing this? I almost quit. But then I told myself I'd never quit anything in my life, and that I'd never forgive myself if I didn't do everything in my power to win a world title."

Now, once again, Howard Davis is on a roll. His comeback began with a ninth-round knockout of Ali Karim Muhammad on January 21, 1988. That was followed by a unanimous ten-round decision over Shelton LeBlanc in March. As always, Davis is in phenomenal condition. On the surface, he doesn't appear to be growing old, but time is running out and everyone knows it.

"It takes a lot of character to do what Howard is doing," says his current manager, Mike Jones. "Not many fighters would go from fighting for hundreds of thousands of dollars a fight to fighting for six or seven thousand, but that's what Howard has done without a word of complaint. That's the type of sacrifice he's willing to make to become a champion."

No one in boxing deserves it more.

Alex Stewart was a fighter with a manufactured record. But he was also a very sweet guy, and I had no hesitancy about writing a program piece on him for Madison Square Garden.

Alex Stewart: Boxing's Dr. Jekyll and Mr. Hyde

Alex Stewart has a split personality. Outside the ring, the popular Felt Forum heavyweight is a young man brimming with charm. More than one observer has likened his buoyancy to that of Sugar Ray Leonard, and there's no one nicer to be around.

But inside the ring, Alex Stewart is a different person. He's "The Destroyer," who has kicked off his pro career by collecting 17 knockouts in 17 fights. In boxing history, only one world champion, Mike Tyson, has had a more auspicious start. Tyson knocked out his first 19 opponents, a record Alex is threatening now. To further the parallel, Tyson and Stewart have faced one common foe, Conroy Nelson, and each man knocked out Nelson in the second round.

In short, anyone in the ring with Stewart faces big trouble. Yet people who have seen him fight and meet him afterward are amazed at how sweet he is. Thus, the question arises: How can someone as nice and likeable as Alex do what he does in the ring?

Stewart was born in England on June 28, 1964. The son of Jamaican immigrants, he grew up in London and was athletically gifted as a child. "I started boxing to please people," he remembers. "It made me feel good to have someone come over to me after I won and say, 'Nice fight, congratulations.' Then I saw Sugar

Ray Leonard at the Olympics in Montreal, and from that day on I wanted to be an Olympic fighter. I told my mum, and she laughed at me. She said, 'You're twelve years old and you're not going to any Olympics in boxing.' But when I was fifteen, my parents moved back to Jamaica and that made me more determined than ever to reach my goal."

Representing Jamaica, Stewart won a bronze medal in the 1983 Pan Am Games. Then, fighting under the Jamaican flag at the 1984 Los Angeles Olympics, he fulfilled his dream.

"I love boxing," he says now. "The competition, the one-on-one." It's the only sport in the world where, if you want it bad enough, you can go out and take it. As far as hurting my opponent is concerned, that's not what boxing is about to me at all. I just want to win. I don't need anger or hate or the other things some fighters use to motivate themselves. I'm a professional. In the ring, I take care of business; that's all. Some fighters, when they knock an opponent down and see him struggling to get up, they want him to make it so they can hit him again. I'm not like that. I want the guy to stay down so I can win. Hey, if I wanted him standing up, I wouldn't have knocked him down to begin with.

"In the dressing room before a fight," Stewart continues, "I feel all sorts of things, but I control them. I'm like a time bomb waiting to explode. Then, when the fight starts, when I hit someone, what goes through my mind is, I'm winning. If you hit me with one punch, I want to hit you with three. Like my mum used to say, I'm a sleeping lion. And you don't want to wake a sleeping lion, because it makes the lion mad."

In the past, Alex Stewart hasn't always won. As an amateur at the Pan Am Games, he lost in the semi-finals to a more experienced opponent. At the Olympics, he scored a second-round knockout in his first bout, but lost by decision to his next foe.

"I hated losing," he says now. "It's not a nice feeling, and I don't plan on letting it happen again. I still make mistakes. Sometimes I don't let my punches go as fast as I should. And when I hit an opponent, I have the tendency to wait for a receipt instead of moving on. But I'm learning, working on my flaws, getting better as I go along."

What does the future hold for Alex Stewart? At this point, it's hard to tell. But Mike Tyson's trainer, Kevin Rooney, says Alex is "one of the few guys out there who might give Mike trouble down the road." And Stewart concurs. To make the point, he harkens back to his second pro fight, a May 7, 1987, bout against Eric Mitchell at the Felt Forum.

"Mitchell was a puncher," Stewart remembers. "He hit me hard, but I came back and knocked him out in the first round. At least, that's what I thought. Then, afterward in the dressing room, my manager and trainer were talking about how I'd knocked him out in the third round. I thought they were kidding, but they swore it was true. I said, 'Wait a minute! You mean, we really had rounds two and three?' Then one of the commission inspectors came into the dressing room. I asked him what round I won in, and he said the third. That told me something. It meant I had the instincts and the heart of a champion."

And then Alex Stewart adds with a wink, "After all, in the ring, it's what you do after you can't remember that counts."

Prior to Alex Stewart's 1989 fight against Evander Holyfield, *Boxing Illustrated* asked me to write a pre-fight piece about the bout from Stewart's point of view. Alex actually did better than expected, staggering Holyfield several times before being knocked out in the eighth round.

At 24–0, All KO's, Alex Stewart Is Unbeaten, Untested, and Unknown

Boxing people know it all, so it's no surprise that those in the know have strong opinions on the upcoming bout between Evander Holyfield and Alex Stewart. Showtime thought so little of Stewart as an opponent that it tried to substitute "Big" Art Tucker, who has yet to appear in a scheduled ten-round fight. Holyfield's adviser, Shelly Finkel, says, "The only question in my mind is whether Stewart can take a punch. If he can, Evander knocks him out in three or four. If not, it ends in the first round." And Caesars Palace was so distressed by the thought of Stewart that it let the bout go to Donald Trump.

So how does Stewart feel about the situation?

"I know Holyfield is good," Alex answers. "But I want to see what he does when I hit him. I think I can knock him out."

Stewart's credentials are suspect, but they can't be entirely ignored. The 25-year-old Jamaican, who grew up in London and now lives in Brooklyn, has had 24 professional bouts and won them *all* by knockout. That eclipses the string of nineteen consecutive KO's at the start of Mike Tyson's journey, and ties him for the most KO's ever by an American heavyweight at the start of his career. Stewart and Tyson have had four common foes and, on paper at least, the results are comparable. Both men knocked out Conroy Nelson in two rounds and Dave Jaco in one. Tyson dispatched Eddie Richardson and Lorenzo Canady in two minutes each, and those opponents went three and five rounds respectively with "The Destroyer."

But records aside, can Alex Stewart fight?

"No," say the critics. Stewart, they claim, has never fought a world-class opponent. In fact, he hasn't even fought a good club fighter. Fifteen of his twenty-four knockouts have been against soft touches at Madison Square Garden's Felt Forum, and the rest of his foes have been equally non-competitive. His most impressive victories were a one-punch third-round knockout of Eddie Richardson and a four-round demolition of Arthel Lawthorne. But Richardson came into the ring, in the words of one writer, "looking like a homeless person from the New York Port Authority Bus Terminal," and Lawthorne weighed in at twenty pounds heavier than for his previous fight. By his own admission, Stewart hasn't even sparred with a world-class heavyweight other than Michael Spinks, and none of his opponents have extended him past four rounds.

All in all, it brings to mind the wisdom of Mickey Duff, one of Great Britain's premier managers, who once opined, "I've managed ordinary fighters through thirty or forty wins without a loss, because I found worse opponents and that was the way it seemed right to do things at the time. But sooner or later, you're faced with a moment of truth when your guy has to fight a real fight. That's when you realize it's a lot easier to be successful with a quality fighter. It's the difference between managing Frank Sinatra and managing some guy who sings at weddings and bar mitzvahs."

So where does all that leave Stewart?

"I know I've got some questions to answer," he admits. "But so does Evander Holyfield. Holyfield beat Dwight Muhammad Qawi, but Qawi was an old cruiserweight. He beat Michael Dokes, but Dokes isn't what he used to be. He beat Adilson Rodrigues, and if I'd fought Rodrigues at the Felt Forum, it would have ended like all my other fights."

The way most of Stewart's fights have ended lately is with the crowd booing a succession of overweight foes, all still standing erect at the moment the referee mercifully intervened to stop the bout. "I've heard the boos," Stewart acknowledges. "And each time, I was unhappy when the fight was stopped. If I was a spectator, I'd have booed too. As a fan, I want to see two men fight until one of them drops. But I'll tell you something, they would have dropped if the fights went longer, and these are the same people that Tyson and all the other heavyweights have fought."

Household names or not, those 24 opponents are now part of Stewart's record. And a trivia buff might pose the question: "Who are Terry Sorrels, Miguel Paez, Ted Gullick, Clarence Boone, Murphy Goodwin, Luis Pires, Ollie Wilson, Leroy Caldwell, Vic Scott, Gregorio Peralta, Stamford Harris, and Charlie Boston?" The answer is, they're the twelve guys George Foreman fought right before he demolished Joe Frazier to win the heavyweight championship of the world.

"Holyfield is a good fighter," Stewart continues, "but I'm looking to take away what he's got. It makes me mad, the way people are talking. Showtime said they wanted a different fighter (Art Tucker) because the other guy killed someone in a knife fight when he was young and that was a better story-line than I was. Holyfield's people said they wanted me because I'd be the best victory for Holyfield. Well, forget the best story-line; forget the best victory. I'm going to put up the best fight. Determination makes a small man strong and a big man invincible, and I'm a pretty big guy. Before I pay thirty dollars to see Evander Holyfield in the ring against Mike Tyson, I want to see if Holyfield can stand up to my punch."

Stewart is a definite long-shot, but the bout against Holyfield will offer him the opportunity to prove himself against an already-established foe. And equally important, the fight will put Stewart on a world stage, which means people will get to know him. And fighting aside, Alex Stewart is a lovely guy. Everyone who meets him likes him. Indeed, to paraphrase a well-known confectioner's slogan, "Everyone doesn't like someone, but nobody doesn't like Alex Stewart." Contrast that with another heavyweight of note who knocks everyone out but seems given to periodic fits of "wilding," and one comes to the conclusion that, if the impossible were to happen and Stewart conquered both Evander Holyfield and Mike Tyson, he'd become one of the most popular champions ever.

But all that is highly speculative and a long way off. "I'm not ready for Tyson yet," Steward admits. "Before Tyson, I'll have to be in at least one war. So if I beat Holyfield, *when* I beat Holyfield, it will be another step up the mountain, that's all."

Mike Tyson was still on his honeymoon with the American public when I wrote the following cover story for *Boxing Illustrated*. In the article, I gave Tyson credit—perhaps too much credit—for his ample ring skills. But I also raised questions that hadn't been previously raised regarding Tyson's character.

Will Mike Tyson Become the Most Unpopular Athlete in America?

Mike Tyson lives to fight. There was a time when many families believed the noblest thing a person could do was become a priest. For Cus D'Amato, who brought Mike into the ring, being a fighter was the best way to serve God. More than any fighter practicing his craft today, Tyson appears to believe in himself. . . . No robe. . . . Black trunks. . . . The Tyson aura is that of a great white shark, an efficient killing machine. His opponents face instant annihilation for every second of every round. Fighters go into the ring against him scared; not the normal fear fighters endure, but something more. Tyson is there to hurt his opponents, and he knows how. To any foe who doesn't bail out early, he administers a beating. He never touches gloves with an adversary at the end of a round.

Tyson is one of those rare fighters who, more than money or glory, is fighting for a place in history. Much has been made of the fact that many of today's heavyweights think heavyweight means "fat." They fight like union members with seniority on featherbedding jobs. Any great heavyweight of the past would stand out among them, but Tyson is something more. His hand-speed is superb; his power awesome; his defensive abilities on a par with the best. He can hurt an opponent with any punch in his arsenal at any point in a sequence whether he gets off first or counters. He's thirty pounds heavier than Dempsey or Marciano; fifteen more than Joe Louis in his prime.

Right now, the only person who can beat Mike Tyson is Mike Tyson. If he gets bored, if personal problems rob him of discipline and motivation, if he loses control over his wilder side; it could happen. Meanwhile, unless Tyson changes course, in a few years he may well be the most unpopular athlete in America.

Wilt Chamberlain once complained, "Nobody roots for Goliath," but in boxing the contrary is often true. Seemingly unbeatable champions like Joe Louis have been revered by the public, and Tyson has been perfectly positioned for a love-in with the American people. Thanks to shrewd management and market-ing, all America knows the heartwarming saga of "Cus and the Kid"—an image reinforced by a series of television commercials for products ranging from Kodak to Diet Pepsi. It's hard to be unpopular when corporate America is pouring tens of millions of dollars worth of airtime into making you look good. Indeed, Tyson's visibility is such that, in one dizzying week last month, he appeared on the cover of *Life*, *Time*, *Sports Illustrated*, and *People*.

Still, all along there have been rumblings that Mike Tyson is not a nice person. In the ring, there have been too many head-butts, elbows, and punches after the bell. Comments about "crying like a woman" and "pushing the bone of his nose into his brain" have been cause for concern. In contrast to fighters like Muhammad Ali and Larry Holmes, who would beckon referees to stop fights against disabled foes, Tyson punches in the manner of Gerry

Cooney versus Ken Norton, trying to destroy opponents who are already beaten and on their way down.

This ferocity is condoned because boxing is a brutal business and Tyson practices it well. However, Mike's conduct outside the ring is more difficult to excuse. More and more, he seems willing to go beyond the bounds of acceptable behavior. There have been incidents of violence and ugly rumors of sexual misconduct that might land a lesser personage in jail. Someone who is rich and has skilled people looking out for him can often get things papered over. But it's becoming increasingly difficult these days to feel good about Mike Tyson. Yes, he came from hard surroundings. Yes, he has some good qualities in him. But too much ugliness is showing.

I write this now because Mike Tyson is at a crossroads in his development as a human being. In the ring, he appears like a Frankenstein creation who outstrips his opponents' worst nightmares. Future adversaries may well decide to bring paramedics with them instead of cutmen. But outside the ring, Tyson's future is less clear. His co-manager Jim Jacobs died on March 23rd of this year, igniting a bitter struggle for control of the champion and his ring earnings. It's too early to predict the ultimate outcome of that battle. But looking at the dispute in terms of its major players, several things seem clear.

DON KING: Don King is a man who kicks people in the groin and then wants to have sex with them. Bill Cayton and company have learned that the hard way this year. King, of course, wants to promote Tyson. "Tyson don't need no manager," is his present cry. "Why give all that money to Bill Cayton when, with me as promoter, Tyson can keep it all."

Anyone who wants to see how King looks after his fighters should sit down and listen to Muhammad Ali talk for five minutes.

After that, they can speak with Tim Witherspoon. Out of a recent $700,000 purse, Witherspoon's "manager", Carl King, took $350,000. Once various loans and miscellaneous expenses were paid, Witherspoon wound up with a reported $43,000.

If Tyson had signed with Don King when he turned pro, he'd be paying fifty percent of his earnings to Carl King today, not one-third to Bill Cayton and company. And that would be after King took his cut off the top. Jacobs and Cayton had to do business with King to get Mike into the HBO tournament, and option requirements tied them together through the Tyson-Spinks bout. But Tyson is on top now, free to deal with whichever promoter he wants. And if he trusts Don King, he's making a big mistake.

ROBIN GIVENS AND RUTH ROPER (the new "Dynamic Duo" of boxing): Givens, age twenty-three, was the only member of her class at Sarah Lawrence to be booed at graduation. On her first date with Tyson, her entourage included two publicists (love at first sight). Previous "boyfriends" have included Michael Jordan and Eddie Murphy. In some circles, this is known as star-fornicating. Her credentials as a Harvard Medical School student equal those of Rosie Ruiz as a Boston Marathon runner. Many people also question whether she was really pregnant, which is reportedly why she and Tyson got married in the first place.

Momma Roper is a "dignified, caring, honorable" woman, who says she contracted an unspecified venereal disease from Yankee slugger Dave Winfield. Together, she and Robin have spent quite a bit of Mike's money; with his consent, of course. Robin has a Mike Tyson power of attorney (her most treasured autograph) among her belongings.

Not long ago I asked Sugar Ray Leonard if he would give his own wife an unrestricted power of attorney. Ray's answer: "First, let me say that I love my wife and I trust my wife. We've been together for a lot more years than Mike Tyson and Robin Givens. Would I give my wife a power of attorney? Man, you've got to be crazy."

Robin and Ruth now want to take over Mike's financial dealings. In boxing, a fighter gets hit when he makes mistakes. At present, Mike Tyson is in the ring with his hands down and chin up, sharing space with two devious power punchers. Maybe the Tyson-Givens encounter will go the distance, but I doubt it.

BILL CAYTON: This is where one starts to question Mike Tyson's decency and loyalty, not just his judgment. Jim Jacobs and Bill Cayton advanced Mike's career together. They invested literally hundreds of thousands of dollars and years of effort to help put him where he is today. So what do we hear now from Iron Mike: "Bill Cayton caused all my marriage problems. . . . Bill Cayton went to a priest to try to get us divorced. . . . I hold Bill Cayton responsible for my wife's miscarriage." Next, we'll hear that Bill Cayton gave Ruth Roper herpes.

Then there's the matter of Tyson and his wife claiming that Cayton hasn't been financially honest. Muhammad Ali and George Foreman fought in Zaire, one of the poorest countries in the world, Mike tells us, and each man got five million dollars. Yet when Iron Mike fought Tony Tubbs in Japan, one of the world's richest countries, he was paid less than either of his predecessors. This is the observation of a man who is not a great financial analyst. By Tyson's illogic (which sounds suspiciously like the babbling of a former numbers czar turned fight promoter), Marvin Hagler should have been paid equal amounts for fighting Juan Domingo Roldon and Sugar Ray Leonard, since both bouts were held in Las Vegas. Who does Mike think made the deals that got him where he is today; the deals that made him richer at age twenty-one than Sugar Ray Leonard or Muhammad Ali?

KEVIN ROONEY: "The one thing I wish Mike would remember," says Kevin Rooney, "is that he has an honest manager." Kevin is a better trainer and much smarter fellow than a lot of people give him credit for. And unlike some people in this soap opera, Rooney hasn't forgotten the meaning of the word loyalty. Not long ago, Mike asked Kevin to discharge Steve Lott. Steve began working for Jim Jacobs and Bill Cayton in the 1970's. When Mike was getting started as a professional, he lived in Steve's apartment for almost two years. Steve talked with him, gave to him, and shared with him. But Robin didn't like Steve, and rather than wield the ax himself, Iron Mike asked Rooney to do it (There's more than one way of showing cowardice, and this is one of them). Kevin's response was the proper one: "No way, Mike. Do it yourself."

In sum, it's time that Mike Tyson stopped feeling sorry for himself. It's time he stopped making ugly statements like, "Bill Cayton will be dead and gone in ten years." It's time he grew up. We already know that Mike Tyson is a great fighter, but the jury is still out on what kind of person he is. Can he grow and learn; can he exhibit loyalty and listen to criticism? If so, more power to him. But if Mike Tyson reverts to being a bully, if he gives in to his lesser instincts, then he will become the most unpopular athlete in America.

As 1988 progressed, Mike Tyson's image in the media began to change. Soon, getting product endorsements for Iron Mike was more difficult than beating him. *Sports, Inc.*, a fledgling magazine devoted to the economics of sports, asked for an overview.

Selling a Troubled Champ

On Friday, August 26, Mike Tyson picked up the telephone and called his manager, Bill Cayton. Tyson and Cayton haven't been getting along lately. Cayton is regarded as one of the most honest businessmen in boxing, and the manner in which he and Jimmy Jacobs co-managed Tyson to superstardom is well known. However, when Tyson married actress Robin Givens, the Tyson-Cayton relationship fell on hard times. Thereafter, Tyson accused Cayton of causing his wife's miscarriage, stealing money from him, committing fraud, and more.

So how was their telephone conversation?

"It was very friendly," Cayton reported. "We chatted for a while, and then Mike asked, 'When are you gonna start making some more [commercial endorsement] deals for me?' I told Mike I'd do my best, but it would be harder this time around than before."

"Harder than before" is an understatement. In less than a year, Mike Tyson has gone from being a rising star with virtually unlimited commercial appeal, to a superstar athlete whose commercial viability is on the skids. That's because the public is starting to see a side of Tyson that it doesn't like.

Why is Mike Tyson having image problems? Isn't this the man who was destined to star in the heartwarming true-life saga of *Cus and the Kid?*

Well, it turns out that life with Cus wasn't exactly like living with the Waltons. And the house in Catskill, New York, where Tyson trained, was far from the Little House on the Prairie. A young man named Teddy Atlas knows, because he was there. Atlas is one of the most respected trainers in boxing. A street kid from Staten Island, he moved to Catskill in 1975 at age nineteen to live and train with Cus D'Amato. Fighting as a 139-pound amateur, Atlas won a Golden Gloves championship and planned to turn pro, but vertebrae and disk problems ended his career. That was when D'Amato convinced him to become a trainer, and Atlas lived with Cus for six more years.

Tyson walked into Cus D'Amato's Catskill gym for the first time in 1978. A former fighter named Bobby Stewart was working with incorrigible youths at the state reformatory and wanted D'Amato to teach Tyson to box. Cus told Stewart and Tyson to get in the ring so he could see what Tyson had. Stewart was in his late twenties, overweight at 175 pounds, but still a former professional fighter. Tyson was twelve years old, 190 pounds.

"Bobby dominated," Atlas recalls. "Mike didn't have the technical skills to cope with him, but through raw strength and desire he forced Bobby to open up and punch hard just to control him. After the first round, Mike's nose was bleeding heavily, but he kept pressing, punching, furiously attacking, attacking, attacking, because that's all he could do."

Looking back, one wonders if the experience wasn't a bit scary for Stewart; staring into the face of a foe who was battered and bruised but simply spat blood and kept coming. Perhaps, inside, he began to fear that, like a trainer in a cage with a wild animal, he wasn't really the stronger of the two, and if this beast could take away his jab or hook or whatever it was that kept him at bay, the beast would destroy him. From that day on, once a week, Stewart brought Tyson to the Catskill gym, and a year later, Tyson was released into D'Amato's custody.

Tyson's first fight in the ring was at a "smoker"—an unlicensed amateur bout—in the South Bronx. He still weighed 190 pounds, but now the weight was molded solid. It was hard to believe he was only thirteen.

"The opponent was a 17-year-old Spanish kid who knew how to box," Atlas recalls. "It was a great fight, just about even. Then, in the third round, Mike caught him with a left hook and hurt him. The other guy was helpless. He couldn't go down, because he was tangled in the ropes, and the ref was slow coming in. That was when Mike flat-out destroyed him. He hit the Spanish guy again, and knocked his mouthpiece out so hard it splattered off the wall in the back of the room. The crowd didn't like it; most of them had bet on the other guy. But I think that night in the ring was the first time in his life that Mike heard people cheering for him."

Tyson had twenty more smoker fights and won all of them, but outside the ring there were problems. "Cus was a wonderful man," says Atlas. "But he failed to discipline Mike, which made it inevitable that Mike would have difficulties later on. When Mike started living with us, everything was 'yes sir,' and 'no sir.' He was polite in the institutionalized way prisoners are polite to prison guards; the way people are polite to other people who can help them. I think he was afraid that if he did something wrong he'd be sent back to the reformatory. But as he progressed as a fighter and started winning amateur titles, he got contemptuous of rules and authority all over again. Lots of young fighters lived with Cus, and over time there came to be two sets of rules; one for Mike, and one for everyone else. Outside the ring, if it didn't affect boxing, Cus's way of disciplining Mike was to not discipline him at all. If Mike's left hand dropped when he brought back his jab, Cus would have him throwing a thousand jabs a day until he got it right. But when it came to disciplining him around the house or for something that happened at school, Cus would say, 'Let him alone. He's going to be heavyweight champion of the world.'

"After his workouts," Atlas continues, "Mike usually refused to shower. It was his way of defying authority. All he'd do was splash a little cologne, but Cus let it go. When Mike got in trouble for assaulting a teacher at school, Cus told him, 'Don't worry. If they expel you, I'll get you a tutor.' I thought it was wrong. I felt, as long as we had Mike under our supervision, we had an obligation to develop him as a person as well as a fighter, but Cus wanted a champion. He felt Mike was his right. He wanted his monument at any cost. Cus put up with an incredible amount of crap from Mike, and do you know why? Because Mike punched harder than anyone else, and Cus was afraid that, if he tried to discipline Mike, to make him a better person as well as a better fighter, Mike wouldn't take well to that discipline. Cus didn't want to test those waters."

Tyson's current trainer, Kevin Rooney, disputes Atlas's portrayal. Atlas and Rooney were boyhood friends on Staten Island, and later lived together with D'Amato. "Cus disciplined all the boys," says Rooney. "Every day, if you did right, he praised you, and if you did wrong, he wouldn't talk to you. He never beat us. That wasn't his way. But if you loved Cus, the silent treatment drove you crazy. Cus didn't have special rules for Mike. The only exception he made was, Cus had a rule that, if you had trouble in school, you couldn't come to the gym. That's because he wanted to motivate everyone to do well in class, and he didn't want the parents of kids he was training to blame boxing for their children's problems. Mike sometimes had trouble in school because he came from such a different environment, but through it all, Cus kept him boxing. That was the only difference."

Former light-heavyweight champion Jose Torres, another D'Amato protégé, stakes out a piece of middle ground. Torres, who watched Tyson grow up, acknowledges, "Cus concentrated on boxing. That's because Cus felt that boxing discipline superseded everything; that if he could discipline Mike in the ring, eventually it would carry over outside. Mike was a bad kid. Because of Cus, he's a better person now, but I don't know how much better."

Regardless of who one believes, third parties report that, in 1983, when Tyson was sixteen, he sought to impose himself sexually on a younger girl. For Teddy Atlas, it was the final straw. He confronted Tyson, the fighter got out of hand, and Atlas pulled a gun. In the aftermath of the incident, Cus found Mike in his bedroom packing a suitcase, ready to go. Forced to choose between his protégé trainer and his protégé fighter, D'Amato chose the latter. Atlas left and has refused to publicly acknowledge, confirm, or deny the incident since then.

Meanwhile, in the ring, Tyson's needs continued to be met. Then, in 1985, he turned pro and an extraordinary marketing blitz was put in place by his co-managers, Bill Cayton and Jim Jacobs. After each Tyson fight, "knockout highlight" cassettes were sent to a hundred sportswriters and television stations nationwide. Over 4,500 cassettes were distributed in this manner. The story of *Cus and the Kid* was told to countless media representatives again and again. ABC highlighted Tyson in its 1986 Statue of Liberty Centennial television extravaganza. And, of course, in the ring Tyson was awesome. By age 22, he had become a great heavyweight champion. The next step was to turn that greatness into cash.

Big purses in boxing are hardly new. Muhammad Ali, Sugar Ray Leonard, and many others have reaped extraordinary rewards for their ring skills. However, what separated Tyson from his predecessors was the money he stood poised to earn outside the ring. One month before Tyson's June 1988 bout against Michael Spinks, he had earned endorsement income of $2,675,000. But the best seemed yet to come. Just prior to the Spinks bout, Cayton negotiated a deal that guaranteed Tyson $1 million for a series of Diet Pepsi commercials. Negotiations were underway with four more multinational corporations, and Pepsi was leaning toward a proposal to make Tyson its world spokesman for a fee of $8 million to $10 million.

So what happened?

"The second Pepsi deal fell through," says Cayton. "With the possible exception of Nintendo, none of the major contracts will be renewed, and no significant new deals are pending. Mike is still the top superstar athlete in the world, and I believe that someday, hopefully in the near future, he'll be commercially in demand again. But for the moment, the endorsements we would like to see simply aren't there."

Why not?

"No one incident has been responsible for the drop," explains Cayton. "Rather, all of the incidents you've read about have had a cumulative effect. Mike's recent car accident (on September 4th in Catskill) was the last straw, but even before that, nothing major was in the works."

The incidents, of course, are well-catalogued:

A scuffle in a Los Angeles parking lot that occurred when Tyson tried to kiss a woman parking attendant.

Several bizarre automobile accidents.

A curbside brawl with heavyweight boxer Mitch Green.

A ruckus in an Albany department store.

Plus, the public-at-large is growing to dislike certain things about Mike Tyson, namely:

His conspicuous consumption.

His disloyalty toward those who helped develop him as a fighter.

His sometimes dirty ring tactics.

Whispers that Tyson's sexual conduct is beyond the pale of acceptability.

The feeling that Tyson is excessively brutal, that he *needs* to beat people up, if not in the ring then somewhere else.

In sum, the public perception of Mike Tyson is becoming that of a man outside the boundaries of society. Is it an image problem?

"No," says Teddy Atlas. "Mike's problem isn't image. It's that the image is wearing off. All this stuff about what a sweet guy Mike is, the stories about how he became a generous loving person because of Cus; that was image. Now the public is starting to see what Mike is really like, and they don't like what they see. People say, 'This wouldn't have happened if Cus was alive; that wouldn't have happened if Cus was here.'" Atlas pauses, reflecting on the loss of his own father figure, mentor, and friend. "Believe me, it would have happened. Sometimes I think Cus died because he knew what was coming. If he'd been here to see what's going on with Mike now, who knows what it would have done to him. He would have been proud of what Mike has accomplished in the ring, but there's more to life than knocking other people out."

After Tyson lost his title to James "Buster" Douglas, *The National* asked me to set the stage for his comeback bout against Henry Tillman, which was the second half of an HBO doubleheader co-featuring George Foreman versus Adilson Rodrigues.

Mike Tyson: The Way He Was

It must feel strange, at age 23, to have people talk about you in the past tense. But since Mike Tyson lost to James "Buster" Douglas, he's heard a lot about "Tyson, the way he used to be."

The way Tyson used to be was scary. Witness Trevor Berbick reeling around the canvas; Michael Spinks caving in; Larry Holmes going down like he was on roller skates. There were suspicions that Tyson needed to beat people up in order to sleep well at night, and sweet sayings like, "I tried to push the bone of his nose into his brain." And then suddenly, Tyson was on the canvas, groping for his mouthpiece and sticking it in his mouth backwards. "What do you think people will say now," Muhammad Ali asked rhetorically, "if someone asks who was greater, Mike Tyson or me?"

Mike Tyson might still be the baddest man on Earth, but he won't prove it this Saturday night. Sure, he'll knock Henry Tillman out. But Tillman is a blown-up cruiserweight, who's lost to the likes of Willie DeWitt and Dwain Bonds. Rumor has it that he was knocked cold by a sparring partner last month. The only reason for Tyson-Tillman is that it's the bout Don King favors. And these days, the man who wears his hair in the air usually gets what he wants. It's sad, really. Don King has taken the baddest man on earth and turned him into a walkout-bout fighter for George

After he knocked out Michael Moorer to regain the heavyweight championship of the world, George Foreman was honored by the Boxing Writers Association of America as its "Fighter of the Year." The following article was written for the program distributed at the annual BWAA Dinner honoring "Big George."

George Foreman— Fighter of the Year

Boxing inspires wonderful fantasies.

During the course of my life, I've fantasized about getting in the ring and beating heavyweights from Sonny Liston to Mike Tyson. I've snapped my jab. My straight right has been on target. I've put all of my opponents on the canvas. And I'm sure I could give a great post-fight interview. The problem is, I don't have what it takes to get there. But on November 5, 1994, George Foreman blurred the lines between fantasy and reality, when he knocked out Michael Moorer at 2:03 of the tenth round to capture the heavyweight championship of the world. For that achievement, he is honored tonight as the BWAA's "Fighter of the Year."

Foreman's comeback might seem like a combination of miracle and luck, but he has worked long and hard to get here. To put things in perspective, his first pro bout was on June 23, 1969. Seven years and nine months later, he retired from boxing after losing to Jimmy Young. His comeback began against Steve Zouski on March 9, 1987. That was more than eight years ago. In other words, Foreman's second ring career has lasted longer than his first. And during the past eight years, he's suffered more than punches. He's been the butt of jokes and taken a lot of abuse.

When Foreman climbed into the ring against Zouski, he was ridiculed as "a poster-boy for a Maidenform bra ad." His early comeback opponents were a mix of has-beens and never-weres. George raised a few eyebrows in 1990 by demolishing Gerry Cooney. But common sense reminded us that Cooney had won only once during the previous five years. Then Foreman lost to Evander Holyfield, and the dream seemed at an end. After that, times got harder. There was a questionable majority decision over Alex Stewart, in a bout that left George's face distorted beyond recognition. A lopsided loss to Tommy Morrison followed. And now—

Yeah; it was one punch. But so was Sugar Ray Robinson's fifth-round knockout of Gene Fullmer. Sure; George was way behind on points when he pulled it out. But so was Mike Weaver when he coldcocked John Tate. So what if there are ten guys out there who'd be favored over Foreman if they fought tomorrow? The Soviets were a better hockey team than the United States in 1980, but the Americans won at Lake Placid. Georgetown was a better basketball team than Villanova in 1985, but Villanova won the NCAA crown. Secretariat was a better horse than Onion. Ben Hogan was a better golfer than Jack Fleck. In sports, it's not who's "better" that counts; it's who wins. That's why they play the games.

So what has George Foreman accomplished? For starters, he's the oldest man ever to capture a world boxing championship. For over a century, fighters have tried unsuccessfully to do what George has done. But more important, if one looks at the sweep of Foreman's career, it's apparent that he has become a fighter for the ages. When he prevailed at the 1968 Olympics, Lyndon Johnson was President of the United States and Michael Moorer was less than a year old. George has fought through the terms of seven Presidents, touching on four decades. He's been a flag-waving Olympian, a menacing despot, a preacher, a joke, and finally, at age forty-six, a beloved champion.

For twenty years, this immense lumbering man was forced to endure memories of Zaire. He was the "dope" in Muhammad Ali's "rope-a-dope." Now Zaire is in the past. Instead of "rope-a-dope," we have "munch-and-punch," "eat-and-beat," "snack-and-whack," and whatever else George wants. Twenty years ago, he was heavy-weight champion of the world, and it wasn't much fun for the rest of us. Now the entire world can share in the enjoyment of this remarkable man's championship the second time around.

For two decades, George Foreman has been regarded as part of the Muhammad Ali legend. But in 1995, it's at long last clear that Muhammad Ali is part of the George Foreman legend as well.

I met Roy Jones, Jr. in 1996, when I interviewed him for *Penthouse*. Initially, his management team was reluctant for him to do it. *Penthouse* wasn't the image they wanted for Roy. But eventually, they relented and I got my interview.

Roy Jones, Jr.

Boxing is in a state of crisis. The sport has four major sanctioning organizations and seventeen different weight divisions. That's 68 titles, and even the sport's most fervent fans have trouble keeping track of who the "champions" are. Indeed, individual titles have been devalued to the point where they don't mean much anymore. What counts is which fighters are "special."

Roy Jones, Jr. is special. At age 27, he has a record of 32 wins and no losses with 28 knockouts. He's the International Boxing Federation supermiddleweight champion (168 pounds) and the best fighter in the world today. It's not just that Jones is undefeated; it's the way he wins that's so impressive. With an arsenal that includes blinding speed, lightning reflexes, uncanny timing, and devastating power, Jones does things in the ring that no one has done since Muhammad Ali in his prime.

Roy Jones, Jr. first stepped into the spotlight at the 1988 Seoul Olympics. In the gold-medal bout, he battered South Korea's Park Si Hun around the ring for three rounds, inflicted a "standing eight count" on his opponent, and landed 86 punches to Park's 32. Yet inexplicably, three of the five judges voted for Park. The decision was worse than incompetent. It reeked of corruption. The judges who voted for Park were relieved of their Olympic duties and banned from officiating international amateur boxing matches for two years. Jones, despite his "loss," was voted the outstanding boxer of the 1988 Olympic Games. Yet the decision against him still stands.

After the Olympics, Jones turned pro with his father Roy Jones, Sr., who had guided his amateur career, as his trainer. In 1992, father and son parted company, and Alton Merkerson (who had been an assistant coach for the United States Olympic boxing team at Seoul) assumed the trainer's role. Meanwhile, Jones's fortunes outside of the ring were being guided by two brothers from his hometown of Pensacola: Fred and Stan Levin.

Fred Levin is one of the most successful personal-injury trial lawyers in Florida. Stan Levin is an attorney whose primary expertise is in trusts and estates. In the mid-1980's, Stan Levin was on the Board of Directors of the Pensacola Boys Club. Jones was in the club's amateur boxing program, and Roy Jones, Sr. was training the youngsters. Then the Boys Club decided to eliminate its boxing program for financial reasons. "It was only a matter of a couple of hundred dollars," Stan Levin remembers, "so I took the money out of my pocket and gave it to them. That's how I met Roy, and it changed my life."

When Jones turned pro, he turned to the Levins for assistance, and they formed a corporation known as Square Ring to manage his affairs. Square Ring has kept Jones free from longterm contractual entanglements with the sport's more unsavory promoters. It also negotiated the most lucrative non-heavyweight contract in the history of boxing for Jones with HBO.

But it is Jones who must deliver in the ring, and so far he has done that to perfection. In 1993, he won the IBF middleweight title with a convincing 12-round decision over Bernard Hopkins. Then, after four more bouts, he faced IBF supermiddleweight champion James "Lights Out" Toney. For Roy Jones, Jr., this was supposed to be "The Test." Toney was a skilled boxer and fearsome puncher, unbeaten in 46 fights. James Toney didn't just knock out his opponents; he beat them up. Boxing's intelligentsia were evenly divided as to who would win the fight. And it was no contest. Jones toyed with Toney for twelve rounds, en route to a lopsided unanimous decision. *Ring Magazine* called his triumph "the most dominant big fight performance in twenty years."

After disposing of Toney, Jones knocked out Antoine Byrd in one round. Then, against Vinnie Pazienza, he took the clock back almost three decades. In a performance reminiscent of Muhammad Ali's 1966 destruction of Cleveland Williams, Jones KO'd Pazienza in the sixth round. In round four of that fight, Jones's defensive skills were such that Pazienza landed zero—count them, zero—punches.

Within the past year, Jones has scored knockout victories over Tony Thornton, Merqui Sosa, and Eric Lucas. At the same time, he has rekindled a childhood dream by playing professional basketball for the Jacksonville Barracudas of the United States Basketball League. This has led to criticism in some circles that Jones isn't living up to his full potential as a fighter and is jeopardizing his chance to be remembered as one of the greatest fighters of all time. But Roy Jones, Jr. is an uncommon young man as demonstrated by the following interview.

Q: What sort of fantasies do you have? When you're daydreaming, what goes on in your mind?

Roy Jones: I fantasize about basketball most of the time. It's a crucial time in an NBA game; a situation where I have to make something happen. Sometimes I hit a jump shot from the corner, but most times it's an assist. I'm penetrating, going to the hole. And all of a sudden, I dish it off to someone like Michael Jordan or Penny Hardaway or Shaq, who comes down the middle and tears the whole rim down.

Q: When did you realize that you could make your dreams about boxing come true and basketball might be beyond your reach?

Roy Jones: In high school. They only have a few players under six feet in the NBA, and I knew I wouldn't get to six feet. So I realized that my body size was more suited to boxing, and that was okay because even then I had much more time invested in boxing.

Q: If you could choose between being regarded as one of the greatest fighters of all time and playing basketball in the NBA, not as a gimmick but on merit, which would you choose?

Roy Jones: That's hard to say, because in boxing I think I'm already on the list of greatest pound-for-pound. And it's not like I think I couldn't make it to the NBA. If I put down boxing and put the same amount of work I've put into boxing into basketball, I'd get there. I believe that. But I've put too much into boxing to walk away from it.

Q: When were you first aware that you were gifted as a fighter?

Roy Jones: When I was a little kid. I understood it from the beginning. The first time I ever fought, people were saying, "Man, that guy's just like Sugar Ray Leonard." He was the man then, and they used to call me "Little Sugar." So I knew there was something different about me, because they didn't talk about anyone else on my team like that.

Q: You've said in the past that your boxing style was influenced by a number of ring greats. What did you learn from each of those fighters?

Roy Jones: From Muhammad Ali, I learned confidence and the value of using everything I have to the best of my ability. From Ray Leonard, the ability to entertain and excite a crowd. From Tommy Hearns, the right hand. Sugar Ray Robinson, combinations. Eusebio Pedroza, body punching. Wilfred Benitez, defensive movement; he was a great defensive fighter. Willie Pep, the same thing; he was another great defensive fighter. Salvador Sanchez, feinting, how to keep my opponent on the defensive all the time. Marvin Hagler, consistency and the fact that Hagler was prepared to perform every time he came into the ring.

Q: Who do you think are the great fighters in the world today?

Roy Jones: Me, Oscar DeLaHoya, Pernell Whitaker, Felix Trinidad, Ike Quartey, and Mike Tyson.

Q: Tell me about the Seoul Olympics.

Roy Jones: Well, I won the fight. Everybody knows that. But after I won, I knew they were going to steal it. I saw a bunch of Koreans at the table where they brought the decision. They were smiling and laughing, and I said to myself, "Yeah, they got me." I listened when they announced it just to make sure, but I knew what they'd done. And it was like, you give it your best effort and you win and then someone steals it away from you; why should you even do it. I still think about it, every day. But I try not to think about the bad part. I think about the days leading up to the fight and performing well; the good things.

Q: When were you at your best as a fighter?

Roy Jones: You might not believe this, but I think in some ways I was as good at the Seoul Olympics as I am now. The big difference is, since then I've become more experienced. But all that means is, when I step into the ring today, I use less of what I know. You see, a man can only do so many things each time he steps into the ring, so I focus on what will work for me against a particular opponent. That's economics; supply and demand. I have a supply of skills, but unless a particular skill is demanded for a particular fight, I don't use it. For example, when I was fighting James Toney, I didn't use my jab because he likes to counter the jab. So even though the jab is in my supply room, I left it home that night. If I'd fought Toney when I was an amateur, I'd have used the jab because, when I was an amateur, I rushed out and used everything I had. But now, I just go to my supply room, take out what I need for a particular fight, and bring a couple of extra tools with me in case there's a surprise. It's like, if a doctor is going to operate on your knee, he knows what tools he should have with him to perform that operation. If he's operating on your knee, there's no need for him to bring the tools he uses for open heart surgery.

Q: What are the best weapons in your supply room?

Roy Jones: Speed, power, and combinations. But that's not all there is. My supply room is stacked.

Q: How good are you?

Roy Jones: I'm pretty good. Right now, I'm the best in the world pound-for-pound, but I could be better. I used to be more skillful technically about the way I boxed. I was more careful. When I got hit with a big shot, I'd pull back and say, okay, let me take my time; refocus on what I'm doing; then I'll get you. Now I open up and take more chances. If a guy hits me with a big shot, I don't wait for my chance to get even. I hit him back fast, hoping I can knock him out. And most of the time, I do. Now, if you hit me with a big shot, it's, "Oh yeah? Okay!" BOOM. "Now I got you back."

Q: Which do you think of as your best fights?

Roy Jones: The Toney fight was a good fight. Pazienza and Sosa were good fights. Bernard Hopkins was a good one-handed fight. Against Hopkins, the middle knuckle on my right hand was injured the whole fight.

Q: Tell me some more about those fights.

Roy Jones: All right. The fight that meant the most to me was James Toney, because so many people thought he could beat me. But after a couple of rounds, Toney realized he couldn't outbox me, so he decided to lay back and try to get me with one shot the way he knocked out Michael Nunn. That's all he really tried to do. The fight of mine that was the most crowd-pleasing was against Vinnie Pazienza. And my best performance, although it didn't last long, was against Merqui Sosa. I train game roosters, so I know how it is when a chicken is out there just fighting as opposed to when a chicken is out there really trying to kill. When a game rooster is going for the kill, he bites down hard. Well, Sosa bit down hard on a right hand and tried to take me out with one punch. Almost hit me, too. I said to myself, nice try but it won't happen tonight. He's got to go. Then I took him out. I stood in there and risked taking something to give something, and people had never seen me take chances like that before and fight that type of a fight.

Q: What did you key on in the Toney fight?

Roy Jones: His right hand. And instead of jabbing, I led with my left hook. If you jab at Toney, he's going to counter. But if you lead with a hook, he's got to block that with his right hand and he can't come back at you.

Q: Of all the people you've fought so far, who came the closest to beating you?

Roy Jones: Nobody. I'm the only one who can beat me.

Q: Which fight did you come closest to beating yourself?

Roy Jones: Probably the Lucas fight, because I played basketball that day and didn't do much jogging in training, so I wasn't in the shape I'd normally be in. I wasn't in danger during the fight, but it could have been a dangerous situation.

Q: Do you watch tapes of an opponent before a fight?

Roy Jones: Just enough to see what I need to bring to win the fight.

Q: One of the complaints you've obviously heard is that you're not fighting the best available—

Roy Jones [Interrupting]: Who's the best available? James Toney? I already beat him. Bernard Hopkins? I already beat him. I've offered to fight Virgil Hill over and over, and he doesn't want me. I'll fight anybody. Frankie Liles, Steve Collins. None of them would be a problem.

Q: You've been talking about fighting heavyweights. Is that something you're serious about?

Roy Jones: If I talk about it, I'm serious about it. It's something I'd do for the challenge. But I don't want to fight a big tall heavyweight.

Q: Would you fight Mike Tyson?

Roy Jones: If the money was right. But you have to understand, if I did it, I'd go in there to win. I'm not the kind of guy who says, "If they pay me enough, it's all right if I lose." When I fight, I fight to win.

Q: What would you key on if a Jones-Tyson fight came about?

Roy Jones: First, I'd key on his power, because if Tyson catches me with a big punch, I'm losing out. I'd have to avoid his big punches and make sure I landed all my punches so he couldn't counter. That wouldn't be easy, because Tyson bobs and weaves and he's quick. One area where I'd have an advantage is, I'd work on his footwork; make him chase me, because his footwork is ordinary. If I get past three rounds, Tyson's in trouble. I doubt if I'd knock him out, but if it goes past three rounds, I'd win a decision.

Q: What's your view of Mike Tyson as a person?

Roy Jones: Life is tough for Tyson, because so many things have happened and so much has come out about him that he has a reputation and he has to be very careful. It must be tough being him in the situation he's in now, where people are waiting to attack him. Probably, he doesn't know who he can trust. He has to be afraid of every move he makes. He has to do certain things to keep people from being able to do things to him. It must be hard living that way. I never want my life to be like that, which is one of the reasons I try to stay out of the limelight. When I see trouble coming, I walk away. I haven't been in a fight outside the ring since junior high school. I'm careful about how I deal with women. I try to treat everyone I meet with respect, and hope they treat me the same way.

Q: You mentioned training game roosters, and I know that cockfighting is an interest of yours. Tell me about that.

Roy Jones: The most interesting part to me isn't the fighting. It's taking the time to breed roosters, so you get to where you have an almost perfect bird. That's what I like about raising roosters; the breeding. And I can learn as much about fighting from watching a chicken-fight as I can by watching people box. A chicken can be way ahead and—WAP—one blow and he's dead. Same thing with boxing. That tells me something. As long as you've got the energy to fight, you've got the energy to win. As long as you've got the will to fight, you've got the will to win. Watch the chickens, and you'll learn a lot.

Q: Are you still involved with cockfights?

Roy Jones: I still raise chickens, but I haven't had time to take them to fights for about two years. Taking them to fights means I have to travel, because chicken-fighting is against the law in Florida. It's legal in Louisiana and Oklahoma, but not in Pensacola where I live. And I miss going. There's a lot of good guys who bring chickens to fights, and I miss sitting down and talking with them. Some of the best people I've met, I've met at chicken-fights. They don't have a lot of money, and for most of them, it's the only competitive thing they can afford. I miss being there, watching the guys, seeing the expression on their face, trading roosters with them. To me, that's a beautiful world.

Q: I assume you've had birds killed at fights. What does it feel like when one of your birds is killed?

Roy Jones: Hey, it happens. The head is a hard place to kill a chicken, because their brain is so small. I've seen a chicken take a spike through the head and come on like nothing happened. So usually, it happens through the body, and you can't see it. The feathers cover up the blood. You don't know that anything is wrong until, all of a sudden, your bird is dead. And you say, "Dang!" You hate to lose him. But you understand that this is what those animals want to do. If you don't lock them up, they'll go out in the yard and kill one another anyway, so you might as well get them in shape and let them fight it out. You see, game roosters are a different species, a different breed from the chickens you eat. Game roosters have a desire to kill. All you have to do is feed them, and they'll fight on their own. And if you try to cook them, they're no good to eat. That should tell you something. Besides, if you look at what happens to other chickens; at least fighting chickens have a chance to win. I see truckloads of fried chicken being sold every day. Those chickens live for a few months, and then they get killed. They never have a chance. And nobody complains about what happens to those chickens.

Q: Tell me a bit more about Roy Jones as a person. What's your lifestyle like?

Roy Jones: Laid back, country-like. I travel a lot when I'm playing basketball; but I'm happiest when I'm at home. I've got a three bedroom brick house on eighty-one acres with horses, dogs, chickens, and a fishing pond. No drinking, no smoking, no drugs. I'm a very down-to-earth person. If I can help someone else, I'll try. I can't help every person, but I do my share. The one thing I hate—and I really hate it—is prejudice. I don't like prejudiced people, and I feel like human beings should be able to overcome that. There's good people of all races and bad people of all races. If you say to me, I don't like that person because he acts a certain way; fine. But you've got to understand that not all people of that race act that way.

Q: What kind of prejudice have you experienced?

Roy Jones: I'm from the South. You *know* what kind of prejudice I've experienced.

Q: Do you consider yourself a role model?

Roy Jones: Absolutely. If you're in a place where kids see you and look up to you, you have to accept that responsibility. Because if kids see a person they look up to and that person is doing things that their parents talk about at home, good or bad, kids learn from that. I want parents to be able to say to their children, "Look at Roy Jones, Jr. He doesn't curse. He treats everybody with respect and stays out of trouble. He's a good person. He conducts himself like a champion." The main problem I have with a lot of successful people is attitude. They think they're better than the rest of the world, and they don't treat other people right.

Q: What sort of things make you happy?

Roy Jones: Riding horses, driving my four-wheeler, going fishing and hunting, fighting, watching fights, and playing basketball

Q: How do you feel about martial arts disciplines besides boxing?

Roy Jones: I love watching fights. Kung fu, kick boxing, no-holds-barred fighting, all that stuff. If a fight is good, I enjoy watching it. The same for all those old karate movies on television.

Q: How about women boxers?

Roy Jones: Like I said; if a fight is good, I enjoy watching it.

Q: What sort of things make you sad.

Roy Jones: Funerals; sometimes weddings; and seeing other people hurt and sad.

Q: What sort of things frustrate you and make you angry?

Roy Jones: I get angry when things at Square Ring don't work right. We'll have a little problem here, and that leads to a problem there, and it frustrates me because I don't understand why people can't get along and work together and do things right. And I feel it's my responsibility to lead and keep things straight, so if things aren't going well, it's like I'm not doing my job. So I'll get angry and stay angry until the problem is worked out, but then I'm fine. And it's the same way with family. I've got my mother and father, a brother, three sisters, eight aunts, six uncles, a thousand cousins. And sometimes I see my family doing things, where I feel responsible for them because I can sit back and see things from a different angle. But I can't live for them; they've got their own lives. So even if I think they're doing something wrong, I have to let it alone sometimes.

Q: Tell me some more about Square Ring; its structure and what it does for you.

Roy Jones: Square Ring is a corporation. I own most of the shares. The other shareholders are Stan Levin, Fred Levin, and Alton Merkerson. I've been independent all my life, and I took a chance when I turned professional. I knew I wanted to stay independent, so I put together a team, and we've made the best of it. That's what Square Ring does for me. It keeps me independent. I don't mind doing business with the big promoters, but I don't want to sign up with any promoter for a long period of time. Don King has come down and talked to me a couple of times. Same old, same old. I asked him, "If I sign with you, how long is this contract going to last?" And he told me, "As long as you're champion." I don't want that, so I'm getting by without him. Square Ring does everything that's necessary to get me in the ring at my best and also to handle my business activities outside the ring. And it does the same thing for all of the other fighters it handles [Square Ring's bestknown fighters other than Jones are Al Cole and Derrick Gainer]. There's about twenty-five people who work for Square Ring. Alton Merkerson does the training and runs the gym. Stan and Fred handle the legal work and business negotiations. But I have final say over all the decisions. And because of Square Ring, I've been able to stay pretty much away from the slimy side of boxing. Because of Square Ring and my ability, I've been able to tell people, I'm going to do things my way.

Q: How are Fred and Stan Levin paid?
Roy Jones: Everything works off of percentages.

Q: One of the complaints I'm sure you've heard from the media is that you aren't as attentive to promotional events as some people would like. What's your comment on that?
Roy Jones: I don't have to satisfy the media. I have to satisfy me. The media is cool. I like the media. But my job is to win, and I have to do what's comfortable for me and gets me ready. If I win, the media has something to write about. And you and I both know that, if I lose, the media won't be interested in me.

Q: Why do you think there was so little criticism of Michael Jordan for giving up basketball and trying his hand at baseball, but people are constantly criticizing you for playing basketball?
Roy Jones: Because Michael Jordan had done all he wanted to do in basketball, so people could understand. And it was Michael Jordan, and people know they'll look bad if they talk bad about Michael Jordan. Plus Roy Jones is a boxer, and boxers aren't supposed to do things like that. But my job isn't to satisfy other people. My job is to satisfy Roy Jones. And right now, I like the challenge of basketball, because I feel like I've done everything I want to do with boxing.

Q: How do you compare yourself with some of the other stars like Bo Jackson and Deion Sanders, who've made it big in two sports?
Roy Jones: Well, it's like this. Deion is a superb football player, but he's not the best at one position. And he's a good baseball player, but he's not the best at one position. Bo Jackson was a pretty good football player and a pretty good baseball player, but he wasn't the best at either sport. Right now, Roy Jones is the best boxer there is, but I need to work at my basketball.

Q: You say that, right now, you're the best boxer there is. Who in your opinion, pound-for-pound, is the greatest fighter of all time?

Roy Jones: Number one, Sugar Ray Robinson. And number two—this might surprise you—Salvador Sanchez. Sanchez was from Mexico and he died young [Sanchez was killed in a car crash in 1982 at age 23], so a lot of people don't understand how great he was. But Sanchez had power; he was a great defensive fighter. And most important, the way he moved: he had the ability to control a fight so what his opponent did almost didn't seem to matter. The opponent was always reacting to Sanchez.

Q: Suppose you got into the ring, and standing across from you was Sugar Ray Robinson in his prime. How would you fight him?

Roy Jones: I'd throw body punches, because Sugar Ray Robinson threw body punches. And I'd throw only one or two punches at a time, because Sugar Ray Robinson's best move was to punch between your punches. If you threw punches in numbers, you were doing what he wanted you to do. Throw three or four punches, and he'd hit you between your punches every time.

Q: And against Marvin Hagler?

Roy Jones: Against Hagler, I'd use combinations because, even at his best, Marvin Hagler couldn't stand combinations. He'd try to block all the punches or dodge them instead of punching back in between. Hagler was strong, very durable. So I'd also bring a lot of conditioning and speed. Not much power. Speed, combinations, and conditioning are the three main things I'd bring to deal with Marvin Hagler.

Q: Where do you see your own place in boxing history?

Roy Jones: I don't. I mean, I care in a way, but in a way I don't. I hope people remember me as being one of the greatest fighters of all time. But if they don't, I won't be disappointed. I know what I can do, and that's what's important. I'm good; I know that. And if I think I can beat someone, I'll tell you about it. But I never know for sure until I step into the ring; because God created this world; God is in charge; and the minute God says so, I'm gone.

Boxing is always on the lookout for the next great heavyweight prospect. In recent years, no one has broken away from the field. But hope springs eternal —witness the powers behind Michael Grant.

Michael Grant: Boxing's Renaissance Man

Michael Grant is 25 years old, stands 6-feet-7-inches tall, and weighs 250 pounds. He's articulate, personable, and bright. On the surface, he makes most things look easy, but Michael Grant is a study in contradictions.

Grant turned pro in mid-1994. After his eleventh pro bout, Craig Hamilton (one of his advisors) brought him to Bill Cayton. Cayton and Steve Lott became Grant's co-managers, and his record has blossomed to 25–0 with 18 knockouts. Grant's most recent victory was his most impressive—a tenth-round stoppage of Al Cole that was nationally televised on ESPN. Also, he has sparred seventy rounds with Ray Mercer, and to hear Cayton tell it, "Mercer was fighting to protect his life."

Grant's physical gifts are prodigious. As a high school football star in Chicago, he was an all-city tight end. At Fullerton Junior College in California, he started at power forward for the school basketball team. And he was a good enough pitcher to be granted a tryout by the Kansas City Royals. Some observers call him the best pure athlete to come into boxing in a long time, while others marvel at his strength, speed, power, and coordination. But in the ring, something seems to be holding him back.

Grant's initial problem is that there are times when he isn't sufficiently focussed on boxing. "Michael is a talented athlete in several sports," says Hamilton, stating the obvious. "He's a good piano player. He sings; he has a nice voice. And there are dozens of other things he does well. The difficulty is, he's so good at so many things that sometimes he seems to forget that his chosen profession is boxing." Cayton echoes Hamilton's concern, adding, "Michael has all the courage in the world, but so far, he hasn't shown the requisite fire in the belly. He's so talented in so many different areas. . . ." Cayton's voice trails off before picking up again. "Unfortunately, sometimes I think Michael likes music more than he likes boxing."

Also, because Grant had only twelve amateur bouts, he's a "project" insofar as boxing is concerned. His early pro fights were the equivalent of amateur experience. And so far, his physical skills haven't developed into boxing ability as quickly as some might like, which has led to a certain amount of controversy.

Donald Turner has been Grant's trainer since his first pro bout. Turner is one of the most respected men in boxing. Like most trainers, he has his own ideas about the sweet science. And often, those ideas are at odds with Cayton's, who believes fervently in "the Cus D'Amato method." Turner, for his part, calls Cayton "a good person and probably the best manager I've known in my lifetime." But he also notes, "Bill Cayton was mesmerized by the success he had with Mike Tyson, and he keeps looking for the next Tyson. But you can't take a six-foot-seven inch guy and turn him into Mike Tyson any more than you could take Tyson and turn him into Muhammad Ali. Also," Turner continues, "regardless of what you hear about how Tyson deteriorated before he fought Evander, Tyson always had flaws that an opponent could exploit. He might have been the greatest offensive force in heavyweight history. But if the opponent had courage and knew what he was doing, Tyson was always easy to hit."

Controversy aside, what it comes down to for the moment is

that, too often, Michael Grant looks like an awkward fighter. That's understandable because of his lack of amateur experience. But worse, Grant has been labeled a "boring" fighter. And that label is troublesome, because in boxing, as far as the people who make big-money fights are concerned, the most important consideration is how entertaining a fighter is; not how multifaceted or nice.

Still, Grant has the potential to become a great fighter. Will he realize that potential? Turner thinks he will, that his charge is four or five fights away from being the best heavyweight in the world. Cayton hopes that Turner's assessment is correct, but feels compelled to add, "So far, Michael has done just enough to win. He wants to win and, when he fights against someone who can hurt him, he rises to the occasion. But Michael is at a point now where, very soon, he'll be facing opponents who have better boxing skills than he does. So it will be their boxing skills against his physical gifts, and that's a pretty tough challenge."

And what does Grant think of it all?

"I've been blessed with certain physical gifts," Michael Grant says. "I feel I can do anything that pertains to boxing. But sometimes, I get so caught up in the mechanics of the sport, trying to do things the correct way, that I'm not myself. You see, guys like Ali, Tyson, and Evander started boxing when they were kids. I've been in this game for less than five years, starting when I was twenty. Sooner or later, it will become more natural for me; but no one can put ten years into five, so I've got to be patient. As for people saying I'm not mean enough or not focussed enough, that doesn't bother me. Fighters are motivated by different things. Ali was motivated by his own talk. Tyson was motivated by playing the bully. Evander is motivated by his faith. I still haven't found the source that will work for me to maximize my ability, but I will."

And as for those who think he isn't exciting enough in the ring, Grant's answer is simple: "As long as I do my job and keep win-

In December 1996, I spent a day with a young man named Eric Esch, better known as "Butterbean." Is Butterbean a great fighter? No. Is Butterbean even a good fighter when judged by professional standards? No. But the truth is, he's a very sweet guy.

"Butterbean" Comes To Madison Square Garden

Boxing returned to Madison Square Garden on December 15th. Oscar DeLaHoya knocked out Jesse James Leija. Arturo Gatti decisioned Tracy Harris Patterson. And then there was "Butterbean."

Butterbean a/k/a Eric Esch is 5-feet-10 inches tall and weighs 300 pounds. He looks like Gert Frobe (who played Auric Goldfinger in the third James Bond film), and shaves his head. During the first eleven months of 1995, Butterbean built up a record of 14 wins and 0 losses with 9 knockouts. He also became a cult figure of considerable proportions.

Butterbean's first major TV exposure came in September, when he fought Adam Sutton on the undercard of Oscar DeLaHoya vs. Genaro Hernandez. Sutton knocked Butterbean down when he caught him off balance with a jab in the first round. In round two, he bloodied Butterbean's nose, and the blood flowed freely from then on. Still, Butterbean continued to move inexorably forward, and won a four-round majority decision. Meanwhile, as the fight progressed, there were non-stop fat jokes from TVKO's Jim Lampley and Larry Merchant:

Lampley: These are heavyweights, in case you haven't noticed.

Merchant: He looks like one of those guys on an afternoon talk show who came down from 600 pounds to 315 and is very proud of it.

Lampley: Ah, the sweet science. And Liebling rolls over in his grave.

Merchant: Butterbean may be the first fighter to get a bra commercial.

Lampley: I thought I saw Jenny Craig lurking in Butterbean's corner.

Merchant: Do you think he does roadwork?

Lampley: Roadwork? Do you mean hiring himself out as a grader?

After a while, it got to be a bit much. Of course, the fact that Esch had the name "Butterbean" emblazoned across his ample waistband sort of encouraged the commentary.

So who is Butterbean? And what's he like?

Well, Eric Esch is a likeable, softspoken, 27-year-old, self-described "regular guy, who likes country music and family." He was born in Michigan, but raised in Jasper, Alabama. During his senior year of high school, he married his high school sweetheart. They have three children, ages 2, 7, and 10. After graduation, he took a job on an assembly-line in a factory that manufactured mobile homes. "Then, about eight years ago," Butterbean recalls, "I entered a tough-man contest. I was real big, 429 pounds. I didn't train or anything, just got in the ring and fought. I won my first fight, and it was kind of a high, all those people cheering for me, so I kept at it."

Over the next six years, Esch continued entering tough-man contests, recording 67 wins (40 by knockout) and four losses. "Meanwhile," he remembers, "people kept asking, 'What about turning pro?' And finally, I figured, why not?"

In 1994, after finishing second in an event billed as "The World

Tough-Man Championship," Butterbean decided to take the plunge. In 1995, he moved back to Michigan, and began training under the tutelage of Murray Sutherland. "I think he's doing pretty well," Sutherland said of his charge shortly before Butterbean fought at Madison Square Garden. "He's improving, getting in better shape, and learning how to fight. I'd like to see him come into the ring around 270, but right now, the weight is a big plus from a promotional point of view. If Butterbean comes in at 270, people will think he's just another fat slob. But at 300, he stands out. Butterbean will never be a world class fighter, but I can see him going to 20 and 0, 22 and 1, something like that, and getting a big money fight. That's what I want; to get him into a position where he can make some money."

And Butterbean himself opined, "I think it's going real well. I'm learning and improving all the time. The biggest joy for me in all of this has been the way people take to me. I'm meeting so many people now, and I don't know who most of them are. But I try to be nice to everyone I meet, and most people are nice to me. I know I have limitations as a fighter. What I do now is fifty percent fighting and fifty percent promotion, but I give a hundred percent to both of them. And the fat jokes don't bother me. All they do is give me the opportunity to prove people wrong, and I love proving people wrong, especially when they look down on me."

Of course, it hasn't all been smooth sailing. On September 29th, Butterbean was on ESPN's Top Rank card against 3–6–1 (1 KO) Kenny Meyers from Spartenburg, South Carolina. Lateral movement is a problem for Butterbean; both his and his opponent's. You can't miss him with a jab. Head movement is hard when you don't have a neck. Meyers dominated round one with his jab, bloodied Butterbean's nose in round two, opened a cut over Butterbean's eye in round three, and pummeled him in round four. Butterbean kept coming forward and hurt Meyers occasionally with clubbing blows, but the majority decision for Butterbean was questionable at best. "Kenny Meyers won that fight," commentator Al Bernstein told the national television audience. Even Sutherland later agreed, acknowledging, "It wasn't a good decision. But outside of that one fight, Butterbean has deserved every decision he's gotten."

Four weeks later, Butterbean was back on ESPN; this time against an out-of-shape 273-pound novice named Pat Jackson. It was another victory for Butterbean, whose best punch of the night was a wild right that landed flush on the cheek (unfortunately, it was the referee's cheek) as the ref moved in to separate the fighters at the end of round three. Butterbean's punches are like that; roundhouse blows you'd expect from a toughman contestant. And the truth is, he's at his best when he reverts to his old bar-room-brawl style. The ref was up at the count of seven.

Then it was on to the undercard of Gabriel Ruelas versus Azumah Nelson. Butterbean's opponent was Louis Monaco, who had absolutely no idea how to block a punch. Butterbean rushed across the ring at the opening bell, and decked Monaco with a roundhouse right three seconds into the round. Two more knockdowns followed; the last one leaving Monaco unconscious on the canvas. This time, Bernstein was moved to opine, "Hey, Butterbean's a big guy. If you stand in there and let him crank up his best punch, he's going to hurt you. I'm not saying he's going to beat anybody great, but he's fun to watch."

All of which led to Butterbean's Big Apple debut at Madison Square Garden. The opponent was Mitchell Rose, a carefully chosen Brooklyn resident with a record of 1 win, 6 losses, and 1 knockout. Rose is now 2 and 6 with 2 KOs. There were no knockdowns, but Butterbean got pummeled pretty good. Rose exposed Butterbean's inability to slip a jab. Then he started landing right hands. Referee Joe Santarpia stopped the bout at 48 seconds of the second round. A standing eight-count might have been in order, but it probably wouldn't have made any difference.

After the loss, Butterbean was philosophical. "It happens. I lost. So what I have to do now is learn from the experience." Yes, he was disappointed that his fans might feel let down. No, there was nobody to blame but himself. And then Butterbean did what a class act would do. He walked back into the main arena to watch the rest of the fights, shaking hands, posing for pictures with fans, and smiling through his tears.

Butterbean might never achieve true single-name status like Madonna, Liberace, or Prince. But he fights with dignity and all the intensity he can muster. Butterbean isn't a great fighter, but he is a professional fighter.

Round 3

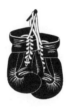

The Fights

George Foreman's comeback to boxing was taken seriously for the first time in January 1990, when he knocked out Gerry Cooney.

George Foreman vs. Gerry Cooney

Gerry Cooney was knocked out at 1:57 of the second round. At what would have been 1:58 of that round, Bob Arum was on the ring apron, praising George Foreman to the skies. "Did you see that!" Arum proclaimed. "He'll knock the shit out of Mike Tyson."

Before one gets too carried away with this hyperbole, it should be remembered that Bob Arum once called Gerrie Coetzee "the greatest white heavyweight" he'd ever seen. (Presumably, Rocky Marciano couldn't have carried Coetzee's jockstrap.) Of course, Arum had promotional ties to Coetzee, as he does now with Foreman. One might also observe that, while Arum has promoted some great fights over the years, he's also given us Muhammad Ali against Antonio Inoki and Evel Knievel versus the Snake River Canyon. Still, the fact remains that, off his performance against Cooney, a large number of people regard George Foreman as a serious challenger for the heavyweight crown; so let's put it all in perspective.

Foreman-Cooney was an entertaining fight; a barroom brawl between two big-name power-punching heavyweights. But in addition to serving as entertainment, boxing is supposed to be a test of skill. And by that standard, Foreman-Cooney was woefully out of place as the first big fight of the nineties. The 1970's could have been Foreman's decade, but for an encounter with Muhammad Ali in Zaire. The 1980's would have belonged to Cooney, if only he'd gotten by Larry Holmes. But both men stumbled, and their time has passed.

"The Geezers at Caesars" was part exciting and part just plain sad. Both men were once quality fighters. Foreman was a true heavyweight champion, demolishing Joe Frazier and Ken Norton in their prime. Cooney took Larry Holmes into the thirteenth round of a competitive fight on a night when Holmes was as good as he ever was. But on January 15th in Atlantic City, one could imagine Ali shouting, "Call it off! I'll whup 'em both at the same time."

Why not? Ali has been out of boxing for eight years, which is two years less than Foreman laid off. And prior to the Foreman bout, Cooney had fought a total of twelve rounds since being knocked out by Holmes in 1982, and won one fight in five years.

Against Foreman, it was Cooney's fight to win or lose. At 41, no matter how powerful and determined George might be, he's too old, too fat, and much too slow. But Cooney hasn't been able to put it together for years. During much of the past decade, he was plagued by alcoholism and persistent rumors of drug abuse. Reports of a "new Cooney" would surface periodically. But the "new" Cooney, like the "new" Nixon, was always a figment of the imagination.

It could have been different. The night Gerry lost to Larry Holmes, Ray Arcel was in Holmes' corner. "When the fight ended," Arcel recalls, "I looked across the ring at Cooney, and right away, I thought of Joe Louis against Max Schmeling the first time around. I thought Gerry had it in him to come back, beat Holmes, and become one of the most popular heavyweight champions of all time."

It never happened. There are no believers in Gerry Cooney as a fighter anymore. And I suppose, for me, the memory of Cooney that will remain is of a moment, not in the ring, but at the Concord Hotel on May 16, 1984. We were in the coffee shop; Cooney, myself, and Cooney's co-manager, Mike Jones. The subject was Gerry's proposed bout against Philip Brown, which CBS wanted to televise in July.

"I want it before June 23rd," Cooney said.

"Gerry, the money's not there," Jones told him. "CBS wants it in July."

"I don't care. I'll take less. They can cut my purse by fifty thousand dollars, but it has to be before June 23rd."

Ultimately, Cooney and Brown fought on September 29th; Gerry's first bout since losing to Holmes. The reason he wanted it before June 23rd was that his ten year high school reunion was on that date. Gerry didn't want to face his high school classmates thinking of himself as a "loser."

That was Gerry Cooney; haunted by his failures far more than he allowed himself to enjoy his success. Now he's been reduced to a promotional prop; a man who gives "credibility" to fighters who knock him out before negotiating to fight Mike Tyson.

When Razor Ruddock and Michael Dokes did battle at Madison Square Garden in 1990, it was my job to report on the featured undercard fight.

James "Bonecrusher" Smith vs. Mike Weaver

First, the kudos. On April 4th, Madison Square Garden put on a great show. For the first time in years, if you were in boxing, the Garden was the place to be. The main event between Razor Ruddock and Michael Dokes was a boxing rarity; a good competitive heavyweight fight. Most of the undercard was exciting. The crowd was enthusiastic.

Now the bad news. On the same card, Mike Weaver and James "Bonecrusher" Smith, as the joke goes, almost got into a fight.

Smith and Weaver are nice men. Once upon a time, they were quality fighters. But Weaver is pushing thirty-eight; Bonecrusher is thirty-five; and both have seen better days in the ring. Weaver has reverted to the form he showed early in his career, when he went six-and-six and was knocked out by Howard Smith, Billy Ryan, and Duane Bobick. Bonecrusher has trouble breathing after three rounds, and weighed in at 247 pounds. They were the opening bout on the pay-per-view segment of the show, and it was a homecoming of sorts; two former champions returning to the scene of past glory. Smith captured the WBA heavyweight championship four years ago in the Garden by knocking out Tim Witherspoon in one round. The main arena was also where Weaver burst upon the scene, losing to Larry Holmes in the twelfth round of a hard-fought battle in 1979. But those days are long gone, and both men have been embarrassingly mediocre in recent bouts. In truth, the match-up figured to be a stinker.

Actually, I had a rather creative solution to the assignment of covering Smith-Weaver for *Boxing Illustrated*. I was planning to score the bout from underneath the ring.

That's right! Under the canvas! Moments before the bout, I planned to crawl beneath the ring with a flashlight, yellow pad, and pen. Then, from that unique vantage point (which would be closer to the action than any other reporter), I intended to score round-by-round, based on what I heard. Cheers, boos, bells, eight-counts, whatever. I figured the first two rounds would belong to Bonecrusher, since he usually comes out strong. But a good judge operates without prejudice or predisposition, so I was prepared to make judgments based strictly on what I heard. And while some nitpickers might have questioned my ability to score reliably from a subterranean view, there's no doubt in my mind that I would have done a better job than Ken Morita (who had Mike Tyson ahead of Buster Douglas after nine rounds in Tokyo), or Masakazu Uchida (who voted for Jose Luis Ramirez over Pernell Whitaker 118–113 in their first championship bout). And to be honest, I kind of liked the idea of being the answer to a trivia question fifty years from now ("Who was the nut who crawled under the ring to score. . . .")

At the last minute, I chickened out. I was afraid the Garden would take away my press credentials. Also, there were a lot of cables underneath the ring, and it occurred to me that I might inadvertently snag my leg and pull the plug on the entire pay-per-view production. So I watched the fight the normal way. And it was awful.

Afterward, Wally Matthews called the bout "a sloppy lumbering stupefying affair." Mike Marley said it was "a pathetic sideshow." Bob Raissman branded it "a dreary slow-motion waltz." They were being polite. It was worse than all that. Weaver went down briefly in the first round, and thereafter simply tried to survive. Bonecrusher ran out of gas in the third round, which was when fans in the know ran out for hot dogs.

What followed was sad—two once-noble warriors who simply don't have it anymore. By round five, the boos were cascading down. One round later, the crowd was chanting, "Boring! Boring!" In round seven, that changed to, "*Very* boring!" Then Bonecrusher began to drool, which he does a lot when he's tired. If the bout had been on network television, a creative producer would have gone to commercials at the two-minute mark of each round and returned a minute later to give viewers a look at the round-card girls.

When it was over, Bonecrusher was awarded a unanimous decision. He made the fight, such as it was, and carried the action to the end. After the bout, Weaver announced his retirement from boxing. Bonecrusher should follow suit; but he won't.

Sugar Ray Leonard has retired and come back more times than anyone cares to remember. But the world knew he was through as a fighter when he lost to Terry Norris at Madison Square Garden on February 9, 1991.

Sugar Ray's Bittersweet End

The downfall of a great fighter is always sad to behold, and Sugar Ray Leonard was a great fighter. Ray Robinson would have beaten him at any weight; but it wouldn't have been a walk in the park. Leonard was a worthy successor to the original Sugar Ray's name.

Leonard fought Wilfred Benitez when Benitez was 39–0–1 and stopped him in the fifteenth round. He fought Thomas Hearns when Hearns was 32–0 and TKO'd Hearns in fourteen. He fought Ayub Kalule when Kalule was 36–0 and knocked out Kalule in nine. He fought Roberto Duran when Duran was 73–1 and forced Duran to plead "no mas." And he fought Marvin Hagler when Hagler was 62–2–2 and flurried his way to a twelve-round decision.

That's five wins against five opponents with a combined record of 242–3–3.

That's greatness.

But like all great fighters, Ray Leonard got old. The relevant numbers for his bout against Terry Norris weren't Ray's career mark of 36–1–1 or Norris' 26–3. They were 34 years 9 months versus 23 years 8 months. Indeed, in the eyes of many, Ray Leonard had long been semi-retired. He'd had 33 fights in his first five years as a professional. But in the nine years leading up to Norris, there had been only five. And in four of those five, the erosion of

Leonard's skills showed. Journeyman Kevin Howard knocked him down before succumbing in round nine. Donny Lalonde decked Ray and hurt him several times. Roberto Duran cut him badly. And Thomas Hearns "dominated to a draw." Only against Marvin Hagler was Leonard's greatness confirmed. No matter how one scored Hagler-Leonard, Sugar Ray shook up the world.

Like Leonard, Madison Square Garden has long had an aura of its own. Although it's no longer "The Mecca of Boxing," it still enjoys a hallowed name. Leonard had never fought before as a professional in the Garden, and good story lines make for good boxing marriages. Hence, Leonard-Norris: a once-great fighter in a great arena against a very good young foe. Give Sugar Ray credit for going in tough. But almost always in that kind of match-up, the good young fighter prevails.

It was a sad night, for Leonard and the Garden. High ticket prices, the fading economy, a mediocre undercard, and Showtime's live TV broadcast contributed to a disappointing turnout of 7,495. Before the bout, Ray talked like a young fighter; but in the ring he was old.

The first six rounds were competitive. The last six were one-sided to a fault. Ray Leonard got beaten up. His face was swollen; he was bleeding from the mouth. By night's end, he looked forty, not three months shy of 35. He fought with courage, but that was all he had. The moves that once made him great weren't there anymore. The trademark flurries that intimidated Hagler were gone. In round two and then again in round seven, Leonard found himself on the canvas; an all too familiar venue lately in his career.

Sugar Ray Robinson might have pulled this one out. At age 36, the original Sugar Ray fought Gene Fullmer for the middleweight championship of the world. Trailing badly in round five, he knocked Fullmer out with a perfect left hook; possibly the best knockout punch ever thrown. But that was a different Sugar Ray. And against Norris, Ray Leonard no longer had what it takes. The best that can be said about Leonard-Norris is that Ray finished his career in Madison Square Garden on his feet; not face down on the Budweiser logo in some casino in Las Vegas or Atlantic City.

The judges' scoring was more one-sided than the fight. Bill Costello got it right at 116–110. Barbara Perez and Sid Rubenstein went overboard at 120–104 and 119–103. After the bout, Leonard announced his retirement. "It took this kind of fight to prove to me that it's no longer my time," he said.

And so Ray Leonard moves on, from an active fighter to the ranks of the immortals. He gave us all a lot of pleasure and bequeathed the world some truly great fights. It was a privilege to watch him in the ring, and one wishes him well in the years ahead.

In the 1980's, big fights occurred only sporadically at Madison Square Garden. Then, in January 1992, MSG reopened what had once been the Felt Forum as a renovated facility known as "The Paramount."

Fight Night At The Paramount

Once, New York City was the capitol of boxing, and Madison Square Garden was its showcase arena. Jess Willard, Jack Dempsey, and Joe Louis defended their heavyweight championships within its walls. Sugar Ray Robinson fought there in his prime, as did Muhammad Ali and Joe Frazier. But in recent decades, MSG boxing has fallen on hard times. For years, because of antitrust concerns stemming from old legal difficulties, Garden officials were unable to sign quality fighters to option contracts. High state and city taxes drove big fights away from New York. Casinos in Las Vegas and Atlantic City began paying huge site fees to lure name fighters. Television networks refused to broadcast fights from the Garden, since doing so often required blacking out the New York metropolitan area. And most important, top Garden management deemphasized the sport. The people in charge didn't care. Boring fights and pathetic mismatches became the rule rather than the exception. In 1985, Madison Square Garden boxing reached its nadir. Rumors of kickbacks from fighters to a Garden official were rampant. Average attendance at the Felt Forum dropped to 737 spectators per card. Many observers questioned whether MSG boxing would survive.

Fortunately, it has. Since January 1986, when Bob Goodman took over as Director of Boxing, there have been three major bouts in the main arena—Camacho-Rosario, Ruddock-Dokes, and

Leonard-Norris. The Garden has developed and maintained pro-motional ties with a number of world-class fighters, including Aaron Davis, Glenwood Brown, and Buddy McGirt. But until recently, one very important element was missing. For two years, as a consequence of major construction renovations, there were no regularly-scheduled fights at Madison Square Garden.

On January 10, 1992, that drought came to an end with MSG Boxing's inaugural fight card at The Paramount. Built on the site of the old Felt Forum, The Paramount is described by Garden offi-cials as "an ultra-modern, state-of-the-art theater." In truth, it was-n't built for boxing. It's more like a concert hall than an arena, and the aisles are too narrow to accommodate the constant crowd movement that accompanies a multi-bout fight card. But on the plus side, The Paramount is clean and comfortable, with nice sight lines from all of its 5,190 seats.

The first bout of the night began at eight o'clock, and ended 37 seconds later when heavyweight Brian Watson knocked out Webster Vinson. It was an ominous start, because the heart of the evening was a TVKO tripleheader that wasn't scheduled to begin until 10:00 P.M. All totalled, the five preliminary bouts consumed a mere 30 minutes and 59 seconds of pugilism, which left consid-erable downtime while the crowd waited for Roy Jones to step into the ring against Jorge Vaca. But once the major bouts began, "Fight Night At The Paramount" was golden.

Jones, who was deprived of his due at the 1988 Olympics by a ludicrous gold-medal-bout decision, was 15–0 as a professional with 15 knockouts. Vaca, a former alphabet-soup champion now campaigning at 157 pounds, was on the card as a measuring stick for Jones. He lasted until 1:45 of the first round, when a picture-perfect left hook put him down. But give Jones credit. Vaca isn't a bum. He was coming off wins over Quincy Taylor and Mark

Breland. And one has the feeling that, in Roy Jones, we are witnessing the emergence of a potential superstar.

The next major bout was the most intriguing matchup of the night. 1984 Olympic gold-medal-winner Frank Tate versus 1988 Olympic gold-medal-winner Andrew Maynard. The #1 IBF light-heavyweight contender against the #1 WBA challenger. Maynard stalked his foe throughout the fight, but Tate generally got off first, controlling the bout with his jab and a right uppercut that landed more often than it should have. Finally, in the eleventh round, Maynard went down from an accumulation of blows, punctuated by a right hand high on the forehead. He rose and then, when the referee beckoned Tate in, decided to return to the canvas, resting on one knee like a kick returner downing a football in the end zone for a touchback. Wrong sport! Several observers later noted that the scene was similar to Maynard's only other professional defeat; a seventh round loss to Bobby Czyz, when many felt he simply quit.

Then came the main event. Darrin "Schoolboy" Van Horn versus Iran Barkley for the IBF super middleweight crown. Or as promoter Dan Duva billed it, "The University of Kentucky versus the University of South Bronx." The South Bronx won. Van Horn, who turned pro at age sixteen, entered the ring with a record of 47 wins and 2 losses. But both of those losses were to Gianfranco Rosi, and one had to wonder how good someone who lost twice to Rosi might be. Also, he was carrying the added burden of a father-trainer-manager, who undoubtedly loves his son and is probably a very nice man, but who insisted upon raising Barkley's level of motivation to greater and greater heights. In the days leading up to the fight, the elder Van Horn repeatedly referred to the challenger as "Iraq," and voiced the view that his son was in for an easy night. Then, just in case Barkley wasn't mad enough, G. L. Van Horn entered the ring wearing a white leisure suit, looking very much like a professional wrestling manager. At that point, whether or not father Van Horn had put his foot in his own mouth was subject to speculation, but Barkley clearly wanted to put his fist in Darrin's. And to compound all his other problems, Van Horn Jr. decided to punch with Barkley from the opening bell, which, despite his college education, wasn't very smart. Perhaps he thought a fast early pace would tire Barkley in the late rounds, but there weren't any late rounds. Referee Arthur Mercante, Jr. stopped the fight when Van Horn went down for the third time at 1:33 of round two.

It was a good night for boxing. Two underdogs—Barkley and Tate—won exciting fights. And if Roy Jones continues to progress, his bout in retrospect might be the most memorable of the lot. But MSG Boxing isn't out of the woods yet. The Garden has yet to demonstrate that it can accommodate champions once they grow to superstar stature. And despite hopes for a spring bout between Julio Cesar Chavez and Buddy McGirt, there's still no natural transition from The Paramount to the main arena. Also, despite having taken place at the Garden, the January 10th fight card was primarily a Main Events - TVKO production.

So what happens next? "Let's take things one step at a time," says Bob Goodman. "First we have to build up The Paramount. Then we'll tackle the main building."

Fair enough! And with that in mind, I suggest the following:

1. *A regular schedule*—At present, boxing at Madison Square Garden is largely a programming tool for MSG Cable. That means, instead of fans knowing they can go to the fights on a predictable basis such as the first Thursday of each month, scheduling is dictated by the Knicks, Rangers, and Yankees. Indeed, MSG Boxing doesn't even enjoy a preferred position with The Paramount. It must compete for dates with Barry

Manilow, Kool and the Gang, and anyone else who wants to rent the theater. Goodman says that The Paramount will have at least one live fight card per month. Looking ahead, the next four dates penciled in are February 18, March 11, April 16, and May 11. But look closer, and that's a Tuesday, a Wednesday, a Thursday, and a Monday. More continuity would lead to more ticket sales and less fan confusion.

2. *A little creativity*—I once spent an hour with Sonny Werblin (then President of Madison Square Garden). *Rocky IV* was opening in a matter of months, and I was trying to convince Werblin to book the premiere with a live undercard in the main arena. Think of it! The event could have been sold like a closed-circuit fight—Rocky Balboa versus The Russian. Twenty thousand fans would have shown up for a gala media event. The Garden could have featured fighters it was grooming on the undercard. And I suspect the main event would have been reported the following morning in every tabloid in the country: "ROCKY KO'S COMMIE!" Werblin wasn't interested. By then, he'd given up on MSG boxing. But comparable opportunities for creative promotion still exist, and one hopes that management will take advantage of them.

3. *Good fights*—In the end, matchmaking is what counts most. People come to the fights to see the fights. In its previous incarnation at the Felt Forum, MSG Boxing featured too many local heroes who triumphed in mismatches and sold tickets to their friends. But as a general rule, when the going got tough, they deflated in competitive fights. Unemployment is very high in boxing. And if a manager doesn't want to put his fighter in tough matches, the Garden should let someone else fight. After all, great fights, not a great facility, make an arena great.

> The present Madison Square Garden opened for business in 1968. Twenty-five years later, to commemorate MSG's "silver anniversary," I catalogued what I judged to be the twelve greatest fight nights at the "new" Madison Square Garden.

Historic Nights At The New Madison Square Garden

There's an important anniversary coming up—the 25th anniversary of the first fight night at the "new" Madison Square Garden. Like most of us who were around for that inaugural event, the Garden isn't so young anymore. But it has aged well over the past quarter-century and developed a tradition of its own. So here's one person's view of boxing's twelve greatest nights at the "new" MSG.

1. *March 8, 1971—Muhammad Ali vs. Joe Frazier*: This wasn't just Madison Square Garden's greatest night. Given the blend of action and social significance, it might have been the greatest fight of all time. Frazier won a unanimous decision. But Ali returned the favor in the same arena on January 28, 1974, when he and "Smoking Joe" went at it a second time.
2. *March 4, 1968—Nino Benvenuti vs. Emile Griffith*: Benvenuti climbed off the canvas to win a decision in the rubber match between two great champions. And in a co-feature, Joe Frazier moved toward title recognition with an 11th round knockout of Buster Mathis for something called "the New York State World Heavyweight Championship."
3. *June 26, 1972—Roberto Duran vs. Ken Buchanan*: Duran savaged Buchanan over thirteen brutal rounds to begin an

unparalleled reign of terror as lightweight champion.

4. *May 24, 1968—Bob Foster vs. Dick Tiger*: Foster struck with sudden fury in the fourth round to capture the light-heavyweight title, which he would hold for six years. For Tiger, it was the only knockout loss of an 81-bout career.

5. *July 21, 1982—Salvador Sanchez vs. Azumah Nelson*: Nelson was a virtual unknown, who had fought all but two of his thirteen bouts in Ghana. Sanchez was a superstar, with victories in nine consecutive featherweight title fights. Sanchez won on a 15th round TKO in what would be his farewell to boxing. Twenty-two days later, he was killed in an automobile accident in Mexico.

6. *February 6, 1970—Joe Frazier vs. Jimmy Ellis*: Jimmy Ellis was Muhammad Ali's sparring partner and friend. Jimmy Ellis was managed and trained by Angelo Dundee. Jimmy Ellis had won the WBA elimination tournament while Ali was in exile. But when Ellis met Frazier in their "title unification" bout, it was no contest. Frazier destroyed him in five rounds.

7. *May 11, 1981—Gerry Cooney vs. Ken Norton*: After 54 seconds, Ken Norton was lying on the canvas, unconscious, his eyes wide open and unfocussed. And Gerry Cooney had become the biggest draw in boxing.

8. *June 16, 1983—Roberto Duran vs. Davey Moore*: Moore was young and undefeated; the WBA junior-middlewight champ. Duran was 32 years old. He'd quit against Sugar Ray Leonard, and begun losing decisions to the likes of Kirkland Laing. Duran was washed up, right? Wrong! He beat Moore as badly as a man can be beaten and knocked him out in the eighth round.

9. *September 29, 1977—Muhammad Ali vs. Earnie Shavers*: Ali had reached the point in his career where he was fighting

from memory and not much more. Shavers was considered the hardest puncher in boxing, with 52 of his 54 wins coming by knockout; twenty in the first round. It was a war, but Ali took the best Shavers had to offer and captured a decision over fifteen rounds.

10. *February 9, 1991—Sugar Ray Leonard vs. Terry Norris:* In the past, Leonard had shown skill and courage. But on this night, more than any other, Sugar Ray showed his heart. Whether or not Terry Norris will become a great fighter remains to be seen. But in going the distance in what one hopes is the last bout of his career, Ray Leonard did nothing to tarnish his own place in boxing history.

11. *June 13, 1986—Hector Camacho vs. Edwin Rosario:* Rosario won the fight. At least, that's what most ringsiders thought. But the judges gave the decision to Camacho, and neither man was the same again.

12. *June 22, 1979—Larry Holmes vs. Mike Weaver:* This was the last major heavyweight championship fight at Madison Square Garden. And Weaver made it tough for Holmes before succumbing in the twelfth round.

There have been other great fighters who did battle at Madison Square Garden. Marvin Hagler, Carlos Monzon, Wilfrid Benitez, Antonio Cervantes, Victor Galindez, Mike McCallum, Wilfredo Gomez, and Alexis Arguello are among those who emerged victorious from Garden title fights. And 1984 Olympians Evander Holyfield, Mark Breland, Pernell Whitaker, and Meldrick Taylor began their respective professional careers on the same card in the Garden on November 15, 1984. But in terms of great fights and historic nights, I'll go with the twelve bouts listed above.

Is there room for argument? Sure! But, hey; that's what boxing is all about.

The small fight clubs died in New York City a long time ago. But one promoter, Ron Scott Stevens, has tried to bring them back in various incarnations, one of which was Powerhouse Enterprises.

What I Wish For Powerhouse Enterprises

Several years ago, I had dinner with Angelo Dundee and asked about his "greatest moment in boxing." Was it Ali-Liston? Leonard- Hearns? The Thrilla-in-Manila?

None of the above.

"My greatest moment in boxing," Dundee reminisced, "was with a club fighter named John Holman. Every time we were together, John would tell me about his dream. He wanted a house with shutters on the windows and a white picket fence around the lawn. One night, John wasn't doing well. He was getting the you-know-what kicked out of him. After the eighth round, I told him, 'You're blowin' it, son. That man on the opposite side of the ring, the one you're fighting, he's taking away your house with the shutters and white picket fence.' John went out and knocked the son-of-a-bitch out in the ninth round."

Dundee's story bears repeating now because a new fight club is opening in New York. Under the guidance of president and match-maker Ron Scott Stevens, Powerhouse Enterprises is inaugurating a monthly fight card at Gleason's Arena in Brooklyn. And hopefully, Powerhouse will be fueled by what boxing is most about; not championship glitz, not made-for-television "name fighters," but good honest competitive bouts.

"The preliminary fighter," Jimmy Cannon once wrote, "works forty hours a week as a gas station attendant. He fights about eight times a year, but he thinks of himself as a fighter and that's how he describes himself when asked his occupation. He trains constantly in the evening at a gym and gets up at six in the morning to do his roadwork. He lives alone in a furnished room, and recently was jilted by a girl who married a salesman with a better income. He has never had a story written about him in a newspaper, never appeared on television in a fight, and never been asked to go on the interview programs. He was never a prospect. He has won as many fights as he has lost. The guys he beats are like him."

But put an honest club fighter in a competitive bout and he'll fight his heart out.

I hope Powerhouse Enterprises succeeds. I really do. And what I wish for it most are competitive fights. I want Gleason's to be a place where someone says, "Let's go to the fights." And if someone else asks, "Who's fighting?" the answer will be, "It doesn't matter; Powerhouse always makes good fights."

Matchmaking is what counts. People come to the fights to see the fights. And if Powerhouse gives us competitive bouts, it will be the best sports buy in New York.

◆　◆　◆

[From the opening bout of one of Ron Scott Stevens's later shows]: The first fight of the night was a guy in white trunks with an 0–3 record against a guy in blue trunks who was 0–1. They were lightweights. And for every second of four rounds, they went at each other with everything they had. The guy in the white trunks won, and the overflow crowd gave both of them a standing ovation.

I like punchers, and I like knockouts. But I don't like to know who will be knocked out before a fight starts. Thank you, Ron Stevens, for bringing back the tradition of "Teddy Brenner fights"—the quaint notion of years ago at Madison Square Garden where, if you wanted to fight for matchmaker Teddy Brenner, you had to "go in tough." The fighters who opened happened to be named Pedro Cotto and Lenny Mars. But that didn't matter. What mattered was they were fighters and this was a fight!

On February 6, 1993, Riddick Bowe defended his heavyweight title for the first time. But Bowe's choice of an opponent and the undercard fights left a lot to be desired.

Bowe-Dokes: The Circus Comes to Madison Square Garden

It's not often that there's a fight card where the star is the arena, but that's what happened recently in Madison Square Garden. Fans paid up to $400 each to see a bout for the heavyweight championship of the world. But what they got instead could have been labeled "Rock Newman's Traveling Rock and Roll Show." The Garden had a record gate. Riddick Bowe rocked. And Michael Dokes looked like he'd eaten too many rolls. But more on that later. Suffice it to say for the moment that, as the fans filed out at evening's end, they could have been forgiven if they'd imagined a voice whispering, "This is embarrassing. That's the same ring where me and Joe Frazier fought. A Bowe ain't nothing. It's the arrow that does the damage, and my jab was like an arrow."

But back to reality. The evening began when Gerard Jones (now 12–0–1) stepped into the ring against Sylvester White (10–18). Why the New York State Athletic Commission would sanction the bout is anyone's guess. Maybe it thought the Bowe–Dokes matchup would look good by comparison. Regardless, fifteen seconds into the fight, White was on the canvas; and 26 seconds after that, it was over. The second bout—Raul Marquez (6–0, 6 KO's) versus Tyrone Heyward (4–10–1)—lasted four times as long as its predecessor; 166 seconds, to be precise. Next, Sean "The Chosen

One" Daughtry lost a four-round decision to Adrian "Handzov" Stone.

Then the heavyweights lumbered in. Ray Mercer and Jesse Ferguson were first on call. Mercer had a late start in boxing. But instead of hurrying to make up for lost time, in recent fights he's come into the ring overweight and under-trained. On this occasion, he tipped the scales at 238 pounds; 23 more than when he won the WBO title from Francesco Damiani in 1991. Ferguson had won only one fight in the past three years. But as the bout unfolded, it became clear that at least Ferguson had come to fight, whereas Mercer expected to win just by showing up. The high point of the contest occurred when Jesse Jackson walked into the arena and took his seat. Soon after, the crowd was chanting, "Jesse! Jesse!" Jackson's chest swelled with pride, and he stood up to wave—at which point the guy behind him tapped the good reverend on the shoulder and pointed toward Jesse Ferguson in the ring. Score a unanimous upset decision for journeyman Jesse Ferguson.

Next on the agenda were Alex Stewart and Wimpy Halstead. Stewart is one of the nicest men in boxing. His problem is, no one can cite the biggest win of his career because, despite compiling a 31–4 record with 31 knockouts, Stewart has never had a big win. In fact, he hasn't even had a medium-sized win, or beaten any fighter who was ranked in the top twenty by any world sanctioning body. Halstead, who hasn't won since 1991, was the quintessential Alex Stewart opponent. If you look up the definition of "shot fighter" in the dictionary, you'll see a picture of Wimpy Halstead. So it wasn't surprising that Stewart wore Halstead down and knocked him out at 1:46 of the seventh round.

Now the stage was set for Riddick "Big Daddy" Bowe versus Michael "Dynamite" Dokes. Bowe, we're told, dreamed long and hard of fighting for the heavyweight championship in Madison

Square Garden. And as "Big Daddy" himself recently said, "I already fulfilled one of my dreams last November when I rode on a float in the Macy's Thanksgiving Day Parade. Now I'm ready to fulfill another." On fight night, Dokes engaged in some serious one-upsmanship by coming into the ring looking like a 244-pound balloon from the same parade. And while the challenger had proclaimed himself "fit as a fiddle," Tubby Tuba seemed to be a more appropriate musical analogy. Anyone who bet low on the "over-under" (which was 485 pounds) lost by two pounds.

The fight itself was short and to the point. The last time Dokes beat a top-ten fighter was 1982. TimeWarner, which has a longterm contract with Bowe, had hoped "Dynamite" would put in a few competitive rounds from memory. But Dokes went against Bowe with nothing at all. Referee Joe Santarpia stopped the mismatch at 2:19 of round one, after which the loser protested that he could have continued. But the last time Dokes fought in Madison Square Garden's main arena, he lay on the canvas unconscious for seven minutes after being knocked out by Razor Ruddock. Santarpia made the right call. And as for the fans who had paid good money—hey, it's not like they weren't forewarned.

One month after Riddick Bowe and Michael Dokes capped a less than inspiring fight card at Madison Square Garden, Pernell Whitaker and Buddy McGirt showed that boxing can be a class act.

Whitaker-McGirt: The Ugly Ducking Turns into a Swan

On November 15, 1984, boxing's brightest stars from the Los Angeles Olympics made their professional debut at Madison Square Garden. They came as a package, carrying the Main Events banner. Mark Breland; the most heralded amateur of his time. Meldrick Taylor; the flashy 17-year-old Olympic gold-medal winner. Evander Holyfield; everyone's longshot candidate for greatness. Tyrell Biggs; the gold medalist in boxing's glamour division. And Pernell Whitaker; the Ugly Duckling of the group. No one knew quite what to make of Whitaker. He had talent. But he weighed in at 132 pounds; not exactly a glamour weight. He was a southpaw, who ran rather than punched. And there was no glowing personality; no Ali charisma or Ray Leonard smile.

Now, eight-and-a-half years later, the Ugly Duckling has turned into a swan. The transformation became complete on March 6th, when Whitaker returned to Madison Square Garden and captured Buddy McGirt's WBC welterweight crown. It was a bout that showcased boxing at its best. No blustering or phony bravado; no grudges or claims of hate. Just two men with great skills and great records squaring off to see who was the better gladiator. The fighters themselves said it best.

McGirt: "If we get ugly and hostile with each other before the fight, it don't make sense."

And Whitaker: "The fans deserve to see great fights; not fights where the champion is a 25–to–1 favorite."

The bout itself was a tactical fight. Both men deserve credit for going in tough; particularly Whitaker, who came into McGirt's home town despite the fact that he could have made HBO money against a lesser foe someplace else. After the fight, McGirt said that his left shoulder had bothered him from the fourth round on. But by now, one has to assume that Buddy McGirt will go into a fight the way Jim Abbott goes into a baseball game—with one arm. And regardless, Whitaker won the first three rounds. What it came down to was, McGirt neutralized Whitaker's speed, but Whitaker was the aggressor for most of the night and landed a few more punches throughout. In the end, the judges agreed on nine of the twelve rounds, scoring those rounds 6 to 3 for Whitaker. That left three rounds in dispute. Dalby Shirley gave all three to Whitaker, making his final tally 117–111. Rudy Ortega (115–114) and Chuck Giampa (115–113) were closer to the mark.

So the question now becomes not, "How good is Pernell Whitaker?" but "Is Pernell Whitaker great?" As an amateur, he won gold medals at the Olympics, the World Championships, and the Pan American Games. He has already reigned as undisputed lightweight champion of the world. And he deserves to be ranked ahead of Crisanto Espana and Maurice Blocker, the current WBA and IBF welterweight titleholders. That means Whitaker can legitimately be joined with Barney Ross, Henry Armstrong, and Roberto Duran as the only men ever to win both the world lightweight and welterweight crowns. Whitaker has fought through pain, including two broken hands suffered in the ring. And his only defeat as a professional came at the whim of two judges who were either incompetent or worse. That loss, a 1988 split-decision defeat at the hands of Jose Ramirez in a WBC title fight, was later avenged. And it's not a stain on Whitaker's record. Rather, it stains the WBC, just as the last-second loss of Whitaker's stablemate, Meldrick Taylor, to Julio Cesar Chavez stains boxing.

Whitaker and Chavez are now scheduled to meet in the ring this autumn. It should be a historic night.

Tim Witherspoon has been around a long time. But as Al Cole found out in January 1996, when they took part in the second of a series of major fight cards at Madison Square Garden, "Terrible Tim" is not to be taken lightly.

Tim Witherspoon Redux

January 12th witnessed the second act of Madison Square Garden's comeback drama. This time, the main event was Roy Jones, Jr. versus Merqui Sosa. And most of the pre-fight stories revolved around whether Jones (who hails from Pensacola) would be adversely affected by the cold weather (as if Sosa grew up in Alaska instead of the Dominican Republic).

Anyway, Jones was great; and Sosa was so-so.

End of fight.

Tim Witherspoon versus Al Cole was a more intriguing drama.

Witherspoon was the best of the heavyweights during that dreary era between Larry Holmes and Mike Tyson. In 1983, with only fifteen fights under his belt, he challenged Holmes for the heavyweight championship and lost a disputed 12-round decision. He rebounded to score championship victories over Greg Page, Tony Tubbs, and Frank Bruno, but two more title-bout losses were thrown into the mix—a decision defeat at the hands of Pinklon Thomas, and a first-round knockout by James "Bonecrusher" Smith at Madison Square Garden.

My own personal memories of Witherspoon date to 1990. SONY was sponsoring a series of events in Indonesia, and invited Muhammad Ali to Jakarta as a guest of honor. I was researching a biography of Ali, and went along for the ride. One of the scheduled events was a fight between Witherspoon and a heavyweight from Kansas named Greg Gorrell. Gorrell had already been knocked out by Wimpy Halstead and Seamus McDonagh, so his prospects for victory were not good.

Ali and I had already boarded the plane in Los Angeles when Witherspoon entered the cabin. For the fun of it, I walked over to Tim, stuck out my hand, and announced, "Hi. I'm Greg Gorrell."

Witherspoon's eyes lit up like it was Christmas. And stifling a laugh, he said in a rather friendly way, "Don't worry; I won't hurt you. It's all about making money. When the fight comes, we'll go out and spar a few rounds. Third round, I'll hit you a shot to the body. You go down, and it'll be over."

"I'm not afraid of you," I countered bravely. (It's easy to be brave when you're planning to watch a fight from the press section).

At which point, Witherspoon's smile turned to a rather intimidating glare. "Is this guy for real?" he asked Ali.

"Before you got on the plane, he called you a nigger," Muhammad said helpfully.

In the end, everything got straightened out. The real Greg Gorrell came on board and Witherspoon seemed satisfied that he was even less formidable than I was. Meanwhile, during our two weeks in Indonesia, I got to know Tim pretty well. He's a nice man. He has genuine compassion for people. And ultimately, it was Tim Witherspoon who had the courage to stand up to Don King in court and, when push came to shove, face King down. That battle took a lot out of Witherspoon. But now, after years of bondage, he's legally, and emotionally, free of King.

It showed in his performance against Al Cole.

Witherspoon-Cole was an honest fight between two honest fighters. Cole's strategy was to tire out his 38-year-old opponent by forcing him to work for three minutes of every round. But Tim was too big and hit too hard for the strategy to succeed. Early on, he took away Cole's jab by jabbing with him and doing it better. Then he began landing power punches; 211 of them over ten rounds. Cole displayed a heavyweight chin, but Witherspoon was the dominant fighter throughout. Two of the judges gave Tim every round; the third judge, nine out of ten.

Prior to the bout, Gil Clancy had opined, "The winner of this fight might not be the best heavyweight in the world, but I'd pick him over any of the three alphabet soup champions."

That statement might have to be amended now, with Mike Tyson's victory over Frank Bruno. But with Tyson honing his skills against mediocre opposition and Riddick Bowe fighting on occasion like a Greg Page clone, on any given night Tim Witherspoon could test the best in the world again.

On May 10, 1996, Madison Square Garden was the site of a heavyweight triple-header. But the most important players were HBO and Madison Square Garden Boxing.

HBO, Madison Square Garden, and the Future of Boxing

The names change. On December 15th, the marquee featured Oscar DeLaHoya, Jesse James Leija, Tracy Harris Patterson, Arturo Gatti, and a walk-on actor known as "Butterbean." On January 12th, the cast included Roy Jones, Jr., Merqui Sosa, Tim Witherspoon, and Al Cole. On March 23rd, it was Gatti again, Wilson Rodriguez, Orlando Canizales, and Junior Jones. But make no mistake about it. The principal actors in the drama unfolding one block from Broadway are HBO and Madison Square Garden Boxing. Act Four of that drama was played out on May 10th, and it was symbolic of the current alignment of forces in boxing.

The first fight ever on HBO was Joe Frazier vs. George Foreman in 1973. That bout was shown live on experimental home systems in Pennsylvania and Florida, and on closed-circuit in theaters throughout the rest of the world. Since then, HBO has become a major player in boxing. It was the most significant media force in the development of Mike Tyson, and one is hard-pressed to think of a great fighter in the past two decades who hasn't appeared on HBO. Indeed, HBO now has Roy Jones, Oscar DeLaHoya, and Pernell Whitaker under contract; pound-for-pound, the three best fighters in the world.

In recent years, HBO has become the most credible of the "alphabet soup" organizations. How out-of-it are the world sanctioning bodies? The IBF ranks Corrie Sanders and Vaughn Bean ahead of Lennox Lewis. The WBC ranks Zeljko Mavrovic ahead of Tim Witherspoon and Michael Moorer. Not to be outdone, the WBO ranks Scott Welch ahead of Witherspoon, Moorer, and Evander Holyfield. The WBA lists Orlin Norris as the third-ranked heavyweight in the world. And that's just the heavyweights. The other divisions are worse. But for true comedy, one should look to the presentations at the WBA's most recent annual awards dinner:

- Promoter of the Year—Don King
- Executive of the Year—Dana Jamison (Vice President of Operations for Don King Productions)
- Manager of the Year—Carl King (son of Don King)
- Comeback of the Year—Mike Tyson (who, as we all know, fights for Don King)
- Trainer of the Year—Aaron Snowell (who happens to be affiliated with Don King)
- Network of the Year—Showtime (the TV home of Don King)
- "Dynamic Duo"—Scott Woodworth (Director of Field Operations for Don King) and Michael Marley (Director of Publicity for Don King)
- All-Time Matchmaker—Al Braverman (Chief Matchmaker for Don King)

Most honest people would be embarrassed by awards like this.

Of course, it shouldn't be forgotten that, like Don King, HBO is in business to make money. After all, these are the folks who gave us Bowe-Ferguson and Bowe-Dokes; not to mention Julio Cesar Chavez vs. Scott Walker. And if Don King walked into Seth Abraham's office with Mike Tyson tomorrow. . . . Well, who knows what evil lurks in the hearts of men?

Still, with the WBA, WBC, IBF, and WBO all vying to become

the WWF of pugilism, HBO is an oasis of honesty and sanity in boxing. It has enough power that it doesn't have to follow other peoples' rules. And at this point, coverage on HBO gives a fighter more credibility than a world title belt.

Madison Square Garden has a glorious history and, when it comes to boxing, a less-than-glorious recent past. However, since it opened in 1968, the "new" Madison Square Garden has witnessed some historic fights. Muhammad Ali, who fought three times in the "old" Garden, graced the present arena on five occasions—against Oscar Bonavena, Floyd Patterson, Earnie Shavers, and Joe Frazier (twice). And MSG, if it so chooses, can still be a major player in boxing. It has (1) the name, (2) the facility, (3) enormous financial backing, (4) its own television network, and (5) the attention of the media. That last point is particularly important because New York is New York and, as Lou BiBella of Time Warner says, "A big event is bigger if it's at Madison Square Garden. New York is a large, sophisticated, jaded city, so it takes more to get New York buzzing than any other place. But if you can get it buzzing, no place buzzes like New York."

New York was buzzing on May 10th for Tim Witherspoon vs. Jorge Gonzalez, Lennox Lewis vs. Ray Mercer, and Evander Holyfield vs. Bobby Czyz. In truth, these were relatively old heavyweights, with an average age of 33-1/2. But by and large, they were quality fighters, and the 17,401 fans in attendance got their money's worth.

At 6-feet-7-inches 250 pounds, Jorge Gonzalez is a menacing figure. No one makes Tim Witherspoon look small, but Gonzalez makes him look normal-sized. Still, Witherspoon is a guy who, in his sixteenth pro fight, stood up to Larry Holmes, so he's not easily intimidated. And Gonzalez, who won eight world amateur championships, still fights like an amateur. He's slow; he carries his left hand too low; he has trouble pulling the trigger; and he takes a good beating, but not a great one.

Witherspoon was the aggressor throughout their fight. Gonzalez landed 44 jabs to Tim's 17, but that was where the Cuban's advantage ended. Both fighters continually loaded up for right hands. Witherspoon's landed; Gonzalez's didn't. Tim won every round; knocked Gonzalez down in the third with a sharp left followed by an overhand right; and KO'd Gonzalez in the fifth with a heavy barrage of punches.

The story-line on Lennox Lewis vs. Ray Mercer was obvious. Two-and-a-half years ago, Mercer lost a multimillion-dollar payday against Riddick Bowe when he was upset by Jesse Ferguson at Madison Square Garden. Now Mercer was returning to the scene of the crime (Oops; no crime, according to the Manhattan jury that found Mercer "not guilty" of offering Ferguson a $100,000 bribe during the fight) in an attempt to deprive Lewis of a title bout against Mike Tyson.

Lewis's credibility comes largely from his 1992 destruction of Razor Ruddock and the fact that, ever since that fight, Riddick Bowe has ducked him. Neither of these credentials is of cosmic proportions. Thus, more intriguing as a lead-in to the Mercer bout was the fact that Lewis had only gone the distance three times in his career; the last time against Tony Tucker in 1993, when Lennox tired in the late rounds en route to winning the WBC crown.

Mercer came out hard at the start, and forced the action for most of the bout. The best round of the fight—and maybe the entire night—was the fourth, when Lewis landed his hardest shots and hurt Mercer, but Mercer fought back. That was when Lennox learned firsthand what everyone in boxing has known for a long time; that Ray Mercer is a tough SOB and very hard to knock out. The fourth round (which all three judges gave to Lewis) and the sixth (which they gave to Mercer), were the only rounds that were scored unanimously during the fight. That presaged the controversial majority decision for Lewis, although the view from here is that the decision was a fair one.

The fact that Evander Holyfield was matched against Bobby Czyz only makes sense if one views the bout as a gift to Holyfield from HBO—a thank you for Evander's long and meritorious service to boxing; and also, an attempt to keep Holyfield away from Showtime and Don King.

Holyfield is a seriously depleted fighter. Coming in against Czyz, he'd lost three of his previous six bouts and hadn't scored a knockout since stopping Bert Cooper in 1991. Still, Czyz had never fought, let alone beaten, a quality heavyweight. His plan was to take Holyfield past the fourth round on the theory that Evander now gets exhausted in the middle of each fight. But Czyz couldn't take David Izegwire past four rounds. And not only is Holyfield bigger and stronger than Czyz, he's also a better boxer.

Holyfield did pretty much what he wanted to do throughout the fight. After getting hit by the likes of George Foreman and Riddick Bowe, getting whacked by Czyz must have seemed like a walk in the park. After the third round, in which Czyz was given a standing eight count, Bobby complained to his corner about a burning sensation in his eyes. Tommy Parks then poured water on Czyz's head. Given Bobby's much-publicized Mensa IQ, one would think he might have told Parks, "No; not my head; my eyes." Regardless, Czyz's eyes kept burning, and Parks's concern for his fighter's well-being led him to stop the fight after five rounds.

As for the future, Tim Witherspoon is clearly the guy that no one near the top wants to fight. "I'm not gonna mess up my life anymore," he told reporters after the fight. No; from now on, Witherspoon plans on messing up other peoples' lives; people with top-ten rankings. At 38, Tim would be competitive with anyone. But the other side of the coin is, Witherspoon has beaten only one top-ten heavyweight in the past ten years, and that was Carl Williams in 1991.

Regarding Lennox Lewis, the Mercer bout tested Lewis's heart in ways that his one-punch loss to Oliver McCall didn't. By the late rounds, Lennox's face looked as though someone had inserted a golf ball beneath his right eye, but he did what he had to do to win. A word of warning, however, is in order. Lewis made Mercer look better than he is. And Mike Tyson can do everything Mercer does, only Tyson does almost everything better.

And then there's Holyfield; a proud warrior, who with every passing fight looks more and more like an aging Matthew Saad Muhammad. Evander should retire, but he won't. And speculation regarding his future includes everything from Holyfield-Tyson to Holyfield-Roy Jones, Jr.

However, more important than the future of any individual fighter is what May 10th meant to the sport and business of boxing. The night showed that there are more than enough players to provide an alternative to chaos and corruption. Main Events is carrying on nicely under Dino Duva. Bob Arum still puts on good fights. And promoters like Cedric Kushner are becoming increasingly important. HBO (along with TVKO) has become the most credible of the alphabet-soup organizations. And Madison Square Garden is Madison Square Garden; an invaluable link between boxing's past and boxing's future. Whatever Atlantic City has, it can never lay claim to Muhammad Ali and Joe Louis. And whatever transpires in the casinos of Las Vegas, they'll never be home to the ghosts of Rocky Marciano and Sugar Ray Robinson.

On July 11, 1996, Riddick Bowe and Andrew Golota met in the ring for the first time. It was an ugly night. Golota pummeled Bowe for most of the bout, but was disqualified for low blows, and a riot followed.

Bowe-Golota In Perspective

First the fight.

Riddick Bowe versus Andrew Golota was as one-sided as the experts thought it would be, except it was Golota who dominated. At 252 pounds, Bowe came in sloppy and out-of-shape; the heaviest of his ring career. By contrast, Golota, at 243 pounds, was focused and physically primed.

Golota is strong, tough, and big. So big, in fact, that when he's backed up against the ropes, it's hard to see what's happening in the ring beyond him. When he gets hit, he does two things. He drops his hands (which is bad) and he fires back (which is good). To say Golota is a rough fighter is putting it politely. His biting and head-butting in past fights are a matter of record. If nothing else, Golota puts to rest the notion that all Eastern European fighters employ a straight-up "amateur style" of boxing.

Still, against Bowe, except for the low blows, Golota fought a smart measured fight. Bowe might have won the second round, but that was it. Make no mistake about it, Riddick Bowe got beaten up. And looking back at the way manager Rock Newman has matched Big Daddy against weak opponents while studiously avoiding tougher foes, one has to wonder if Newman knows something about the limits of his fighter's ability that the rest of us don't. All that saved Bowe from defeat at the hands of Golota was a questionable disqualification at 2:33 of round seven.

The fouling began in round one, when, on several occasions, Bowe held Golota around the waist with his left arm and whacked him on the back of the head with hard rights. He did it twice more in round two, and then Golota went low on him. In round four, Bowe took a blow well below the waist and sank to the canvas. The punch was low, and referee Wayne Kelly's deduction of a point was appropriate. But when Bowe went down, he looked like a man thinking seriously about quitting. In round six, Kelly deducted a second point from Golota under dubious circumstances. The punch in question was near the border, and Bowe was wearing his trunks high. The third deduction, in round seven, was as debatable as the second. The final low blow, like the two that preceded it, was the kind of punch that most fighters fight through. But by that point, Bowe was looking for help. And it was here that Big Daddy went into an act worthy of Laurence Olivier. As fight maven Johnny Bos later noted, "When you get hit in the proverbials, you go into a fetal position, but Bowe lay flat on his back." Regardless, at that point, referee Wayne Kelly stopped the bout. My own view is that Kelly, who's a pretty good referee, overreacted.

The punch-stats told at least part of the story. Golota landed one hundred more punches than Bowe. He outjabbed him 106 to 72, and scored 66 more power punches. But what those numbers don't fully show is that Andrew Golota gave Riddick Bowe the beating of his life. And what Golota has to do now is learn to fight within the rules. He didn't bite Bowe (he didn't have to). But his history of biting and head-butting worked against him in this bout. He has huge potential, and he shouldn't waste it.

As for Bowe; he got off lucky. For much of the night, he fought like a man who didn't want to fight. And each time he was hit low, he acted like a man who didn't want to continue. In 1994, when

Bowe fought Buster Mathis, Jr., Big Daddy whacked Mathis while Buster was on the canvas and was immediately disqualified by referee Arthur Mercante. But that call was overturned and the bout declared "no contest" because, before the foul, Mathis had acted like a man who didn't want to continue. Sound familiar? "No contest" would have been a more equitable ending for Bowe-Golota.

However, July 11, 1996, will be remembered not so much for the fight itself as for what happened afterward. There was a riot. And it came in waves. The first wave hit immediately after the disqualification, when Rock Newman and other members of Bowe's entourage (who were in the press section during the fight) stormed the ring. Bernard Brooks, Sr. struck Golota from behind. Golota turned and confronted his assailant. Several would-be peacemakers held Golota back. And while the fighter was being restrained, Jason Harris (another member of Bowe's entourage) whacked him three times on top of the head with a walkie-talkie, opening an ugly gash. It was an unprovoked assault, with several members of Bowe's entourage looking very much like the thugs who beat Reginald Denny at a street intersection in Los Angeles and the cops who assaulted Rodney King.

Then came the second wave, with partisans of both sides storming the ring from outside of the press section. Bowe's "fans" wanted to join the action. Golota's supporters saw their fighter being beaten by a mob. And because Madison Square Garden's security personnel weren't protecting him, they decided to do the job themselves. At this point, the riot was still limited to the ring and press section. But in the third wave, people in the crowd away from the ring began assaulting each other, and the disturbance became a racially motivated series of black-white confrontations.

The incident began at 10:43 P.M. Eighteen New York City police officers had been assigned to detail outside the Garden, but none were inside the building when the trouble started. MSG's fifty ushers and seventy security personnel were quickly overwhelmed, and five minutes passed before the police were notified. The cops arrived nine minutes later. At its peak, 150 police officers were assigned to the operation. Finally, at 11:19 P.M., the officer in charge of the site declared the disturbance "under control." Fifteen spectators and nine cops were treated for injuries at local hospitals. There were sixteen arrests.

As for who's responsible, there's plenty of blame to go around. The primary culprits were members of Riddick Bowe's entourage. Bowe himself seems like a basically decent person. His biggest vices appear to be undertraining and overeating, but too many of the people around him are thugs. The acted like thugs when they beat up a photographer after Bowe-Holyfield I in 1992. They did it again in 1993, when they employed brutally excessive force to subdue the idiot who parachuted into the ring during Bowe-Holyfield II. And Bowe himself has gone overboard in and out of the ring, suckerpunching Elijah Tillery, Buster Mathis, and Larry Donald.

Inadequate control over the area immediately around the ring—which was the shared domain of Spencer Promotions (Rock Newman's promotional company), Madison Square Garden, and the New York State Athletic Commission—was also a factor. The press section is for the press. That's why it's called the "press section." Properly set up and secured, it serves as a moat to protect against this type of incident. It should be reserved for members of the media, plus a small number of cornermen and working officals of the NYSAC, but that wasn't the case on July 11th. Instead, an inordinate number of Bowe partisans were given credentials and allowed to hover inside the security net by the ring apron. And although their behavior grew more and more raucous as the fight progressed, nothing was done to put a lid on them.

And then there's the New York State Athletic Commission. The NYSAC didn't cause the riot, but it certainly contributed to the climate in which the riot occurred. In recent years, the NYSAC has become a microcosm of governmental incompetence and corruption. Its chairman, Floyd Patterson, was a courageous fighter. But Patterson has serious memory problems, and is no more qualified to head a governmental agency than Mike Katz is to be heavyweight champion of the world. Patterson doesn't run the NYSAC. He's being used as a cover by political operatives, who are filling most commission jobs with people of questionable competence who know next-to-nothing about boxing. It's the cruel cynical exploitation of a man who deserves better. And the result is that no one in power is protecting the fighters and no one in power is protecting the public, because no one at the Commission knows what's going on.

The NYSAC has one referee who doesn't know how to stop a fight when a fighter is in trouble. It has another referee who let a fight continue when most of the lights in the arena went out in the middle of a round. It has as inspector who let a fighter enter the ring and begin a bout while wearing an earring. It has administrative personnel who allow a manager's wife to take extra slices from his fighters' purses in the form of "booking fees." And, oh yes! It also has a lot of loyal Republicans on the public payroll, who are enjoying junkets and cashing checks at taxpayer expense.

On the night of July 11th, 75 credentials were issued to the NYSAC. How many of those people actually worked that night? Didn't commission personnel know about Rock Newman and Lou Duva's reputation for incendiary behavior? As the fight progressed, the people in Bowe's corner grew increasingly unruly. What did Commission officials do about it? The New York State Athletic

Commission is a disaster waiting to happen. And unless there's a complete house-cleaning, things will get worse.

Meanwhile, July 11th isn't a reason to ban boxing. It's a reason to be more responsible in regulating it. One can take heart from Dave Checketts (President of Madison Square Garden), who told reporters the day after the fight, "We will not let the actions of a few despicable people deter us from our commitment to boxing." And one can also take heart from the conduct of fighters themselves.

There were a lot of professional boxers in the crowd at Madison Square Garden on July 11th. Black and white. And none of them were involved in the riot. Instead, they were telling others to "cool it." At one point, when the rioting was at its peak, I came face to face with Shannon Briggs, one of today's better young heavyweights. And what followed was instructive. Shannon suggested that I walk with him to a corridor beneath the stands so I wouldn't get hurt. And when we got there, I suggested he stay put because his size and dreadlocks would make him an obvious target for some nut with a bottle if he returned to the main arena. So we stood together, out of harm's way, and talked about the craziness that was going on around us. And I felt a lot in common with Shannon, who's a different color and comes from a whole different world than I do. I think he felt the same way about me. And both of us were revulsed by the lunatics, black and white, who were screaming racial epithets and commiting mayhem against one another.

In October 1996, Roy Jones, Jr. returned to Madison Square Garden on the same fight card as Ike Quartey. At the start of the night, both fighters were being touted as "great," and both fighters won. But Jones was the bigger winner.

Roy Jones, Jr. and Ike Quartey: Answers and Questions

It's not often that you have two superb fighters in interesting match-ups on the same card. But it happened at Madison Square Garden on October 4th.

First up was Ike Quartey versus Oba Carr for the WBA welterweight title. Quartey came into the bout with a 32–0 record and 28 knockouts, and has looked good enough doing what he's done lately that boxing insiders were calling him "great." Carr stepped in at 39–1 with 25 KO's; his only loss coming on an eighth-round stoppage at the hands of Felix Trinidad.

Quartey is a confident fighter and he was the aggressor for most of the bout, but it wasn't always effective aggression. He was stronger than Carr and hit harder, but Carr's speed gave him some trouble. Despite outlanding his opponent 400 to 261, Quartey looked a bit one-dimensional at times. Also, his left hand gets very low on occasion, and when that happened, Carr hit him with some solid rights.

The judges' scoring varied widely, and wildly, with the majority decision going to Quartey. I gave him the nod by four points. After the bout, Quartey was being touted as a very good fighter instead of a great one.

Then came the main event—Roy Jones, Jr. versus Bryant Brannon for the IBF supermiddleweight crown. Before the fight, Stan Levin (who, with brother Fred, constitutes Jones's managerial team) stood at ringside with his hands perspiring, and acknowledged, "I always get nervous before a fight. My mind says not to worry, but my hands worry."

Not to worry. Against Brannon, Jones was an artist at work, doing everything right from the opening bell. The truth of the matter is that there are very few fighters in the world today who can test him. Over the course of 5 minutes 23 seconds, Jones landed 102 of 168 power punches; knocked Brannon down three times; and when referee Ron Lipton failed to protect Brannon, who was out on his feet, Jones did Lipton's job too. KO 2.

However, more important than the fights themselves was the fact that they plugged into two of boxing's larger dramas. Drama number one concerns the welterweight division, which has become the sport's glamour division. The prospect of a series of unification bouts between Quartey, Oscar DeLaHoya, Pernell Whitaker, and Felix Trinidad now looms. Will they take place? Three of the four are HBO fighters. And if one of them wants out, there's always Kostya Tszyu to fill in the ranks.

What will happen if they meet? Taking the fighters one at a time:

Pernell Whitaker has never lost a professional fight, and has never drawn one either. Both his 1988 "loss" to Jose Ramirez and his 1993 "draw" against Julio Cesar Chavez were WBC-perpetrated frauds. Once upon a time, Whitaker was the best fighter in the world. A young Pernell Whitaker would have given today's top welterweights trouble. Whitaker isn't young anymore.

If Whitaker has slipped, Trinidad isn't quite there yet.

That leaves Quartey and De La Hoya. Those who favor Quartey over DeLaHoya point to the fact that "The Golden Boy" has been knocked down several times. Oscar's supporters note that, after twelve rounds against Carr, Quartey's luster has noticeably dimmed. Both Quartey and DeLaHoya are relentless in their assaults. If they meet soon, the fact that Quartey is a natural 147-pounder and DeLaHoya a natural 140 might spell the difference; but I don't think so. Oscar is filling out. And regardless of when they meet, I'd choose Oscar.

And that leads to the second story-line that continued to unfold at Madison Square Garden on October 4th; the drama of who's the best fighter in the world today. At the start of the evening, the prevailing view was that the pound-for-pound title would belong either to Roy Jones, Jr. or whoever emerges from the welterweight tangle.

Forget it. Pound-for-pound belongs to Roy Jones. Nobody else can fight like Jones does, and nobody else is as good. At times, his bouts look like a Sugar Ray Robinson highlight film. And if Jones's performance against Bryant Brannon is an indication of what the future holds, the gap between him and the rest of the field is widening.

Boxing fans should enjoy Roy Jones, Jr. while they can. He's a fighter for the ages.

On March 21, 1997, Roy Jones, Jr. stepped into the ring against Montell Griffin. Jones was winning the fight and had Griffin in trouble. But just for a moment, he lost his cool, and it cost him his unblemished record.

DSQ 9

On March 13, 1963, a highly-touted young heavyweight named Cassius Clay fought a blue-collar fighter named Doug Jones. The story-line leading up to the bout was all Clay, but the bout itself was more evenly divided. Cassius fought one of the worst fights of his budding career, and Doug Jones fought one of the best. Clay escaped with a narrow decision and, afterward, his trainer, Angelo Dundee, acknowledged, "I found out something. Don't give away quickness to any opponent. I sacrificed quickness, because believe it or not, Doug Jones was a little quicker than Cassius. And it was a mistake."

Montell Griffin isn't as celebrated as Roy Jones, Jr., but he's just as quick. When the two of them did battle for the WBC light-heavyweight crown in Atlantic City on March 21st, it was a tactical fight. And it was a good fight. Going into the ninth round, two of the three judges had Jones slightly ahead, while the third judge favored Griffin by a point. Then, midway through the round, Griffin was stunned by a series of blows. Jones chased him across the ring, and Montell went to one knee to get out of harm's way. "I could have stayed up if I'd wanted to," Griffin admitted later. "I took one knee because I was dizzy."

At that point, referee Tony Perez was nowhere to be found. There are rumors that Perez was watching the fight from a distant corner of the ring, but equally reliable sources report that Elvis Presley was in the casino playing blackjack that night. Regardless, Jones then did what he shouldn't have done. Knowing that Griffin had taken a breather, and knowing Griffin had the habit of crouching low and coming up punching, he whacked Griffin—not once, but twice.

Roy Jones is a clean fighter. There have been no similar incidents in any of his previous bouts. Indeed, in title contests against Vinny Pazienza and Bryant Brannon, Jones backed off when he had his opponent hurt and urged the referee to stop the fight. Nonetheless, on this occasion, he was disqualified.

A number of vexing issues surrounded the end of the bout. Initially, Perez counted Griffin out, which appeared to make Jones the victor. Then Larry Hazzard (Chairman of the New Jersey State Athletic Commission) climbed into the ring, overruled Perez, and declared Griffin the victor by disqualification. Perez now claims he was counting because he "wanted to see if Griffin could get up. If he'd gotten up," the referee explains, "I would have taken one or two points away from Jones and let them continue fighting." Perez also says that he, not Hazzard, made the decision to disqualify Jones. But when a fighter is knocked down by a low blow or a blow after the bell, the referee doesn't count to ten to see if he can beat the count. He waves the knockdown off and gives the fallen fighter five minutes to recover. If Perez saw the foul and thought there was a chance the fight could go on, that would have been the proper procedure to follow. Moreover, despite what anyone says now, it was Hazzard who appeared to make the ruling. The commission chairman was on the ring apron at the count of nine, shaking his head and gesturing "no." If Perez was really counting to ten to see if Griffin could continue, Larry Hazzard had no business being on the ring apron before the bout was over.

Moreover, one of boxing's proudest boasts is that no fighter can call "time out." A boxer in trouble has two options. Either he gets knocked down, or he keeps fighting until the referee tells him to stop. Montell Griffin chose a non-option. He said "no mas for the time being," and administered his own standing eight-count. Prior to the foul, Jones had clearly become the stronger fighter. And even if Griffin had gotten up and survived round nine, Jones would have been leading on the judges' scorecards going into the final three rounds. Keep adding, and you come to the conclusion that "no contest" would have been fairer and more appropriate than a disqualification. Montell Griffin fought a superb fight. But right now he's wearing a belt he doesn't deserve, and won't deserve, unless he wins a rematch.

The problem of fouling has become all too common in boxing, and intentional transgressions should be dealt with firmly. Thus, one can argue that, if Roy Jones's disqualification is truly the beginning of a universally applied hardline, so be it. But there's also a school of thought that Jones's disqualification had little to do with consistently applied principles and a lot to do with the fact that Jones and his management team aren't on particularly good terms with Larry Hazzard and some of the other powers-that-be in boxing.

Jones-Griffin was no different in principle from the 1994 bout between Riddick Bowe and Buster Mathis, Jr. In that bout, Mathis was taking a beating. And like Griffin, Mathis voluntarily went to one knee to avoid further punishment. Bowe then whacked him, and referee Arthur Mercante disqualified Bowe. What happened next? Larry Hazzard overruled Mercante and declared the bout "no contest." Why the difference this time?

Meanwhile, there's irony in the fact that Roy Jones, Jr. first became interested in boxing while watching Muhammad Ali's second fight against Joe Frazier. "I was five years old," Jones remembers, "and the only reason I paid attention was because my father was fascinated by what was going on, and being a kid, I wanted to know what was so fascinating to my father. Watching what Ali did that night made me want to box. Even though I was only five years old, I saw the whole picture right there in front of me. I knew that what Ali was doing was something I could do, if only I could get someone to teach me how to do it."

Ali, of course, won that fight, but there was one particularly controversial moment. In the second round, Muhammad staggered Frazier with a straight right. Joe was in trouble, but just then, the referee mistakenly thought he heard the bell and sent the fighters to their respective corners, giving Frazier precious seconds to recover.

The referee that night was Tony Perez.

> Every now and then, I put my foot in my mouth big-time. My pre-fight appraisal of Evander Holyfield versus Mike Tyson was one such occasion.

Tyson-Holyfield: A Bad Idea Whose Time Has Come

On November 9th, Evander Holyfield will do battle with Mike Tyson in Las Vegas. It's a bad idea whose time has come.

Holyfield is a courageous fighter who makes a hard sport look harder. He was a great light-heavyweight and cruiserweight champion, but his achievements as a heavyweight have been tinged with luck.

Holyfield won the title with a third-round knockout over an undermotivated out-of-shape James "Buster" Douglas. Defenses against three "old fighters"—George Foreman, Bert Cooper, and Larry Holmes—followed. In two of those defenses, Evander was in trouble. Then he ran into Riddick Bowe. Round ten of their November 1992 bout ranks among the most memorable in boxing history. Bowe had the edge in that round, but it was good enough that the judges could have been forgiven if they'd scored it 11–10 instead of 10–9 for Big Daddy. Evander lost that bout, but won the title back from Bowe a year later.

Since then, Holyfield's ring skills and health have been in decline. He lost a decision to Michael Moorer, after which he was diagnosed as having a heart problem. He was being outboxed by Ray Mercer, before the referee interrupted the flow of the bout and Holyfield rallied to win. In his third bout against Bowe, Evander put Big Daddy on the canvas with a left hook, but was so debilitated that he couldn't follow up with punches and got knocked out in the eight round. His debacle against Bobby Czyz followed.

Tyson-Holyfield is a bout that might have made sense five years ago, but makes no sense today. Mike Tyson is a devastatingly powerful fighter. And there are disturbing parallels between Tyson-Holyfield and another bout that Don King promoted in Las Vegas sixteen years ago—Muhammad Ali versus Larry Holmes:

1. Like Ali, Holyfield is an aging ex-champion, who has all the heart in the world and takes too many punches.
2. There's a strong suspicion that something is physically wrong with Holyfield, as there was with Ali.
3. Anyone who knows anything about boxing can see that Holyfield is not the same in the ring as he used to be, as was the case with Ali.
4. Like Ali, Holyfield will be facing a great champion, one who can really hurt him.
5. And the Nevada State Athletic Commission has told us, "Don't worry about Evander. The Mayo Clinic has given him a clean bill of health."

It's Holyfield's "clean bill of health" from the Mayo Clinic that's the most obscene part of this fight. Prior to Ali-Holmes, Muhammad Ali wasn't talking right; he wasn't moving right. There were serious concerns regarding his health. So before the Nevada State Athletic Commission licensed the bout, Ali checked into the Mayo Clinic, after which the clinic forwarded its report to the Nevada Commission. On the basis of that report, Ali was granted a license to fight.

That raised a lot of eyebrows. As Ferdie Pacheco later said, "Just because a man can pass a physical examination doesn't mean he should be fighting in a prize ring. That shouldn't be a hard concept to grasp. Most trainers can tell you better than any neurologist in the world when a fighter is shot." But of equal significance was the fact that the Nevada State Athletic Commission refused all requests from the media to release the Mayo Clinic's report.

Years later, when I was researching *Muhammad Ali: His Life And Times*, I found out why. Muhammad gave me a letter that allowed me to obtain all of his medical records. I got a copy of the report directly from the Mayo Clinic. Among its finding were: "Ali does not quite hop with the agility that one might anticipate. On finger to nose testing, there is a slight degree of missing the target. . . . A CT scan of the head was performed, and showed a congenital variation in the form of a small cavum septum pellucidum [a hole in the membrane separating the ventricles that can be enlarged by concussive blows to the head]. . . . There is evidence of some difficulty with his speech and memory."

Sixteen years ago, the Nevada State Athletic Commission failed to do its job properly. Lured by Don King's siren call of millions upon millions of dollars for Nevada's gaming industry, it ignored its statutory obligation to protect Muhammad Ali. The result of that misfeasance is now on display for all the world to see. Now it appears as though the Nevada authorities intend once again to neglect their most important responsibility—the physical well-being of the fighter. There's simply too much money involved for it to be otherwise.

Evander Holyfield believes that God has cured him. But one of boxing's axioms is that fighters who rely on The Almighty in the ring have a pretty dismal record. Holyfield versus Tyson will be an ugly spectacle that can only result in physical damage to a decent honorable man. The public and the media should boycott it. Enough said!

Evander Holyfield's upset of Mike Tyson was one of those great moments in sports that it's a privilege to write about.

Holyfield-Tyson: What It Means

It ended the way most people thought it would—with Evander Holyfield sitting on a stool; a doctor at his side and his wife crying. Except the doctor was his wife. Her tears were tears of joy. And a lot of people who thought that Tyson-Holyfield shouldn't be allowed to happen (including yours truly) were exceedingly happy to have been wrong.

The fight was billed as a confrontation between Good and Evil, with the deck stacked in Evil's favor. Showtime was promoting the bout under the banner "Finally," but phrases like "Fatally," and "The Execution" were being bandied about. Holyfield was considered damaged goods; a 34-year-old fighter whose time had passed. Too many beatings had taken their toll. His stamina was questionable; he got hit too much; and there was no way he could take Tyson's punch.

But Evander Holyfield was propelled by a religious fervor. Like Muhammad Ali before him, he found something larger than himself to flow into and elevate his performance. And against Tyson, Holyfield was magnificent.

Holyfield always comes into his fights in shape, but this time he was in fighting shape. He has always taken a good punch; and when Tyson's landed, he survived. He has always been an aggressive fighter—just as aggressive as Tyson—and because he never took a round off, Tyson couldn't either. Plus Holyfield had more speed, skill, and courage than any man Tyson had faced before. As the fight wore on, it became clear that Tyson had little in the way of a fight plan and virtually no help from his corner. And just as important, once Tyson's attempts at intimidation failed, the intimidator became the intimidated.

Give Tyson credit. A brutal body shot in round five took Holyfield out of the fight for a round. And credit Tyson for staying on his feet, except for a flash knockdown in round six. Holyfield whacked Iron Mike with eleven solid shots to the head in the last 22 seconds of round ten, and nine more at the start of round eleven. The hurt that Evander lay on Mike was "vintage Tyson." He beat Tyson up, but Tyson wouldn't go down. Thus, it was left to Mitch Halpern, who did an outstanding job of refereeing the bout, to stop the action at 37 seconds of the eleventh round.

An hour after the bout, Tyson was still dazed. But he was gracious in defeat; more so than he had ever been in victory. In defeat, perhaps for the first time, Mike carried himself like a champion. Meanwhile, the time has come to reevaluate Evander Holyfield's place in history; and that of Mike Tyson.

Whatever Tyson's merits as a fighter—and they're considerable—it's now clear that his ring mystique has outpaced his growth as a boxer. Once, Tyson's name was mentioned with Muhammad Ali, Jack Johnson, and Joe Louis as men who defined their era. Now he must battle in the years ahead simply to be included on the next plateau with warriors like Jack Dempsey, Gene Tunney, Rocky Marciano, Sonny Liston, Joe Frazier, George Foreman, and Larry Holmes. Holyfield, too, will be a contender for acceptance on that level. And ironically, whether or not he achieves it will depend in part on Tyson. If Tyson flourishes in the years ahead, then Holyfield's reputation will grow with it. But regardless of his final ranking as a fighter, Holyfield's place in history is secure.

Boxing is not a gentleman's business. But every now and then, someone comes along and enobles the sport in a way that elevates it above all others. Joe Louis did it against Max Schmeling. Muhammad Ali did it against George Foreman. And Evander Holyfield did it against Mike Tyson. Treasure the memory of November 9, 1996. Great action, between two great fighters, in a bout that transcends boxing, equals a great fight. And Evander Holyfield versus Mike Tyson was a great fight; a glorious night for boxing.

> Larry Holmes was once a great fighter with enormous heart, a deadly righthand, and the most punishing jab in boxing. His time is now long gone, but Larry continues to do what he has done for the past twenty-five years.

I Saw Larry Holmes Fight

The truth is, I've always liked Larry Holmes. We met for the first time in 1984, at a press conference to announce his upcoming title bout against James "Bonecrusher" Smith. I was just getting involved with boxing. When the press conference was over, we chatted briefly and I felt a fan's excitement at being in his presence.

Six years later, I was part of the boxing establishment. And after hearing Larry sing in Indonesia, I had these temerity to write a music review entitled "Larry Holmes in Concert." My critique of Larry's vocal ability was less than complimentary, which didn't exactly endear me to Larry. For the better part of a year, he refused to speak to me. Then he decided he would say hello but not shake hands. But beneath his gruff exterior, Larry Holmes is a softie at heart. Sooner or later, he forgives everyone. He's forgiven Don King a dozen times, and I'm not as bad as Don King. So eventually, Larry forgave me. The past few years, he's been downright friendly.

All of that history was very much on my mind when I saw Holmes at Madison Square Garden on July 29th. This time, our interaction wasn't social. I was going to watch Larry fight. I'd seen fifteen heavyweight champions in the ring at various times in their respective careers. I saw Ali and Frazier do battle against each other twice. I watched Buster Douglas, Evander Holyfield, and

Floyd Patterson when they were at less than their best, witnessed
Mike Tyson when he was young, and contemplated Riddick Bowe
at his peak. And I've seen a host of alphabet-soup champions—
Lennox Lewis, Tim Witherspoon, Ken Norton, Bonecrusher Smith,
Michael Dokes, Pinklon Thomas, Tony Tubbs, and Mike Weaver.
But through it all, I'd never seen Larry Holmes in the ring and I
wanted to experience that magic.

When Holmes was young, he was a great fighter. He's not anymore. His opponent was Maurice Harris who, to paraphrase, could-
n't have carried Larry's jockstrap ten years ago. Harris has some
skills but, prior to July 29th, he had won only 9 of 19 fights and
been knocked out by the likes of Scott Lopeck, John Andrade, Dale
Brown, and Gerald Nobles.

It wasn't a very good fight. Holmes came into the ring at a
career-high 248 pounds. Age has taken a toll on his reflexes, and
whatever drama there was came not from the action but from the
fact that we were watching Larry Holmes.

In the first round, Harris appeared in awe of his opponent and
showed him too much respect. Then he caught on to the fact that
Larry is a shell of his former self and swept rounds two through
four. Round five was Harris's best. He started letting his punches
go inside, instead of tieing up Larry when they got in close. Also,
he started landing righthands, including one that shook Holmes at
the bell. Then Harris got respectful again and Larry sucked it up,
winning rounds six through eight by default. In boxing, ineffective
aggression is better than no aggression at all. Harris came on strong
at the end. The saddest thing about it all was that Harris actually
outjabbed Holmes. That's like a house painter doing ceilings better than Michelangelo.

Outside of the Holmes entourage, only a handful of people in
attendance at The Garden thought Larry won the fight. Unfortunately,

two of those people were judges assigned to the bout by the New York State Athletic Commission. Thus, Holmes was awarded a split decision, even though Harris deserved a unanimous one. In the cosmic scheme of things, that makes up for Holmes-Spinks II when Larry got jobbed, although I suspect Harris feels differently about the matter.

Meanwhile, I don't regret going to the fight. Larry Holmes is old and Larry Holmes is fat, but he's still Larry Holmes. The people who heard Frank Sinatra sing when he was seventy years old knew he wasn't "the real Sinatra" anymore, but he was still Frank Sinatra. And for the rest of my life I can say to myself, "Hey; I saw Larry Holmes fight."

> Larry Holmes over Maurice Harris was a bad decision. Shannon Briggs over George Foreman had all the earmarks of a corrupt one.

Fix ?

On November 22, 1997, 48-year-old George Foreman and 25-year-old Shannon Briggs did battle for what was loosely referred to as the linear heavyweight championship of the world.

Foreman's credentials are self-explanatory. Explaining Briggs is a bit more complicated.

Shannon is articulate, personable, and bright. He's intellectually curious, surfs the internet, and is interested, among other things, in family genealogy. Indeed, he can trace his roots back to his great-great-great-grandparents, who were slaves in Virginia before the Civil War. While much of his adolescence was spent in relative comfort, there was a time when he was forced to deal with a drug-addicted mother and a stint of homelessness on the streets of New York.

Once upon a time, Briggs was touted as a rising star. He was an amateur champion and a top prospect for the 1992 United States Olympic boxing team until a hand injury took him out of the Olympic trials. His manager Marc Roberts has invested a reported $1.4 million in his career and done a good job of positioning him on the way to a 29-1 record with 24 knockouts. But the fact that Foreman was willing to fight him was testament to the disappointing nature of Shannon's progress. There were a lot of questions about him. The mediocre level of his opponents; his refusal to fight Joe Hipp on *Boxing After Dark*; and the big question mark—Briggs's third-round knockout loss at the hands of Darroll Wilson in

1996 when, in the words of HBO's Jim Lampley, Shannon folded
like an accordian." After the loss, the word was, Shannon Briggs
doesn't take a very good punch, and he doesn't want to." Briggs said
the loss to Wilson was due to an attack of asthma in the ring.
Briggs's trainer at the time, Teddy Atlas, said that Shannon had quit.

"I think Shannon has talent," Atlas said recently." And I worked
very hard to give him a foundation, so he'd have the boxing
mechanics and mental strength necessary to face an opponent in
the ring. But Shannon was always more interested in finding the
easy way to do things. Physically, he worked hard, but mentally it
was all a big con with him. He was great at shmoozing investors
with Marc Roberts. You can con investors. But sooner or later in
boxing, you meet an opponent who you can't con in the ring, like
Darroll Wilson. I never said Shannon didn't have asthma. What I
said was, Shannon didn't have an asthma attack that night. But a
weak mind and panic can bring on a lot of things. I tried to help
Shannon become a real fighter. Not a phoney; a real fighter. And
the sad thing is, Shannon could have done all the stuff he wanted
to do outside the ring and still become a fighter. I feel very betrayed
by him."

After Atlas made his comments, Briggs responded, saying,
"Teddy played an important role in my development as a boxer and
as a person. I had a lot of love for Teddy and a lot of respect for
Teddy, and some of the things he said hurt me a lot. You know
what I'm talking about. That I quit against Darroll Wilson; that I
lack character. If you look at the other side of things, I wasn't
always happy with Teddy. Teddy talks a lot about character and
discipline, but he isn't always as disciplined as he should be. If I
did some of the things Teddy has done, if I'd gotten into some of
the fights outside the ring that Teddy has gotten into, he would have
been on me like a ton of bricks and I would have deserved it.

There were lots of times when I thought Teddy was wrong about something. There were lots of times when I felt Teddy was much too into controlling other people and not enough into controlling himself. But whatever problems I had with Teddy, I didn't go public with them. And he did. He said a lot of very negative things about me to the media, and I felt betrayed. It hurt a lot; and it hurt more because he walked out on me after a loss when I was down. Teddy is still part of my thinking. I got some very good things from him, and you don't just break up with someone and forget about them completely. But I have to admit, I'm still bitter about some of the things Teddy said about me."

No one other than Shannon Briggs knows what truly went on in his mind against Darroll Wilson. But everyone knew that Briggs had been handpicked by Foreman, because George felt he could break Shannon's will. If a fighter quits in the ring, one of two things happens afterward: either quitting becomes part of his personality, like a circuit-breaker that trips whenever he's in trouble; or he hates having quit so much that he vows he will never quit again. And that led to three very interesting questions:

(1) Were Briggs's physical skills so superior to Foreman's at this point in their respective careers that Briggs's will would never be tested?

(2) If Foreman tested Briggs's will, would Shannon quit?

(3) If Briggs got Foreman in trouble, would he go for the win or would he lie back content to survive and let the win slip away?

In sum, while the promotion was about Foreman, the crucial questions regarding the fight revolved around Briggs.

"I'm not looking for a knockout," Shannon said hours before the opening bell. If it happens, fine; but my mind isn't set on it. I envision using my jab, using my legs, fighting within my boundaries. If it turns into a test of brute strength, I'm in trouble, but that's not what the fight will be about. People say that George handpicked me as his opponent. But what they lose sight of is, I picked George too." Then Briggs turned pensive. When George goes into the ring, he believes God is behind him, and that gives him strength. I have a different view of religion. I don't think God takes sides in sports contests. This is the biggest fight of my life, and I feel like it's all on me."

At 9:00 p.m. on the night of the fight, there were sixteen people in Briggs's dressing room. An hour later, the number had dwindled to ten. By the time Shannon made his way to the ring, the following was down to his three corner men. Then, finally, he stood alone with George Foreman. He'd watched Foreman on television, but had never seen him fight in person. After their press conference announcing the fight, he'd expressed surprise that George wasn't as big as he'd thought. Now he saw Foreman up close and personal; a massive presence who'd had 32 professional fights before Shannon was even born. And while George no longer enjoys the physical gifts he once possessed, he's far stronger mentally than when he was young.

As for the fight, Foreman moved purposefully and inexorably forward for twelve rounds. Shannon retreated as George advanced whether Foreman was punching or not, which allowed George to rest when he wanted to. There was no trademark Shannon Briggs "swarm." Briggs rarely threw his right hand with conviction. His jab was mostly a stay-away-from-me jab rather than a potent offensive weapon.

In round three, Shannon found himself on the receiving end of some punishment and it looked for a moment as though he might go down. In round eight, Foreman landed a series of sledgehammer blows, but again Briggs survived. Still, time was running out, and it appeared to virtually every onlooker that Shannon never did what he had to do to win the fight.

Then came the decision. When Steve Weisfeld's 114-114 score was announced, there was amazement at ringside. What fight had he been watching? Next, ring announcer Michael Buffer read the scores of Calvin Claxton and Lawrence Layton [116-112 and 117-113 respectively], and it appeared that sanity had been restored until Buffer intoned the words . . . "For the *new* . . ."

The decision was inexplicable by any honest measure. Foreman dominated the fight. He outboxed Briggs. He out-punched Briggs. He landed 284 punches to Briggs's 223, and his were the harder blows. Those looking for a clue as to the scoring might take note of the fact that, subsequent to raising millions of dollars through a 1996 offering of Worldwide Entertainment & Sports stock, Marc Roberts has been involved with two major fights in New Jersey. Foreman-Briggs was the second of those fights. The first was the December 14, 1996, bout between Tim Witherspoon and Ray Mercer [another WWES fighter]. That bout resulted in an absurdly lopsided decision for Mercer, and the most lopsided scorecard was turned in by Calvin Claxton.

Larry Hazzard (Chairman of the New Jersey State Athletic Commission) and several of his judges have a lot of questions to answer. Hopefully, those questions will be posed by law enforce-ment authorities in front of a grand jury.

Meanwhile, the Foreman camp was gracious in defeat. "He's a good kid," George said of Shannon after the fight. "He just lost his mother. He stayed in there with me. I wish him well." And Roy Foreman added, "Shannon Briggs is a nice young man. The deci-sion wasn't his fault. Shannon didn't score the fight."

Briggs, for his part, was equally gracious. "I was lucky," he conceded in his dressing room shortly after the bout. "The judges were nice to me."

Round 4

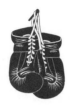

Non-Combatants

When I began researching *The Black Lights* in autumn 1983, the first person I interviewed was Jim Jacobs. His death was a source of great sadness to me, as it was to virtually everyone who knew him.

Jim Jacobs—An Appreciation

Eight weeks before he died, Jim Jacobs called me to say goodbye. Not in those words, but the message was clear.

"I want to apologize for not getting together lately," he told me. "I've been very sick. Please don't be angry with me."

For Jim to say he'd been very sick was out of the ordinary. I'd known since 1984 that he was suffering from leukemia, but we'd never discussed it. Silence was his way. Obviously, I wasn't angry, but I wasn't sure what to say either; whether to press for details I already knew or feign ignorance. Finally, so as not to seem uncaring, I asked what was wrong, and he answered, "It's not important. But I want you to know, you're a very special person. Your friendship is very important to me."

That moment, I realized I might never see Jim again. I did, once more. And then he died. Now I find myself recalling the words of Mark Twain, who once wrote, "Grief can take care of itself, but to get the full value of a joy, you must have somebody to divide it with."

Jim Jacobs was a joy. And he battled leukemia so successfully for so long that the people who loved him were able to lose sight of the harsh reality that all champions, no matter how great, grow old and die in the end. Still, he led an extraordinary life before passing away on March 13, 1988.

Jim and Bill Cayton were best known as the co-managers of

Mike Tyson. However, there's irony in the fact that two men so accomplished in their own right should be known by the feats of a protégé barely old enough to buy a drink at the present time. For long before Tyson came on the scene, Jim Jacobs was recognized as the greatest handball player of all time. He was a world-class skeet shooter and good enough in basketball to be invited to the Olympic trials. Former all-pro quarterback Bob Waterfield called him "the greatest athlete I've ever seen." And working with Cayton, Jim helped amass the greatest fight film collection of all time.

More important, however, Jim cared about his friends and the people he worked with. And he felt a special obligation to the fighters he managed. I remember sitting in on a conversation between Jim and Edwin Rosario in a hotel room in San Juan, Puerto Rico. Rosario had successfully defended his WBC lightweight championship against Roberto Elizondo the night before. Now, through an interpreter, they were discussing the fight, when Jim's voice took on an urgent tone. "There's something I want to tell you," he said. "And this is very important. No matter how long I live, this is the most important thing I'll ever say to you, so I want you to listen very carefully to me." Jim then proceeded to list every world champion born in Puerto Rico and to detail the financial woes that had fallen on most of them. He explained the financial facts of life in a way that Edwin could understand, and concluded by saying, "I'm very proud of what you've accomplished in boxing, and I'm sure you'll accomplish much more before your career is done. But what would make me proudest of all is if, for all your life after boxing, you are a wealthy man."

Jim had detractors, most of whom bring to mind Mark Twain's axiom, "Few things in life are harder to put up with than the annoyance of a good example." But those who knew him best agree that he was a loving person and superb friend. He was compassionate, intellectually alive, and the consummate sportsman. The people he touched will bear his imprint forever and remember him warmly, even his flaws.

And here it must be acknowledged that, as a fight prognosticator, Jim clearly was fallible. "Davey Moore will beat Roberto Duran," he announced confidently before their 1983 bout at Madison Square Garden. "I wish I was as sure of going to heaven as I'm sure Davey Moore will beat Roberto Duran."

Despite that prediction, Jim is assuredly now in heaven. Most likely, he's been watching fight films of David versus Goliath, marvelling at David's footwork and hand-speed. And if ever there's a celestial battle between the forces of good and evil, Jim Jacobs will be a ranking officer in the Army of the Lord.

The ripples from his life could cross an ocean.

Jim Jacobs had died and Mike Tyson had filed suit against his manager, Bill Cayton, when I authored this profile for the Mike Tyson versus Carl Williams fight program.

Bill Cayton: Tyson's Manager

It's no secret; not anymore. As the 1960's song says, "There's Trouble in Paradise." Mike Tyson and his manager, Bill Cayton, are at odds. Hopefully, someday, the war will be resolved. But in the meantime, it's worth taking a look at Bill Cayton.

William D'Arcy Cayton has been involved with boxing since the 1940's, when he began packaging fight films for television. In 1961, he hired Jim Jacobs to assist in building his film empire. Later, they co-managed Wilfred Benitez and Edwin Rosario to boxing stardom. Then came Mike Tyson.

No fighter has ever had better management than "Iron Mike." Most managers are content simply to book bouts with one promoter and send out press releases on behalf of their fighters. Cayton and Jacobs managed Tyson in the truest sense of the word. They arranged for him to fight on network television, cable-TV, even on ABC's 1986 Statue of Liberty Centennial Extravaganza. At Cayton's suggestion, after each Tyson fight, "knockout highlight" cassettes were sent to hundreds of sportswriters and television stations nationwide. The Mike Tyson image was carefully nurtured. People the world over learned the heartwarming saga of *Cus and the Kid*. Soon, corporate sponsors like Kodak, Nintendo, Pepsi Cola, and Toyota were clamoring to get on board. Before

Tyson ever became heavyweight champion, shrewd marketing had made him a media star. No fighter in history ever made so much money so fast. And all this was accomplished without benefit of an Olympic gold medal or a Sugar Ray Leonard personality to sell.

Lately, though, the issue has become "character." While acknowledging Cayton's ability and the success of his efforts, some have questioned his integrity and motives. Money and greed do strange things to people. Often, they lead to outrageous acts and equally outrageous charges.

But the view from here is that Bill Cayton is on safe ground. If the battle turns on character, he has it won. He's not flashy. He doesn't have a swashbuckling lifestyle replete with myriad women and expensive cars. He's constant; he's loyal; and despite everything that has happened, he has never stopped trying to effectively manage Mike Tyson's career.

That's not surprising, though. Cayton has always been someone to count on. He and Jim Jacobs worked together until death did them part. He's been married to the same woman for forty-six years. Whatever else his critics might say, he has never broken a promise or gone back on his word. People talk about Mike Tyson being able to trace his lineage to Muhammad Ali, Joe Louis, Jack Dempsey, and Jack Johnson. And it's true; he can. But Bill Cayton has blue blood too. His brethren are people like Jim Jacobs, Mickey Duff, Jack Blackburn, and Cus D'Amato.

Champions are remembered not by fights that are easy but by the bouts that are hard. I hope Bill Cayton wins this one.

Don King might have hair that stands straight up, but promoter Butch Lewis has been known to cause people to pull their hair out. After Michael Spinks beat Larry Holmes for the IBF heavyweight crown, Lewis pulled Spinks out of a two-million-dollar fight with Mike Tyson, got Spinks stripped of his title, and then put together a deal to pay Spinks $13.5 million to fight Tyson.

Butch Lewis: The Sting

Ronald "Butch" Lewis is on a roll. Operating out of Butch Lewis Productions at 250 West 57th Street in Manhattan, he has taken to wearing silk shirts and diamond rings that would do Don King proud. Lewis is a promoter. Most of his clients (fighters and rock singers) are unknown. Still, he's walking around with a roll of hundred dollar bills that would choke a horse and a reputation that makes Al Davis look like a choirboy. That's because Lewis, who has held promotional rights to Michael Spinks since the fighter turned pro, has pulled off the sports "sting" of the year.

Lewis was born in Woodbury, New Jersey, raised by his maternal grandmother and, by his own admission, "grew up playing lots of cards." After graduating from high school, he took a job as a relief-man machine operator for the Scott Paper Company and shifted to General Motors two years later. Then, at age twenty, he joined his father, John L. Lewis, selling new and used cars. "You better believe I was the best salesman ever," Lewis says of those years. "Before I was old enough to vote I was making sixty thousand, seventy thousand dollars a year."

Soon, though, another interest took hold. In 1964, Joe Frazier came out of the Olympics, and a group of Philadelphia businessmen formed Cloverlay Inc. to launch the fighter's career. Lewis's father was one of them, and before long Butch was traveling with Frazier as the boxer's road buddy. Over time, he parlayed connections made on the road into promotional links with a group of German businessmen. And in 1976, he entered the world of promotion as co-promoter of the Muhammad Ali versus Richard Dunn championship bout in Munich. That same year, Michael Spinks emerged from the Montreal Olympics with a gold medal, and the Spinks-Lewis union was formed.

Nine years later, in 1985, Spinks upset Larry Holmes to become one of three "heavyweight champions of the world." And except for Butch Lewis, no one was satisfied. Having three heavyweight champions was like having three kings of England at the same time. Thus, in early 1986, Lewis, Don King (who controlled most of the heavyweight division), and HBO entered into a contract to stage a heavyweight elimination tournament designed to produce one champion with one crown. Pursuant to that contract, Spinks was paid $2.5 million for a successful rematch against Holmes and $1.2 million to beat up a Norwegian pacifist named Steffen Tangstad. However, as the tournament progressed, a cloud named Mike Tyson appeared on the horizon.

Lewis didn't want Spinks to face Tyson. At least, not for the contractually-agreed-upon $2 million Spinks was to be paid for the tournament's final round. Thus, he opened negotiations for a fight between Spinks and Gerry Cooney, and watched contentedly as the International Boxing Federation stripped Spinks of his title; a move which Lewis claimed erased Spinks' obligation to continue in the tournament since the fighter no longer held the IBF crown.

The Cooney gambit caused consternation all around. HBO feared its tournament would fall apart. The Las Vegas Hilton, which had a contract to stage the tournament finale, foresaw a huge loss in gambling revenue. Tyson's camp was furious, because they wanted to fight Spinks for the undisputed heavyweight crown, and also because they wanted Cooney for themselves.

On December 2, 1986, Tyson's co-managers (Jim Jacobs and Bill Cayton) met with Dennis Rappaport (Cooney's representative) and made him an unprecedented offer. "We wanted a Tyson-Cooney fight," Cayton recalls, "and we promised it to Rappaport for July or August 1987, assuming of course that Mike prevailed in the tournament. It would have been the largest grossing fight of all time."

And how would that money have been divided?

"We were willing to go fifty-fifty with Dennis," Jacobs (who died last month) remembered; "give him half of everything if he was willing to stay away from Michael Spinks."

Cooney's trainer, Victor Valle, wanted the Tyson fight. Money aside, he thought Cooney would fare better against Tyson than against the more elusive Spinks. Cooney's manager, Mike Jones (who had been removed from the decision-making process by Cooney and Rappaport), was pulling his curly hair out, arguing in favor of a Cooney-Tyson bout with its monumental estimated gross. Nonetheless, Rappaport opted for Cooney-Spinks, and Cooney was knocked out for $2.5 million.

Meanwhile, Tyson knocked out Trevor Berbick to win the WBC title, decisioned James "Bonecrusher" Smith and Tony "TNT" Tucker for the WBA and IBF crowns, and annihilated Tyrell Biggs and Larry Holmes. At that point, it began to look as though Michael Spinks might be a fighter left out in the cold. Tyson signed a new contract with HBO, with added revenues for a six-bout schedule that promised to bring him $50 million over the next year, provided he kept winning. Spinks, on the other hand, had no big-money opponent on the horizon except Tyson.

"I wasn't worried," says Lewis. "I figured Jacobs and Cayton would sit down with me. Tyson-Spinks was the fight the public wanted; not Tyson-Bruno or Tyson-Tubbs. There'd been more ink written about why that fight wasn't taking place than most championship fights get for happening."

The day after Tyson beat Holmes, Jacobs and Cayton offered Spinks a guarantee of $10 million to fight Tyson; or if Lewis preferred, one-third of the Tyson-Spinks adjusted gross (estimated at $40 million).

Lewis declined.

"They kept saying that Michael Spinks needed this fight more than Tyson," Lewis recalls; "that it was the only way we could make money. Well, let me tell you something; Tyson needs this fight too. When somebody dangles twenty million dollars under your nose, which is what they're talking about Tyson getting, you take it. I remember when I was with Joe Frazier. After he beat Ali, they offered him five million dollars to fight Ali a second time. That's twice what each fighter got for the first one. Joe was fixing to fight Ali again, but first he figured he'd fight a tuneup against George Foreman for $850,000. The rest is history. Foreman knocked Joe out in the second round. Everyone said I was crazy when I said no to ten million dollars, but I knew Tyson's people would come around."

Michael Spinks is now scheduled to fight Mike Tyson on June 17th. Spinks will be paid $13.5 million—the biggest single-fight guarantee in the history of boxing. "The determining factor in making the bout," says Cayton, "was that Mike Tyson wanted the fight. That's why, financially, we went the extra mile. Mike has always fought the fights Jim and I made for him but, by the same token, we've always tried to be sensitive to his feelings."

Should Spinks fail to cooperate with the pre-fight promotion (as determined by a panel of arbitrators), a contractual provision says he'll be penalized $1 million. "For $1 million, you better believe Michael will cooperate," Lewis promises. The site fee, already contracted for with Donald Trump, is $11 million, far in excess of the previous $6.5 million high paid for Sugar Ray Leonard versus Marvin Hagler. Cayton estimates closed circuit and pay-per-view revenues at $23 million. HBO will pay $3.1 million for delayed TV rights. Foreign sales will bring in another $2 million, and sponsors' fees $1 million more. All totalled, revenues are expected to run slightly more than $40 million.

The major expense will be Michael Spinks's $13.5 million guarantee. Add to that a $3 million fee for Don King and miscellaneous expenditures such as sanctioning fees, undercard fighters, and various commissions totalling $2.5 million. That leaves an estimated profit of $21 million for Mike Tyson and company.

Clearly, Butch Lewis did a masterful job for his fighter (as Jacobs and Cayton did for theirs). Did he breach his contract regarding the HBO tournament? One New York court said "no"; that when the IBF stripped Spinks of his title, Spinks's obligation to the tournament came to an end. But that decision is being appealed and, more ominously, the Las Vegas Hilton is pursuing a lawsuit against Butch Lewis Productions in Nevada, where a trial is expected shortly.

Lewis gets angry when the subject of contracts and lawsuits arises. "Look, man," he argues, "my job is to do the best I can for my fighter. Not for HBO, not for Don King, not for Jim Jacobs, or Bill Cayton, not for Mike Tyson. For Michael Spinks. I didn't rob anybody. I didn't run numbers or beat a man to death like Don King. They say I broke a contract, but you tell me, who got hurt?"

It's a good question. HBO lost the live broadcast of a Tyson-Spinks bout, but kept its tournament intact, got good ratings, and will air a Tyson-Spinks bout far bigger than the one originally planned on delayed tape. Don King came out of the fray just fine. Mike Tyson is the best thing that's happened to him in years. In 1986, King's power was waning. Bob Arum, Dan Duva, and other promoters were cutting into his power base. The heavyweight division, which he controlled, was boring. Now King is promoting Mike Tyson, smoothing the way for the Tyson camp with the world sanctioning bodies, and receiving astronomical paydays in return.

Tyson lost a potential $17 million payday against Gerry Cooney, but he'll make it back with interest against Spinks. The conventional wisdom is that Tyson-Spinks won't be a competitive bout. Lewis argues to the contrary: "I see Michael Spinks frustrating Tyson, giving him angles like he's never seen before, getting in and out, hitting him just like he hit Cooney." Still, there's a growing feeling among boxing's intelligentsia that Tyson is one of the great heavyweights of all-time, and that Tyson-Spinks will be a performance, not a contest. Regardless, people have always been willing to pay for the privilege of witnessing a coronation. $20 million, give or take a few million, should make Tyson happy with his earnings in June.

The real loser then, is Gerry Cooney. He could have fought Tyson for parity; an estimated $17 million per man. Or had Spinks stayed in the tournament and beaten Tyson, Cooney-Spinks would have become a $40 million draw. "We could have been rich," moans Victor Valle. Instead, Cooney got knocked out for $2.5 million. And in the process, Butch Lewis pocketed the Cooney mystique and took it to the bank for his own fighter. Beating Gerry Cooney gave Michael Spinks box office cachet and true heavyweight credentials.

"Yeah, I used Rappaport and Cooney," Lewis acknowledges, flashing his trademark wide-as-a-river grin. "And you know something? Rappaport didn't even know it."

Presumably, he does now.

No one has done more to exploit fighters, steal from fighters, and ruin fighters than Don King. But King is also one of the smartest, hardest working, most charismatic people I've ever known. The following profile was commissioned by *The London Sunday Express*, shortly before Mike Tyson's release from prison in 1995.

King Again

Don King's persona extends far beyond boxing. A tall bulky man with diamond studded fingers, he wears frilled shirts, sequined tuxedos, and a gold necklace embedded with diamonds that spell his name. He's also the possessor of the world's best known "Afro," with graying hair that rises toward the heavens in apparent defiance of the laws of gravity. Federal prosecutors in the United States contend that gravity isn't the only law King has violated. He is currently under indictment for fraud. Other detractors suggest that King, whose exploitation of fighters is legendary, styles his hair to cover up his horns. Regardless, virtually everyone agrees that, when Oliver McCall knocked out Lennox Lewis in last week's heavyweight championship bout at Wembly Arena, the primary beneficiary was Don King. And with Mike Tyson, another King fighter, due out of prison in seven months, King is establishing a stranglehold over professional boxing.

King has done so many bad things in his life that it's impossible to list all of them. He has corrupted virtually everyone and every institution he has ever been involved with. His résumé includes a stint as one of the largest promoters of illegal "numbers" gambling in Cleveland. During the course of conducting that business, he killed two men. The first was Hillary Brown, who King shot to death in 1954 in an incident that the courts ruled "justifiable homicide." The second victim was Sam Garrett; a numbers runner who King thought was stealing from him. King beat Garrett to death in 1966. For that act, he was found guilty of murder (the verdict was later reduced to manslaughter), and sent to prison for four years. After his release, King decided to try his hand at boxing. Now, at age sixty-two, he's not content to be the sport's most powerful promoter. It seems as though he wants to be the *only* promoter in boxing.

King has managed to control his sport by forging alliances with boxing's three world sanctioning organizations, and denying title opportunities to fighters who don't cede portions of their earnings to him. His method of operation is simple. First, he woos fighters with promises of money and fame. He also appeals to black fighters on ethnic grounds, suggesting that only a black promoter will treat them fairly. But King's commitment to racial justice is limited. Indeed, in 1984, Arthur Ashe and Harry Belafonte led a successful effort to force the promoter out of Athletes and Artists Against Apartheid, after it was revealed that King had received a million dollars in return for allowing two of his fighters to fight in Sun City in violation of the international boycott against South Africa.

When promises of wealth and ethnic appeals don't do the job, King has been known to threaten violence to get what he wants. Former heavyweight champion Larry Holmes recounts an incident that occurred in 1977, when King wanted him to fight Young Sanford for $10,000. King's archrival Bob Arum, had offered Holmes $75,000 for the same fight. Holmes recalls, "I tried to get Don to sweeten the pot and told him if he didn't I was going to fight for Arum. I never saw Don's face get the way it got. His eyes turned cold and empty. He said, real quietly, 'If you do, I'll have your legs broke.'" Holmes continued to fight for King for the next ten years.

Of course, not every fighter signs with Don King. But those who don't are often punished severely for their independence. In most sports, it's presumed that the officials are impartial. Their integrity is the bedrock of the game. Imagine, if you will, a World Cup Soccer match between England and Argentina. The game ends with England having scored three goals and Argentina two. The officials caucus. The crowd waits. And the final score is. . . . Argentina 4, England 3. Things like that happen in boxing all the time.

When Oliver McCall defeated Lennox Lewis last week, many observers considered the referee's work suspect. Yes, Lewis had been knocked down. And yes, he was badly hurt. But Lewis was on his feet at the count of six. He wanted to continue. And this was a fight for the heavyweight championship of the world. When Larry Holmes was champion, he was knocked down by punches just as devastating as the punch that floored Lewis. Earnie Shavers did it to Holmes in 1979, and Renaldo Snipes repeated the feat in 1981. But Holmes was a Don King fighter. Both times, the referee allowed the bout to continue; and both times, Holmes won.

Mexican junior-welterweight Julio Cesar Chavez is another of Don King's favorites. In March 1990, Chavez was fighting Meldrick Taylor in a 140-pound title-unification bout. Taylor was leading on the scorecards of all three judges when, with seconds left, Chavez knocked him down. Taylor rose to his feet, ready to continue. But with two seconds remaining in the fight—not enough time for another punch to be thrown—the referee stopped the bout and awarded victory to Chavez.

Three years later, Chavez received a second "gift" when he fought Pernell Whitaker in another title match. In the eyes of virtually every ringside observer, Whitaker clearly won the fight. Yet Chavez escaped with a draw.

Somehow, it seems as though, whenever there's questionable official conduct in a major fight, the beneficiary is a Don King-controlled fighter. It happens time and time again. When James "Buster" Douglas knocked out Mike Tyson to capture the heavyweight championship in 1990, King grabbed headlines with his futile effort to have the knockout overturned. Lost in the shuffle was the fact that, although Douglas appeared to have won at least seven of the nine rounds before the knockout, only one judge had him ahead on points at the end.

The key to King's power lies in the alliances he has forged with boxing's three world sanctioning bodies—the World Boxing Council (WBC), the World Boxing Association (WBA), and the International Boxing Federation (IBF). These organizations were formed to control championships. They make their own rules, designate their own "world champions," and sanction only championship matches and title elimination bouts. To hold a championship sponsored by one of these groups, a fighter must compete against opponents, and under conditions, specified by the sanctioning body. If he refuses, he may be stripped of his title. The sanctioning bodies also appoint the referees and judges for championship fights, and establish their own "ratings."

Ratings are a fighter's future. In order to qualify for a title bout, a fighter must be ranked among the top ten challengers in his weight division. Also, once a year, each champion is required to face the top-ranked challenger in his division. But it now appears as though Don King controls the ratings mechanisms of all three world sanctioning organizations.

A look at boxing's heavyweight division is instructive. When Buster Douglas knocked out Mike Tyson and went to court rather than submit to King's machinations, King temporarily lost control of boxing's flagship division. Douglas then lost to Evander Holyfield, pushing King further out of the loop. Finally, after a series of bouts, the heavyweight championship was divided between Michael Moorer (WBA and IBF) and Lennox Lewis (WBC). That's when King and the ratings committees went to work.

Oliver McCall, a King-controlled fighter with losses to the likes of Joey Christjohn and Mike Hunter, was ranked first by each of the world sanctioning organizations. That meant, eventually, one of the heavyweight champions would have to fight him. Tony Tucker, another King-controlled fighter who had lost previously to Lennox Lewis, was ranked second by each organization. Now that McCall is the WBC champion, Tucker will move up to number one in the rankings of each organization. That means, sooner or later, Michael Moorer will have to fight him or relinquish his crown. After Tucker comes Bruce Seldon, soon to be ranked second by the WBA and IBF. Seldon was knocked out in the first round by Riddick Bowe; yet he's ranked ahead of Bowe by all three sanctioning bodies. If fact, Bowe isn't even ranked in the top ten by the WBC and WBA. Bowe is independent of Don King. Bruce Seldon is a Don-King fighter.

"It's worse now than it has ever been," says Seth Abraham (President of TimeWarner Sports, the preeminent cable-TV and pay-per-view boxing programmer in the United States). "And believe me, things were pretty bad in the past."

Jack Newfield, the American investigative journalist who is in the process of writing a biography of King, concurs with Abraham and adds, "What makes it so bad is the way King steals from his own fighters once he's stolen them from someone else. Jeff Merritt, the first fighter King controlled, is a homeless crack addict in Las Vegas. Muhammad Ali, Larry Holmes, Tim Witherspoon. . . . You can go down the list; King has screwed them all."

Muhammad Ali gave Don King his start in boxing, but King showed no loyalty in return. When Ali was dethroned by Leon

Spinks in 1978, Spinks offered Ali an immediate rematch. At the time, King controlled Larry Holmes, Ken Norton, and Jimmy Young, but not Spinks or Ali. So King encouraged the WBC to strip Spinks of his title and sanction a "title elimination bout" between Young and Norton, with the winner to fight Holmes. Then, two years later, King promoted Ali's challenge against Holmes, despite medical records that signalled Ali's deteriorating physical condition. And after Ali was brutally beaten in that bout, his paycheck from King was a million dollars short.

Tim Witherspoon was the reigning WBA heavyweight champion when he journeyed to London to fight Frank Bruno in 1986. Witherspoon was promoted by Don King and "managed" by King's son, Carl. This is a favorite tactic of King's. The fighters he promotes are often required to pay fifty percent of their earnings to Carl for "managerial services." HBO, which was televising the Witherspoon-Bruno fight in the United States, gave King $1.6 million to provide Witherspoon's services and co-promote the bout. Not knowing the numbers, Witherspoon was cajoled into signing a contract for $500,000. After the bout, he received a check for $90,000.

While Mike Tyson was disintegrating as a fighter, Don King was busy ripping him off. Originally managed by Bill Cayton and Jim Jacobs, Tyson put his faith in King and left his old management team behind. Cayton later obtained affidavits from Joseph Maffia (the former Comptroller of Don King Productions). Among other things, those affidavits revealed:

- King paid excessive sanctioning fees out of Mike Tyson's purses to the WBC, WBA, and IBF for each title bout that Tyson fought while under King's control.
- When Tyson fought Razor Ruddock for the first time,

among the expenses that King charged to Tyson were a $2 million fee to Ruddock's promoter, in return for which King received promotional rights to Ruddock; a 25 percent deduction from pay-per-view revenues collected by KingVision on the bout as a fee for "services rendered;" $750,000 for "overhead" at King's corporate headquarters in New York; and a $100,000 "consulting fee" for King's wife, Henrietta.

■ King also billed Tyson for the cost of maintaining a corporate apartment rented by Don King Productions in New York, a house owned by Don King Productions in Las Vegas, and a duplex apartment rented by Don King Productions in Los Angeles.

And all that was just the tip of the King-Tyson iceberg.

So what happens next? Oliver McCall's first title defense may well be against Peter McNeeley, an inept Boston heavyweight with longterm promotional ties to King. Frans Botha, a King-controlled punching bag from South Africa, is also under consideraton. Meanwhile, King will throw "mandatory" challengers against Michael Moorer until one of them succeeds. And of course, when Mike Tyson is released from prison, Oliver McCall's title will be available for him to fight for.

It's a grim picture, but those who oppose King do have one ray of hope. In July of this year, after a long investigation, King was indicted by a federal grand jury in New York on nine counts of fraud. At the heart of the indictment is the claim that King defrauded Lloyd's of London out of several hundred thousand dollars in connection with a fight between Julio Cesar Chavez and Harold Brazier that was cancelled. More sweeping criminal charges are rumored to be pending. And there is also talk of a civil antitrust suit to be filed by the United States Department of Justice. If these prosecutions succeed, Don King's power will be curbed. But if King prevails in court, professional boxing faces a bleak future.

The "Big Three" of boxing promotion in the United States have long been Don King, Bob Arum, and the Duva family. But in 1996, Cedric Kushner came into the fold.

Cedric Kushner's Magical Mystery Tour

Cedric Kushner's time is coming.

That's a refrain one hears a lot these days.

From Lou DiBella of TimeWarner Sports: "Cedric Kushner is a real professional. He's got a good organization. He's fair to his fighters. We'd like to do more business with him."

From Jerry Izenberg: "Cedric will do business with anyone, and I don't think he cares a whole lot if the other side screws its fighters. But he lives up to his deals and treats his own right. Look at the job he's done for Buster Mathis, Jr. and Axel Schulz."

And Mike Katz: "Cedric Kushner is one of the few people I know who works as hard as Don King. And he's on his way to becoming one of the most powerful men in the sport."

The object of this attention is a portly 48-year-old man with an "I Am The Walrus" mustache and self-deprecating sense of humor, who knows boxing very well.

Kushner was born in South Africa. A self-described "disobedient youngster who had no interest in school," he abandoned academia after failing the American equivalent of seventh grade and worked at a series of jobs, including a stint as a tally clerk on the docks of Cape Town. He left South Africa as a deckhand onboard a freighter in 1970. On his 23rd birthday, he arrived in the United States, where he worked for three months as a laborer in a Boston warehouse. Then the weather got cold, so he hitchhiked to Florida and took a job cleaning swimming pools and handing out towels at the Fountainebleau Hotel. Eventually, he came back north and was employed as a messenger for the Australian Consulate. He also worked briefly as a Ferris wheel operator at an amusement park in New Jersey.

In 1974, Kushner began pursuing his version of "The American Dream." Armed with a $5,000 stake, he formed Cedric Kushner Promotions with the aim of promoting rock concerts. His first effort was a Steppenwolf concert at Plymouth State College in New Hampshire. "And I lost all my money," he recalls. "Financially, the concert was a disaster, but people were satisfied with the job I did and wanted to work with me again." One thing led to another, and soon Kushnner was a prominent industry figure, promoting the likes of Rod Stewart, Joni Mitchell, and Fleetwood Mac. Then, in 1981, he was indicted and pled "nolo contendere" to a charge of "territorial allocation" as part of an antitrust prosecution brought by the federal government. "After that, it seemed like it was time to move on," Kushner remembers. "And that's when the boxing bug bit me."

In 1982, Kushner acquired managerial rights to a fighter named Irish Teddy Mann. But after paying Mann $30,000 in advances against future purses, he came to the conclusion that "the economics of managing a $5,000 fighter were a losing proposition." Around the same time, South African heavyweight Gerrie Coetzee beat Renaldo Snipes all over the ring in Tarrytown, New York, but lost a ten-round decision. Kushner put two and two together and offered his services to Coetzee as a promoter. He and Bob Arum then co-promoted Coetzee's bouts against Stan Ward and Pinklon Thomas, but had a falling out after which Kushner took Coetzee to Don King.

"King talked endlessly about the horrors of apartheid," Kushner remembers, "and how, because of it, I'd never be able to get Coetzee into position for a mandatory title shot. But really, all he was doing was breaking me down to get options on the fighter. Once our promotional deal was signed, Mr. King's moral problems with apartheid vanished."

Kushner's deal with King provided for a bout between Coetzee and WBA heavyweight champion Michael Dokes. Should Coetzee win, King would be his promoter for the duration of his championship reign plus an additional two years. Dokes was a fighter on the decline, wasted by cocaine abuse. On September 23, 1993, Coetzee knocked him out in ten rounds. One of boxing's most memorable images from that era is of Don King stepping over the body of the fighter he "loved like a son" to embrace the white South African victor.

Meanwhile, Kushner was delighted. He'd been in boxing for just eighteen months, and was involved with a heavyweight champion. King had paid him $150,000 as a "co-promotional" fee for the fight, and he had a contract that entitled him to $250,000 each time Coetzee defended his crown. Plus, as the result of a second agreement with King, Kushner was to receive 45 percent of a nonrefundable $750,000 binder that had been paid to King by parties seeking to match Coetzee against WBC champion Larry Holmes. But then, as is often his modus operandi, King refused to pay Kushner his due. That led to a lawsuit. "But I didn't have the staying power to pursue the matter in court," Kushner recalls, "so eventually I settled for $150,000, out of which I had to pay my lawyers as well."

It was a bitter pill to swallow, but Kushner soldiered on. In March 1983, he had promoted his first nationally televised fight— a ten-round bout between Lenny LaPaglia and John Collins on NBC from Chicago. That was followed by more shows in the

Windy City, and then Kushner made another major move in the heavyweight ranks; this time with Tony Tucker.

Tucker was a young heavyweight with twelve knockouts in twelve fights when Kushner became his promoter. Kushner brought him to 34–0, which set up a 1987 IBF championship bout against James "Buster" Douglas after Michael Spinks was stripped of his title for refusing to fight Mike Tyson. Once again, Kushner was forced to deal with Don King. And once again, he was paid $150,000 for delivering the services of his fighter. Tucker won, but in his next bout, lost a twelve-round decision to Tyson. Kushner received a $500,000 "co-promotional" fee for that fight, but was otherwise shut out of the promotion.

Following Tucker's loss to Tyson, Kushner decided to concentrate on the European market. "Europe was five or six years behind the United States in terms of cable," he remembers. "A lot of new companies were starting up, and they needed programming." In 1990, Kushner closed a $2 million promotional deal with Sky TV in England. Before long, he was promoting two shows a month in Europe. And while he still maintains a low profile in the United States, he's one of the most visible promoters in Europe today.

All totalled, Kushner has promoted close to 150 world title fights. His roster of past champions includes Prince Charles Williams, Kennedy McKinney, Orlando Canizales, and Junior Jones. His current roster is headed by Virgil Hill and Henry Maske. Cedric Kushner Promotions now has twelve employees, and packages shows for a global television market through Cedric Kushner Sports Network—a wholly owned subsidiary formed in 1993.

"I'm proud of what I've accomplished," Kushner says, looking back over his journey. "I've had my share of luck, which you have to have to make it in any business. But I've worked very hard to get where I am, and I intend to continue working very hard in the future."

Now and then, I like to write about the people behind the scenes, who are unknown to the public but are an integral part of the world of professional boxing. Ron Katz is one of those people.

A Look At Ron Katz

The best matchmaker in boxing is Ron Katz.

Ask Wally Matthews of the *New York Post*, who says, "No one makes better fights. If I was a manager, I wouldn't let Ron Katz near my fighter, which is the highest compliment I can pay a matchmaker." Or Mike Katz (no relation) of the *New York Daily News*, who proclaims, "Ron Katz is a guy who likes to see good fights and happens to be a matchmaker. Too bad there aren't more like him." Or Jerry Izenberg of the *Newark Star-Ledger*, who says simply, "As a fight fan, I love him."

The object of this admiration is 41 years old with a counterculture haircut and boundless enthusiasm for boxing. Katz grew up in the suburbs of New York, and was talented enough as a high school pitcher to earn an invitation to a Kansas City Royals tryout camp. Then, in his senior year of high school, he was involved in a car accident in which two friends were killed. The accident left him with a dislocated shoulder, broken ribs, and a deep gash on his right foot, but the mental effects were worse. "Mentally, it was devastating," Katz remembers, "and I got into things I shouldn't have done; like cocaine. After that, I went to college for a year, dropped out, started deejaying in night clubs, and the drugs got worse. Finally, I realized what I was doing to myself and decided to turn my life around."

Katz's introduction to boxing came through Lou Falcigno, a

family friend, who was promoting shows at the Westchester County Center and handling closed-circuit telecasts. Katz moved from gofer, to publicist, to matchmaker, relying heavily for advice on Johnny Bos "who kind of broke me in." From 1983 through 1986, he served as matchmaker for the Houston Boxing Association. "At one point, Bob Gutkowski was after me bigtime to become Director of Boxing for Madison Square Garden," Katz remembers. "He called me every day for weeks, but I turned him down out of loyalty to HBA, which was a mistake on my part. Then, in 1987, I went to Top Rank and got to spend a few years with Teddy Brenner. That's when my education really began. Some people today call me 'Young Teddy' because of the fights I make. And to me, that's like being called 'Young Muhammad Ali' or 'Young Babe Ruth.'"

Katz now makes all of the east-coast matches for Top Rank. That means he's responsible for eighty percent of Top Rank's cards on ESPN, as well as many of its network, regular cable, and pay-per-view shows. Most of his work is done by telephone. He gets roughly fifty calls a day from managers asking him to use their fighters. In making matches, he relies more on calls to people he respects and trusts than on video tapes. Bob Arum (President of Top Rank) gives him considerable leeway in the matches he makes, and that's when the Ron Katz philosophy of matchmaking takes over.

"As a matchmaker," explains Katz, "you have to have the best interests of the public at heart. Let someone else look out for the managers, the promoters, even the fighters. My job is to look out for the fans, so I try to make fights that I want to watch myself. On occasion, circumstances might dictate otherwise. But whenever I make a match, I ask myself first, "Do I want to see this fight? Right now," Katz continues, "there are too many mismatches, and it's bad for boxing. No one would watch football or basketball if the powerhouse teams played cellar-dwellers all the time. But in boxing, that's what you have today. Too many people in our sport just don't get it. You have to put on fights that fans want to see; not these awful pathetic mismatches."

Meanwhile, just as fighters with good punching power are known for knockouts, Katz is known for his "knockoffs"—matches he's made where heavily favored fighters have tasted defeat. "It's not that I want to hurt anyone's career," he explains. "It's just that I like good fights." And having said that, Katz savors the recollection of Santos Cardona knocking off Livingston Bramble; Jose Quiñones knocking out Doug Dewitt; Bruce Seldon being stopped by Oliver McCall; Saoul Mamby beating Larry Barnes—all for Top Rank on ESPN. "There was a period," Katz remembers fondly, "where number-one guys got knocked off three weeks in a row. One night, I got the whole Kronk team destroyed."

Is Ron Katz important to boxing? That depends on one's view of the sport. If spectators are paying simply to watch one man beat up another in predictable fashion, then people like Ron Katz are unnecessary. But if that's what boxing is all about, then boxing isn't a sport and it shouldn't be allowed to exist at all. However, if one sees boxing as the purest form of athletic competition, one-on-one, man-against-man, then we should be thankful that Ron Katz is out there making "Teddy Brenner fights."

Michael Katz

Rock Newman is angry. He's on the telephone, complaining about Mike Katz. Katz, according to Newman, has no respect for the truth. He's a biased, lousy, good-for-nothing—sputtering wildly, Newman plays his trump card—"Mike Katz is a racist."

The object of Newman's wrath is a visual mix between Karl Marx and Santa Claus with a shaggy beard, the fringes of which disappear into a neck collar worn to ease the pain of a condition known as spinal stenosis. Katz is widely known for his scowl and reputation as a curmudgeon. He is also possibly the best and most influential boxing writer in America.

Katz was born in the South Bronx in 1939. His father owned a succession of small businesses, including at one time, a jelly donut factory. "The only thing I was ever truly great at," Katz recalls, "was putting jelly into jelly donuts. I did it for maybe three years. It's called punching donuts, and I was the best jelly-donut puncher in New York, probably the world. If there had been a world championship for punching donuts, I would have won it."

After graduating from high school, Katz enrolled as an engineering student at CCNY, intent upon becoming a chemical engineer. But his plans to blow up the world, such as they might have been, were sidetracked when he began writing sports for CCNY's undergraduate student newspaper, *The Campus*. "The minute I began," he remembers, "I told myself, 'This is what I want to do with my life.'"

Katz rose to sports editor and ultimately editor-in-chief of the

student newspaper, attending one hundred consecutive CCNY basketball games along the way. Meanwhile, while still in school, he
become a "stringer," covering CCNY sports for *The New York
Times*, and took a job working nights as a copy boy for journalism's "Gray Lady." After college, he worked his way up the *Times*
ladder from day clerk to news assistant and finally a sports-desk
staff-level editor's job. Then, in 1966, he moved to Europe, from
whence his by-line appeared in *The New York Times* and
International Herald Tribune.

In 1972, Katz returned to the United States and his old desk job
at the *Times*. Soon, his duties were expanded to include writing a
weekly motor sports column (he still doesn't know how to drive)
and covering other sports, mostly in Europe, on a sporadic basis.
"Eventually, they offered me the Yankees and Knicks," he remembers, "but those beats involved too much traveling so I turned them
down. Then they offered me the Giants, and I said 'yes.'"

Meanwhile, 1976 was a watershed year for boxing in the United
States. With the box-office success of *Rocky* and five gold medals
for the United States Olympic boxing team in Montreal, the sport
went mainstream. That same year, Muhammad Ali fought Richard
Dunn in Munich. Katz was already in Europe on another assignment, and his editor asked him to cover the bout. "I won some sort
of award for deadline writing," he remembers, "and then I wrote
sidebar stories for Ali-Norton III and Ali-Shavers. Around that
time, Dave Anderson, who had a regular column and was also the
paper's main boxing writer, asked if I'd take some of the load off
his shoulders. After that, it was just a matter of time until I became
the paper's fulltime boxing writer. And I was happy at the *Times*.
I really was. But in 1985, Vic Ziegel became sports editor for the
Daily News. Vic was one of my closest friends, so when he offered
me a job I figured. 'Hey, why not; it'll be fun to work with him.'"

A dozen years later, Katz is still with the *Daily News*, as its main boxing writer and once-a-week boxing columnist. "I don't really have a philosophy of writing," he says. "I just try to find out what's happening and report it. I write what I find. I roll with the punches. I'm honest with people, so I've been able to develop good contacts. I don't think I'm a great writer like A. J. Liebling, Bob Waters, or Barney Nagler. But I can hold my own with most of the competition."

And as for that reputation for being a curmudgeon?

"I get cranky at times," Katz acknowledges. "And maybe it's something I cultivate a bit. But you know, sometimes somebody will come to me and say, 'You've got to write this; you've got to help me; we're both in boxing.' And I'll say to him, 'No, I'm not in boxing; I'm a newspaper guy.' Also," Katz continues, "some of the sleaziest people I've ever met are in boxing. Don't get me wrong; there are some great people in boxing. Fighters, in particular, have a certain nobility about them. Some of my favorite people in the world are guys like Mark Breland, Larry Holmes, Marvin Hagler, and Roy Jones. And Muhammad Ali is in a class by himself. But then you have people like Don King and Jose Sulaiman. . . ."

And then Mike Katz is off and running. . . . "Dennis Rappaport has been number one on my sleaze list for years. Vinny and Angelo Pazienza make my skin crawl. Al Braverman; I think the guy invented kickbacks. Mike Marley; at least now he admits he's working for Don King. . . ."

So when all is said and done, does Mike Katz *like* boxing? "Yeah; I like it. There are times when I get fed up with the bullshit and the way fighters are exploited, and I feel like walking away from it all. But to me, the only real sports in the world are boxing and horse racing. All the rest are children's games. And when I'm covering a great fight—Leonard-Hearns, Pryor-Arguello,

Holyfield-Tyson—you know which ones the great fights are—I know in my heart that it's an honor and a privilege to be at ringside writing about boxing.

Oh, and by the way. About that charge that Mike Katz is a racist. Here's what a fellow named Muhammad Ali had to say on the subject: "Mike Katz is a good man. The only thing Mike Katz hates is bigotry and injustice. If everyone was like him, there'd be a lot less prejudice. Anyone who says Mike Katz is a bigot doesn't know what they're talking about."

Writing Howard Cosell's obituary presented the problem of how to reconcile the man's enormous contribution to sports journalism with his lesser side.

Howard Cosell

1918–1995

When The Grim Reaper comes, it's best to speak well of the departed. So let it be said first that Howard Cosell changed the face of sports commentary in America. There were talented broadcasters before him, but Cosell brought something new to the game— a willingness to speak the truth in hard situations. That was particularly evident in the 1960's, when Cassius Clay changed his name to Muhammad Ali and refused induction into the United States Army. Cosell wasn't Ali's only defender. Writers like Jerry Izenberg and Robert Lipsyte were equally eloquent in support of Muhammad's cause. But Cosell had access to television; an extraordinarily powerful new medium. And because of that, his name will be linked with Ali's forever.

There was also a time when Howard Cosell was good for boxing. Like him or not, he had the most recognizable voice in America and was boxing's only nationally known commentator. He had the ability to go before a major sports audience, and by virtue of his presence, make almost any event seem important. For two decades, he was integral to the sport. Then, in 1982, he walked away, telling an interviewer, "I now favor the abolition of professional boxing. It's utterly immoral; it's not capable of reformation. You'll never clean it up. Mud can never be clean."

That, of course, was Cosell's prerogative. Just as he urged others, particularly black athletes, to speak their mind, he also had First Amendment rights. But something beyond the Constitution always seemed to be pushing Howard Cosell on. Ultimately, he began to act as though he was more important than the events he covered. Despite an enormously successful career, he became an increasingly bitter and abusive man.

My own first contact with Cosell was a positive experience. It came in 1962. I was a high school junior. He was hosting pre- and post-game radio shows for the New York Mets. I wrote him a letter suggesting that he was becoming a "shill." And I doubt very much that an eleventh grader ever caused more consternation at ABC. When I got home from school several days later, my mother told me, "Someone named Howard Cosell called this morning." The next day, I received a typed two-page single-spaced letter in the mail.

"Dear Tom," the missive began. "Despite a flood of mail, I am answering your letter as immediately as I have received it for one very important reason—I respect it." (The man wrote like he talked). The letter went on to reaffirm Cosell's commitment to truth, and closed with the words, "I shall not change; I assure you of that. I have gone my way regardless of the fact that much of the public seems to prefer bland tripe to forthright exposition, and I shall continue to do so. Meanwhile, I ask that you, as an intelligent listener, bear in mind that life is complex, integrity is precious, and that working before and after the Mets games has been the biggest challenge to my courage—as a married man with children—that I have ever faced."

That was my introduction to Howard Cosell. We met face-to-face twenty-two years later, when I was researching a book entitled *The Black Lights*. I went to ABC for an interview, and was ushered into "The Great One's" office. He was on the telephone with Eddie Einhorn of the Chicago White Sox, and the first words I heard him say were, "Eddie, take your fucking ballclub and shove it up your ass." Then the conversation got ugly. And during my interview, he was just as unpleasant.

Five years later, while researching *Muhammad Ali: His Life And Times*, I had occasion to interview Cosell again. Another time, I was a guest on his radio talk show, "Speaking Of Everything." And he invited me both to the Friars Club and to his home. But it really wasn't worth the price, because the cost of access was non-stop abuse: of me, of the people he worked with, of the world at large. I mean, how can you digest your lunch when you're sitting next to someone who's saying, "Alex Wallau has cancer, and he deserves it."

The last time I saw Howard Cosell was at CORE's annual Martin Luther King Day dinner in 1992. Secretary of State James Baker and Muhammad Ali were the guests of honor. The schedule called for Cosell to make a presentation, after which I would introduce Ali. I arrived at the pre-dinner reception with Ali, saw Cosell sitting alone, and went over to shake hands with him.

"How are you, sir?"

All I got in return was an icy stare followed by the words, "How dare they ruin my presentation by asking the likes of you to introduce Muhammad Ali?"

And that was the last time I saw Howard Cosell. So yes, he was important. And yes, he did some very good things. I just wish he had been nicer about it all.

No sports commentator in America ever had more detractors than Howard Cosell, and none was more respected. Such a man deserves critics no less forthright than he was.

Mike Jones—A Remembrance

I met Mike Jones in 1984. I was researching a book on the sport and business of boxing and thought it would be a good idea to interview Gerry Cooney. Mike, who was Cooney's co-manager, set it up; and Cooney turned out to be a less-than-spectacular person at that point in his life. But along the way, something wonderful happened. I got to know Mike, who became my guide through the Byzantine world of professional boxing.

Ultimately, my book focussed on Mike, Billy Costello (who was Mike's only world champion), and Billy's trainer, Victor Valle. But by then, Mike wasn't just someone I was writing about. He was my friend. We talked on the phone four times a week for the better part of six years. This past January, he told me he was suffering from multiple myeloma. The disease isn't curable. Some people live with it for a dozen years. The statistical average is two to five.

Mike's doctor told him, "It helps to be lucky." Mike wasn't. Six months after the disease was diagnosed, he died at age fifty-five.

Mike's skill as a manager is a matter of record. In addition to his success with Billy Costello, he guided Howard Davis, Gerry Cooney, Wilford Scypion, and Ronnie Harris to world title bouts. When he died, he was co-managing Glenwood Brown, Alex Stewart, and Jade Scott—all fighters with world-class potential. But what always impressed me most about Mike as a manager was the way he blended skill with compassion. He looked after his fighters, physically and financially. And beyond that, he was concerned for the welfare of everyone in the ring.

Once, Mike refused to use the only sparring partner in Billy Costello's camp because the sparring partner had recently been knocked unconscious. Another time, he dismissed a Gerry Cooney sparring partner because the fighter suffered from impaired vision in one eye. Neither of those acts might seem like much. But in the world of boxing, where sparring partners are treated like dead meat and interruptions in training are avoided at all costs, Mike's decency ran against the grain. And, in the end, even when Cooney turned against him and sought to break their managerial contract, Mike never stopped rooting for him. I was sitting with Mike the night Cooney was knocked out by Michael Spinks. Mike looked like a little boy trying hard not to cry.

After I finished writing about boxing, I went on to other things. Then, in 1988, Muhammad Ali asked if I'd be interested in authoring the definitive Ali biography, and I returned to the sweet science. As might be expected, Ali has kept me busy over the past two years, but Mike and I continued our friendship. Several weeks before he died, reflecting on the fact that my only boxing books were about him and Ali, Mike said with satisfaction, "I guess I'm in pretty good company."

"So is Ali," I told him.

And I meant it.

Mike loved boxing. In a business where most people have only allies, he had friends. His word was good; he never walked out on a deal. Now that he's gone, I feel sorry for his wife Stella, his children, his friends, his fighters, and everyone else who loved and relied on him. But most of all, I feel sorry for Mike. He led a good life, and it should have been longer. But if there's a better world, I'm sure he's there.

Round 5

Issues and Answers

World titles have been seriously devalued over the
past two decades with the proliferation of weight
classes and multiple sanctioning bodies in boxing.
The trend was accelerating in 1987, when I took issue
with Thomas Hearns claiming that he was the winner
of boxing's first quadruple crown.

The Quadruple Crown

Thomas Hearns is a nice young man and an exceptionally talented
fighter. But I'm tired of hearing that he's been a world champion
in four weight divisions—because he hasn't. Not unless you
believe that Gary Hogeboom's scab-game touchdown passes put
him on a par with Johnny Unitas, or that Sadahura Oh broke Babe
Ruth's home run record. In fact, by my reckoning, Hearns hasn't
even won world championships in three weight divisions; nor have
several other pretenders to that honor.

The first man to win titles in three weight classes was Bob
Fitzsimmons, who began with a thirteenth round knockout of Jack
Dempsey (no, not that Jack Dempsey) in 1891 to capture the mid-
dleweight crown. Six years later, weighing only 167 pounds,
Fitzsimmons KO'd James Corbett to win the heavyweight cham-
pionship. And after losing to James Jeffries, he returned at age
forty to take light-heavyweight honors by knocking out George
Gardner.

Fitzsimmons's three world titles were legitimate, as were those
of Tony Canzoneri (featherweight, lightweight, junior-welterweight) and Barney Ross (lightweight, junior-welterweight, welterweight). Keep in mind, though, that Canzoneri and Ross each needed
a "junior" title to make the grade.

Next came Henry Armstrong, who was in a class all his own. In

1937, Armstrong captured the featherweight crown with a sixth-round knockout of Petey Sarron. Seven months later, he battered Barney Ross for the welterweight title. And two-and-a-half months after that, he decisioned Lou Ambers for the lightweight championship. For one glorious moment, before relinquishing the featherweight title, Armstrong held championships *simultaneously* in three of boxing's original eight weight classes. Indeed, only a disputed 1940 draw against world middleweight titleholder Ceferino Garcia kept him from winning a fourth crown.

Then came the age of pretenders. Wilfred Benitez was a classy fighter, but his triple crown credentials were suspect. Two of his titles were "junior" championships won against over-the-hill warriors, and one was of WBA alphabet soup vintage.

Roberto Duran deserves credit for being on a par with the greatest lightweights of all time. And in beating Sugar Ray Leonard, he earned the right to be considered world welterweight king. But Roberto Duran as junior-middleweight champ? Forget it! By the time Duran beat Davey Moore for the WBA title, Thomas Hearns was entrenched as the WBC's 154-pound titleholder. And when Duran met Hearns. . . . Well, you remember that last right hand.

Wilfredo Gomez was a superb WBC junior-featherweight champion. None of the five WBA titleholders during his reign measured up to him. But Gomez's featherweight credentials were weak and, despite what the record book might say, he was never really WBA junior-lightweight king. That honor belonged properly to Rocky Lockridge, who was victimized by one of the more outrageous decisions in recent years when they met in the ring. And in any event, the matter is academic, since the genuine world junior-lightweight champion back then was Julio Cesar Chavez, who held the WBC crown.

In truth, there have been only two legitimate triple crown winners since Henry Armstrong. The first was Alexis Arguello. When Arguello was WBA featherweight champ, his WBC counterparts were Bobby Chacon (who he knocked out), and David Kotey (who he would have knocked out if they'd fought each other). As WBC junior-lightweight champ, Arguello's WBA rival was Sammy Serrano (stop laughing). And when Arguello was WBC lightweight king, the WBA champs were Claude Noel (who he knocked out), Ray Mancini (who he knocked out), and Arturo Frias (who Sammy Serrano could have KO'd).

And the other genuine triple crown winner of recent vintage? Sugar Ray Leonard. Leonard became the undisputed world welterweight champion by knocking out Thomas Hearns in 1981. That same year, he KO'd Ayub Kalule to win the WBA junior-middleweight crown. Since the WBC's 154-pound king at that time was Wilfred Benitez (who Ray had knocked out two years earlier), you have to concede world supremacy to Leonard in that division too. Then, in 1987, he captured every world middleweight title in existence by dethroning Marvelous Marvin Hagler.

As for Thomas Hearns; clearly, after beating Duran, he was the preeminent junior-middleweight in the world. But that's all. Ray Leonard won the WBC welterweight title eight months before Hearns toppled Pipino Cuevas for the WBA crown, and Sugar Ray's fourteenth-round knockout of the Hit Man established who was truly king. No one can convince me that a solitary win over Dennis Andries (the weakest of three alphabet champions) established Hearns as light-heavyweight champion of the world. And I won't believe he's the best middleweight around until he beats Frank Tate and Mike McCallum.

Boxing's legends are very special. Let's not tarnish them with promotional hype that Thomas Hearns has won "the quadruple crown."

Call it incompetence; call it corruption. Either way, boxing has a problem. Too often, as highlighted in this 1992 article, its referees make serious mistakes and the decisions of ring judges are just plain wrong.

Ring Officiating

Just when one assumes that boxing can't sink any lower, it sinks lower. Within the past few months, its biggest drawing card has been convicted of rape and sentenced to a lengthy prison term. One of its "young lions" was more muscleless than merciless in being outclassed by 42-year-old Larry Holmes. Holmes, in turn, went twelve dreary rounds with Evander Holyfield. And IBF middleweight champ James Toney was awarded a split decision over Dave Tiberi that had much of the crowd on its collective feet shouting about cow feces. Indeed, after the fight, ABC boxing commentator Alex Wallau told a national television audience that the verdict for Toney was "one of the most disgusting decisions I've ever seen." But as Wallau himself later acknowledged, it wasn't out of character for boxing, and therein lies the problem.

In every other major sport, the integrity of the officials is taken for granted; it's the bedrock of the game. Imagine going to Yankee Stadium. The game ends with the Red Sox having scored nine runs and the Yankees three. The official scorers caucus. George Steinbrenner looks on, grinning like Don King. And the final score is. . . . Yankees 7, Red Sox 5. That's what happened to Dave Tiberi in Atlantic City, and it happens in boxing all the time.

Pernell Whitaker dominated Jose Luis Ramirez from start to finish in their first bout, but lost a split decision with one judge awarding him only two rounds. Before Jeff Fenech challenged

Azumah Nelson for the WBC superfeatherweight title, a knowing observer predicted, "If it's close, they'll give the decision to Nelson." It wasn't close. Fenech beat up on Nelson all night, so Nelson retained his crown on a draw. Buster Douglas savaged Mike Tyson in Tokyo, but one judge had Tyson ahead on points and another had the fight scored even when Tyson was knocked out.

Judging a fight isn't particularly hard. Some of it might be subjective. How many jabs equal a solid left hook? But in most fights, anyone who knows boxing and pays attention will find 75 percent of the rounds easy to score. Why then the discrepancies? Wallau believes, "There's more incompetence than corruption in boxing. Some judges and referees just aren't qualified to do the job." But the fact remains, at the championship level there are a lot of "house fighters" whose victories are intertwined with the financial interests of a particular promoter, world sanctioning body, or state athletic commission member. And invariably, when an outrageous decision occurs, it's in favor of the house fighter.

"You're talking about millions of dollars," says NBC's Ferdie Pacheco, who has witnessed his share of bad decisions. "Sometimes a judge justifies his scorecard by telling himself that it's good for the sport if a particular fighter wins. Other times, it might be a case of knowing that the people who assigned him and paid for his trip to Las Vegas or Monte Carlo have a rooting interest in the fight. You don't need an envelope full of cash for corruption to exist. And no one from the state athletic commissions or world sanctioning bodies tries to improve upon an official's performance. No one sits down with him after a fight, puts a tape in the VCR, and asks, 'How could you score this round that way?' So time after time, you find yourself watching a fight where you say, 'They can't possibly steal this one; it would be too obvious.' And then they steal it."

And it's not just judges. Referee Richard Steele raised more than a few eyebrows the night he called a halt to Meldrick Taylor versus Julio Cesar Chavez, with Taylor hurt but ahead on all cards and two seconds left in the fight. Had the situation been reversed, many observers speculated Steele would have inquired of Chavez, "Are you all right? How many fingers do I have up? Do you want to continue? Are you sure?" Then, a year later, Steele raised eyebrows again with a questionable stoppage of the first Tyson-Ruddock fight. "I like Richard Steele," says Al Bernstein, ESPN's widely respected boxing commentator. "I think he's a great guy. But those calls created a lot of doubt in peoples' minds. They just weren't appropriate."

In sum, boxing today is rife with troubling judgment calls and outrageous decisions. Virtually all of them go in a predictable direction. By-and-large, the industry knows who's incorruptible and whose conduct raises doubts. But the people in charge seem to be shameless, and the rest of the world simply smiles and says, "Well, that's boxing."

So what's the solution? Certainly, at this point, a federal boxing commission preempting—not just coordinating—the fifty state regulatory bodies is worth trying. Perhaps then we'd see some accountability, as well as an end to blatant mismatches and stranglehold option contracts. Also, a few well-placed criminal investigations might encourage boxing to clean up its act. But in the interim, everyone in the media who covers and cares about the sport has an obligation to stand up and call attention to the problem.

Is anybody listening?

Boxing doesn't do nearly enough for fighters once their ring careers are over. The sport could do itself, and the fighters, a favor by employing former boxers as judges.

Let The Fighters Judge

Boxing has a lot of problems these days, and one of them is that the judging stinks. That's not a blanket indictment. There are judges like Harold Lederman and Jerry Roth who understand what they're watching and do their job without fear or favoritism. But all too often, fighters fight their heart out, win a bout, and then find themselves robbed by decision-makers who are either incompetent or corrupt. Hometown decisions and verdicts favoring a particular economic interest have become the norm, and it's wrong.

So what can be done about it? Simple! Let retired fighters do the judging. These are men who've competed in the ring, so they know what they're watching. They're less likely to screw another fighter, because most of them have been shipped down that road themselves and didn't like what they found. And let's face it; a lot of former fighters need work; full-time, part-time. Letting them judge would be a way to lend a helping hand.

In the past, fighters have served with distinction at ringside. Bill Costello was one of the best judges in New York until petty politics deprived him of the job. Now boxing in New York is an embarrassment, with judges' scorecards varying so wildly that no one knows what to make of the situation. When Larry Barnes and Harold Brazier met recently in Madison Square Garden, one judge scored the bout 118–111 for Brazier, while another had it 116–112 for Barnes. And in New York, as well as elsewhere in the country, that's not unusual anymore.

Like everyone else, former fighters should meet certain standards before they're allowed to judge. They should be retired. They shouldn't judge a fight that involves a former opponent or any other potential conflict of interest. And they should be chosen on the basis of their ability to judge, not public relations gimmickry. That means, in giving out assignments, it shouldn't matter whether someone was a six-round club fighter or world-champion superstar.

So how about it? Listen up, all you people who run the various state athletic commissions and world sanctioning bodies. The time has come to give priority in judging assignments to former fighters the same way military veterans once had priority for certain jobs. And if you want to know what instructions to give your new judges, simply ask them, "Did you ever get robbed on a bad decision? How did it make you feel?" Then tell them, "All right; make sure you don't do that to another fighter when you're a judge."

James "Buster" Douglas looked awful in losing his title to Evander Holyfield. But even then, I figured the sporting world owed him something for his performance against Mike Tyson.

An Open Letter to Buster Douglas

Dear Buster,

Let's get the bad stuff out of the way first. Against Evander Holyfield, you looked awful. You came in fat. You hadn't trained properly. Your timing was off, which was to be expected since a fighter has to do some work in the gym to get his timing right. You got knocked down, and if Seamus McDonagh can get up from Holyfield's punch, the suspicion here is that you could have too. But then again, I've never been punched in the face by Evander Holyfield; nor have most of your critics. Besides, none of that matters. What's important is, this past February you gave the world a thrill that will last forever.

Outside of a fellow named Muhammad Ali, no fighter in my lifetime has bestowed a greater moment upon boxing than the one you gave us this past February in Tokyo. Mike Tyson was "unbeatable." In tandem with Don King, he'd subjected the sweet science to a reign of terror that seemed like it would never end. No one had survived Tyson in the ring, and no one had successfully challenged Don King out of it.

You did both. First, you knocked Tyson on his butt. And no matter how people try to explain away that moment, the bottom line was Iron Mike on the canvas groping for his mouthpiece while the referee counted ten. Maybe Tyson hadn't trained right; maybe the rumors about substance abuse were true. Regardless, you did what had to be done. So what if you stayed on the canvas in Las Vegas? You got up in Tokyo, when it mattered most.

Boxing is a strange business, and it's hard to predict what lies ahead. But one thing is certain. If Don King's power is broken, much of the credit will go to you. If you'd signed for the immediate rematch against Tyson that King wanted, the "Only in America Man" would have had options on both of you. Whoever won, he would have controlled the heavyweight crown. Instead, King is on the outside now, with his nose pressed against the glass. The bureaucrats who did his bidding have been exposed for what they are. And boxing shows signs of becoming fun again. That's a pretty big accomplishment for one man, but you did it. You stood up to King in court, when Jose Sulaiman, Donald Trump, and so many others were working on his behalf. Maybe Big Don will make it back; maybe he won't. But one thing is sure—he'll always remember you, because right now he's on the canvas groping for his mouthpiece too.

So thank you, Buster. You gave us a wonderful eight months. And if I may, let me give you some advice in return. Your purse for the Holyfield fight was $24 million. Subtract the money you paid Don King to settle your lawsuit, ten percent for a trainer, John Johnson's managerial share, taxes, miscellaneous expenses, and you should have roughly $7 million.

Save that money! Don't leave it with people who promise to double it, because anyone who promises to double your money can lose it all. Put it in treasury bills, which are backed by the United States government and are free of state and local taxes. $7 million in treasury bills will guarantee you more than $500,000 a year for life. Not many fighters walk away from boxing with a stake like that, but you can. Don't get sucked into fighting again unless you truly want to. And whatever you do, don't fight Tyson again, because it can only tarnish what you've done.

Sleep late, spend time with your family, get involved in community affairs, eat all you want. And enjoy yourself, because you've earned it. You don't owe us a thing; we owe you.

As Always,
Thomas Hauser

Boxing's "senior circuit" is nothing new. Once-great fighters have been making comebacks for decades, most often with sad results.

Why Ex-Champions Come Back

Sugar Ray Robinson was 42 years old, and in the twilight of an unparalleled career. Once heralded as "pound-for-pound" the greatest fighter who ever lived," he'd just fought a ten-round draw with Fabio Bettini, who wouldn't have lasted ten minutes against "the real Sugar Ray." The signs were obvious, and had been for years. Like virtually all boxing "comebacks," this one was doomed to fail. And with that in mind, a fledgling reporter named Stewart Klein telephoned A. J. Liebling to push the notion that Robinson should abandon his comeback and retire forever from the sweet science.

"How old are you?" the dean of boxing writers demanded.

"Thirty," Klein answered.

"Well, you're very young," Liebling told him. "You have a job. But maybe, when you reach Robinson's age, you'll have trouble making a buck too. What right do you have to tell anyone else how he should make a living? What else can Robinson do? What else does he know? Can he teach at a college? Can he be an accountant? The only way he knows to make a living is fighting. A reporter reports. A fighter fights. Get off his back."

Robinson fought for two more years. In his first 131 professional fights, he'd been beaten once. In the final ten bouts of his career, he lost five times. But that was to be expected. Comebacks in boxing virtually always fail. A fighter retires because he can't do what he used to do in the ring anymore, so he can hardly be expected to perform any better when he's two or three years older the second time around. And for every comeback success story like that of George Foreman, there are dozens of great fighters who fail. All one has to do is look at how Foreman's contemporaries in the heavyweight division ended their ring careers—Muhammad Ali, 1–3; Joe Frazier, 3–4–1; Ken Norton, 2–3–1. For almost always in the end, when a great fighter comes back, the result is physical damage and humiliation. Yet they've been doing it since the days of John L. Sullivan.

Why do fighters come back? For starters, no one stops them. Unlike other major sports, boxing has no cuts to make and no rosters to fill. To the contrary, its structure encourages over-the-hill champions to continue on long past their prime. Irresponsible state regulatory bodies license aging fighters. Greedy promoters promote their fights, and greedy managers manage them. Puppet sanctioning organizations rank them in the top ten, so they're eligible for championship bouts. And often, the result is disaster.

Money is on top of the list of reasons why fighters come back. Most athletes, particularly football and basketball players, have some form of education to fall back on when their playing days are over. By contrast, many fighters never graduated from high school. Most sports afford participants an opportunity during the off-season to develop alternative careers. But boxing is a twelve-months-a-year job. When the only marketable skill a man has is his ability to fight, what else does he do to make money?

Also, retired fighters, and former champions in particular, often find life difficult without the fringe benefits of boxing. Being champion is like being the CEO of a small corporation. There's always someone around to serve you. You have a trainer. Someone else runs errands. A third person writes letters for you. But when a champion retires, he loses his work force. And he loses a substantial portion of the adulation he has become accustomed to receiving as well. Former ring greats would be less than human if they didn't miss hearing, "Ladies and gentlemen; in this corner, the undisputed champion of the world. . . ."

No one is immune to that addiction. "I don't care how much money you have," Muhammad Ali once said, explaining why he came back to fight Larry Holmes. "I don't care who your friends are. There's nothing like the sound of the crowd when you come down that aisle, and they're yelling, 'Ali! Ali!' You'd give your life to hear that sound."

And Ali, like many great fighters, had one more motivation for his return to boxing. It was the yardstick he used to define himself. "Muhammad fought again because he wanted to," says his trainer Angelo Dundee. "I've heard all sorts of reasons. He wanted the money. There was this and that. But I'll tell you something; Muhammad was never happy outside the ring. He loved boxing, the gym, the competition. It was in his blood, and win or lose, he loved it to the end."

Still, acknowledging all of the above, one question often asked is, "Do black fighters come back more frequently than whites?"

"I don't think so," says Eddie Futch. "I've been training fighters since 1932 and managing them since 1939, and there's no difference. Black fighters and white fighters come back for the same reasons."

Futch's view, shared by many in the sport, is that the reason we see more comebacks by blacks than whites is simply a question of numbers. That is, the fighters today are overwhelmingly black and Hispanic. And certainly, if one examines the careers of white fighters like Ray Mancini, Jerry Quarry, Gerry Cooney, and Donny Lalonde, they've come back too.

But there's some intriguing evidence that remains to be examined. Without doubt, the most cherished title in boxing is the undisputed heavyweight championship of the world. Set aside Mike Tyson, James "Buster" Douglas, and Evander Holyfield for a moment. No one knows with certainty how their careers will end. Then take a look at the fourteen men who held the undisputed heavyweight crown in the half-century before Tyson. Four of them—Max Baer, James Braddock, Rocky Marciano, and Ingemar Johansson—were white. After announcing their retirement, none of those four came back to boxing. The other ten were black—Joe Louis, Ezzard Charles, Jersey Joe Walcott, Floyd Patterson, Sonny Liston, Muhammad Ali, Joe Frazier, George Foreman, Larry Holmes, and Leon Spinks. Each of these ten attempted a comeback, except for Liston who died of a heroin overdose at age 38 while still an active fighter.

Why?

"White fighters usually haven't accomplished much to come back to," suggests manager Dave Wolf. And certainly, it's true that, in recent decades, black fighters have had more opportunity to come back because they've been more capable and more in demand than their white counterparts. But that doesn't fully explain the situation.

One reason black fighters come back with greater frequency than white fighters is that they need the money more. Wilbert "Skeeter" McClure won a gold medal in boxing at the 1960 Olympics. Now a psychotherapist in Massachusetts, McClure says, "Black fighters have traditionally made less money in the ring than whites, but the real hurt comes when they retire. Black businesses are reluctant to get behind them, and give them jobs or commercial endorsements. White businessmen take care of their former heroes. Unfortunately, most black businessmen don't."

McClure's thoughts are sadly founded on reality. White fighters who were successful in the ring can make a nice living playing the ex-champion. Jack Dempsey opened a profitable restaurant in New York. Rocky Marciano was well-paid for personal appearances long after his career ended. Rocky Graziano and Jake LaMotta parlayed successful movies about their lives into money-making careers as comics. But when a black fighter retires, it seems sometimes as though he has dropped off the face of the earth. Sure, Marvin Hagler has carved out an overseas film career and remained economically solvent. But for every success story like Hagler's, there are a hundred black ring greats who end up carrying luggage in Las Vegas or shining shoes like the legendary Beau Jack.

Wolf sums it up when he says, "Society in general offers lesser economic opportunities to blacks than to whites; so it shouldn't surprise anyone that society offers lesser economic opportunities to former fighters who are black than to former fighters who are white." And on top of all the other financial burdens, black fighters tend to have more people who are financially dependent upon them—family members and members of their entourage—urging them to fight.

But for those who think black fighters are more inclined than their white counterparts to attempt comebacks, the reasons go beyond simple economics. "When I was playing tennis, if someone from a Fortune Five Hundred company came up to me at a tournament, I'd take his card," historian, businessman, and former tennis star Arthur Ashe once said. "That's because I was thinking ahead. Emotionally, as well as economically, I was planning for the future. But most black athletes don't think like that. They look at themselves as athletes first, if not athletes only. And by the time they wake up, it's too late."

And therein lies the rub. A boxer's athletic ability makes him special until he's about thirty years old. Then he begins to lose that ability, and for ex-champions in particular the transformation is terrifying. Look at the contrasts that successful boxers experience in life. While champion, they enjoy broad acceptance, which for most black fighters is a new feeling. There's no name calling in a boxing ring. No one can tell them what to do. They have to be shown with fists, and that's as level a playing field as many black people ever get. Then the same champions retire, and all of a sudden the acceptance is gone. How can anyone expect them not to come back? How do you extinguish the need to be somebody in a man who has it ingrained in him deeply enough to have become a world champion?

The answer is, "You can't." And as a result, as long as other avenues to financial security and self-esteem are blocked, fighters will continue to come back. Perhaps Bartlett Giamatti expressed it best years ago, when he wrote of Muhammad Ali, "I believe he will participate in ring fights longer than he should because he cannot stop until he has fought down the need, compounded of fear and fury, to act out completely what in his view it is to be black in America; to always be living at the margin, on the edge, in a position where despite the pain of your work and the beauty of your play, a man may announce with superb casualness at any given moment that you have been counted out."

George Foreman and Muhammad Ali will be forever joined in the hearts and minds of boxing fans as a consequence of their 1974 championship bout in Zaire. But as the 1990's progressed, a more ominous parallel came to mind.

Parable for the Preacher

Once upon a time there was a great fighter.

He was a former champion.

After a long layoff, he sought to regain his crown.

He was deeply religious.

He charmed with his wit.

The world fell in love with him.

And admired his courage.

He made more money from his comeback fights than he ever had before.

He also took a lot of punches to the head, but his strength was such that he refused to go down.

And the people who could make money off him urged him to keep fighting even though he was getting old.

It would be very sad if, someday, the parishioners in George Foreman's church had difficulty understanding what their preacher was saying. George Foreman should retire from boxing now.

In 1995, I took issue with the induction process for the International Boxing Hall of Fame. A year after this article was published, my criticisms were validated and my fears confirmed. Don King was elected to the Hall of Fame with the meager backing of six electors.

The International Boxing Hall of Fame

On June 11, 1995, fifteen men will be inducted into the International Boxing Hall of Fame. Like other members of the Boxing Writers Association of America, I'm partly responsible for that. Several months ago, I received a ballot in the mail and filled it out. Then I began to question my response. I think I voted wisely, but the issue is whether I should have voted at all.

The doubts I had, and still have, center on the integrity of the the selection process. My sentiments are similar to those of Jerry Izenberg, who says, "I get the ballot; I figure their heart is in the right place; it's a legitimate effort; everyone I know who's been inducted comes back from the ceremony with a good feeling; so I vote." But I also agree with Izenberg's warning, "They're putting too many people in the Hall too quickly, and the standards should be higher."

There are four categories for induction into the International Boxing Hall of Fame:

1. Non-participants—Those other than boxers who have made a contribution to the sport.
2. Pioneers—Boxers whose last contest was prior to 1893.

3. Old-timers—Boxers whose last contest was between 1893 and 1942.
4. Moderns—Boxers who have been retired for five or more years and whose last contest was no earlier than 1943.

But what are the standards for induction? And who determines whether those standards have been met?

The first step in the selection process involves placing the candidates' names on the ballot. That decision rests with a "screening committee" comprised of three boxing historians—Herb Goldman, Hank Kaplan, and Silvio DeChristofaro. Then the "electors" have their say. "Non-participants," "pioneers," and "old-timers" are voted upon by separate panels of "historians." "Moderns" are voted upon by BWAA members and other electors chosen by the Hall's board of directors. The number of inductees in each category is predetermined, and the top vote-getters are inducted.

So where's the problem? For starters, three people is a pretty small screening committee. One might also question the validity of the "historian" panels. For example, the "pioneers" are voted upon by a total of seven electors. And since these seven electors are choosing from many candidates, it's possible for a "pioneer" to be inducted after receiving only two or three votes.

The "moderns" are at the other end of the spectrum. Last year, eighty members of the BWAA and 25 other electors cast votes in this category. But as Mike Katz says, "It's ridiculous for every member of the BWAA to be allowed to vote. I've been writing boxing for thirty years," Katz continues, "and it's only recently that I've considered myself qualified to vote. A lot of our members don't understand the intricacies of boxing. In fact, a lot of our members aren't even writers; they're publicists and promoters."

Ed Brophy is Executive Director of the International Boxing Hall of Fame. He defends the selection process as follows: "We feel the number of inductees so far is appropriate and that our catch-up formula is working well. Boxing has a long history and is international in scope. The candidates on the ballot have outstanding credentials, and it will take years to induct everyone who deserves it."

Maybe so; but one has to question the rush to judgment. Contrast, if you will, the manner in which baseball and boxing select inductees for their respective halls of fame. Baseball requires that a candidate receive 75 percent of all votes cast. That means, in an average year, roughly 350 "yes" votes are required for enshrinement; and in sixty years, only 224 people have been voted into Cooperstown. Yet in six years, the Boxing Hall of Fame has designated 152 inductees.

Let's take Ken Norton, who was inducted in 1992, as an example. Ken Norton was a good fighter. But a fighter of Hall of Fame caliber? Norton's career record was 42–7–1. He became a "champion" by virtue of a disputed decision over Jimmy Young in a "title elimination bout." After that bout, the WBC stripped Leon Spinks of his crown for fighting a rematch with Muhammad Ali, and Norton was designated the WBC's heavyweight champion. But Norton never won a title bout. He was knocked out by Jose Luis Garcia, George Foreman, Earnie Shavers, and Gerry Cooney. And he fought to a draw with Scott LeDoux. His only victories of note were against Young, Jerry Quarry, Duane Bobick, and Muhammad Ali. And yes; the victory over Ali was important. But one win shouldn't put a fighter in the Hall of Fame any more than one win (say, a perfect game in the 1956 World Series) should put a pitcher in Cooperstown.

In sum, the people who run boxing's Hall of Fame have made a good start. But the time has come for them to modify the induction process. I would suggest the following:

1. Increase the size of the screening committee.
2. Increase the number of electors in the "pioneer," "non-participant," and "old-timer" categories to thirty each.
3. Ask the BWAA to select its thirty most-qualified members to be electors, rather than using all of them.
4. And most important, institute the requirement that a candidate be named on seventy percent of all ballots to be inducted.

The time to do all of these things is now. Otherwise, too many inductees will diminish the honor of induction into the International Boxing Hall of Fame. And the giants of our sport deserve better than that.

I'm a big admirer of Roy Jones, Jr.; in and out of the ring. But as 1996 wore on, I felt he was in danger of squandering his chance for ring immortality.

To Roy Jones, Jr.— "You're Blowing It, Son"

Roy Jones, Jr. is a great fighter. He proved it by dominating Bernard Hopkins and James Toney with incredible speed, reflexes, timing, and power. And he's proven it again in the way he has demolished a succession of lesser foes, doing things in the ring that no one has done since Muhammad Ali when Ali was young. If there's a chink in Jones's armor, it's that sometimes he gets wild and misses by a lot. A good counterpuncher might get lucky against him someday. But for now, that's a reach. With Pernell Whitaker fading and Jones's star rising, at the end of last year, the "pound-for-pound" title belonged to Jones. But Oscar DeLaHoya is knocking at the door.

One of the wonderful things about boxing is that a fighter has to prove himself each and every time he performs. Mike Tyson might have been "The Baddest Man On Earth," but when he stepped into the ring against Buster Douglas, they started from scratch. George Foreman earned the heavyweight title by knocking out Michael Moorer. Foreman hasn't lost since then, but he hasn't fought a credible opponent either. No one seriously recognizes George as heavyweight champion of the world anymore.

Like Foreman, Roy Jones Jr. is in danger of losing his crown. Except it's not an alphabet soup title. It's the "pound-for-pound" throne. Since beating James Toney in 1994, Jones has fought

Antoine Byrd, Vinnie Pazienza, Tony Thornton, Merqui Sosa, and Eric Lucas. Enough already! Is there anyone out there under 200 pounds who would be favored over Roy Jones? Probably not. But that doesn't excuse him from his obligation, if he wants to be Number One, to fight the best available foes.

Roy Jones, Jr. is fighting for himself. I understand that. He wasn't put on earth to please you or me. And as long as he doesn't break any laws, he's free to pursue his personal goals, make as much money as he can, and enjoy himself in whatever way he chooses. But by the same token, as long as Jones fights mediocre opponents, while Oscar DeLaHoya lines up aging lions like Julio Cesar Chavez and Pernell Whitaker and truer tests like Felix Trinidad and Ike Quartey, the "pound-for-pound" crown will belong to DeLaHoya. It's not that Oscar is any better than Jones. It's that Oscar seems to want the "pound-for-pound" title more.

And there's another designation that Jones should consider. A year ago, there were serious students of boxing who thought that Roy Jones, Jr. might someday rank among the greatest fighters of all time. But that recognition could be forever fading from Jones's grasp.

Sugar Ray Robinson, Joe Louis, and Muhammad Ali all had long (too long) glorious careers. But like most fighters, they were best when they were young.

Sugar Ray Robinson's name isn't forever entwined with the phrase "pound-for-pound" because of what he did at 160 pounds. Robinson won the world middleweight championship five times, but he lost it on four occasions. Robinson as a middleweight was beatable. The young Sugar Ray Robinson fighting as a welterweight—the man who lost just once in his first 131 professional fights—was close to perfection.

On the night that Joe Louis knocked out Max Schmeling, The

Brown Bomber might have been the greatest fighter who ever lived. Louis was 24 years old at the time. And although he fought for thirteen more years, he never achieved that level of greatness again.

Muhammad Ali scored wondrous victories over Joe Frazier and George Foreman after his exile from boxing. But those who consider Ali to be "The Greatest" point to his youth, when he raced through the likes of Sonny Liston, Floyd Patterson, Cleveland Williams, and Zora Folley. And Ali himself acknowledges, "I was better when I was young."

Roy Jones, Jr. will only be young once. If he wants to be ranked among the greatest fighters of all time, now is the time to prove it. For the moment, though, one can only say to Jones what Angelo Dundee once told Ray Leonard in spurring Leonard to greatness against Thomas Hearns: "You're blowing it, son."

> No fighter, no matter how good he is, "looks great" all
> the time. The opponent can be tough; the opponent can
> be passively cute. And fighters, like everyone else, have
> off nights. Yet some observors of the boxing scene
> seem to forget that fighters aren't computers with the
> ability to perform at a single unchanging standard.

The Need to "Look Great"

Boxing has a problem. Actually, boxing has lots of problems; but
at the moment, one in particular comes to mind. The sport is
blessed with some fine young talent. But when these young men
fight, the focus isn't on whether they win or lose. Rather, it's on
how "good" they look.

HBO, which is the best boxing network with the best fights, is
a prime offender. HBO eats its young. Honest commentary is very
much appreciated, but at times the voices on HBO seem to go
beyond that.

The recent championship bout between Oscar DeLaHoya and
Pernell Whitaker is an example. All DeLaHoya did was beat the
man viewed by many as pound-for-pound the world's best fighter.
That should hardly have been cause for complaint, yet DeLaHoya
was castigated by Larry Merchant. And then, in a paradoxical turn-
around, several months later he was praised for "looking great"
when he knocked out David Kamau in the second round.

"Roy Jones doesn't like to get hit," is another refrain we hear a
lot. Neither did Muhammad Ali, and when Ali was young he
danced all over the ring to avoid it.

There are reasons for today's emphasis on "looking great."
Reason number one is the fact that boxing is entertainment.
Today's fighters are paid to be more than fighters. They're paid for

their value as entertainers and their ability to reach beyond an audience of hardcore boxing fans. That's why George Foreman earns more money in a single night than Joe Louis, Jack Dempsey, and Rocky Marciano made in their entire careers combined. It's why Butterbean is more lucratively compensated than five hundred guys who could beat the crap out of him. Reason number two is that the culture has changed. Traditionally, the honest everyday workman was valued in sports. But like the rest of society, sports has fallen victim to the 360-degree-slam dunk-bank-it-off-the-moon-McDonald's-Reebok-Nike-commercial. A society that demands instant gratification now also demands instant greatness in sports.

The third reason is television. TV tends to magnify each appearance by a fighter and make it a paradigm of his entire career. Also, in the old days, people listened to fights on radio and read about them in newspapers, but they didn't see fights except on newsreel highlights. Now the entire world watches both the good and the boring as a fight unfolds.

And last, let's face it; there are times when fighters don't look good. Has Michael Moorer been awful in the ring lately? You bet he has. Did Roy Jones give fair value when he fought Mike McCallum and Eric Lukas? No.

But let's be reasonable! Decisioning Pernell Whitaker is more impressive than stopping David Kamau no matter how one slices it. Nobody "looks good" against Whitaker, who happens to be one of the great defensive fighters of all time. And not looking good against Mike McCallum is far more acceptable than not looking good against Frans Botha.

Also, to expect greatness from a fighter every time out is unfair. Shakespeare wrote *Hamlet* and *Macbeth*, but he also wrote *Troilus and Cressida*. Elvis Presley sang some real clinkers. There are times when Michael Jordan goes four for twenty from the floor and stinks out the joint. No one looks good all the time.

Sugar Ray Robinson, when he was great, went the distance and looked very ordinary against a lot of ordinary fighters. Joe Louis had trouble with slick boxers. After Muhammad Ali beat Sonny Liston, he defended his title nine times in twenty-two months. No fighter ever defended his championship in such spectacular fashion so often in such a short period of time. Yet Ali's 15-round victories over George Chuvalo and Ernie Terrell were hardly spectacular; and that was when Ali was in his prime.

However, one thing more should also be said with regard to the recent commentary by Larry Merchant and others. There's a difference between a fighter looking great and a fighter digging down to bring out what's best in himself. And viewed in that light, even though criticism of Oscar DeLaHoya's performance against Pernell Whitaker might have seemed unwarranted, Merchant later made a vaid point.

"In DeLaHoya versus Whitaker," Merchant said recently, "DeLaHoya's performance was more disappointing than Whitaker's, because Oscar was a young rising star facing an aging veteran who was past his prime. Whenever two exceptional champions are in the ring, you want the fight to catch fire, and that never happened in DeLaHoya-Whitaker. One reason it didn't happen was Whitaker's style. It's very hard to look good against him. But I thought Oscar could have done more to make things happen and to earn a more convincing victory. The moment was there for the taking. And even though DeLaHoya won that night, he fell short of his potential by a far greater margin than Whitaker. That's why I was disappointed with his performance. And that's why Oscar himself acknowledged being disappointed after the fight."

Fair enough.

But let's not forget the sage advice of George Benton, who on more than one occasion has cautioned his fighters, "Win this one. Look good next time."

Making Weight

On October 4, 1997, Arturo Gatti rallied to knock out Gabriel
Ruelas in the fifth round to retain his IBF junior-lightweight crown.
It was a great fight. Gatti displayed extraordinary courage and
heart. The problem is, he wasn't a junior-lightweight. He'd been
allowed to weigh-in the day before the fight, and came into the ring
at 146 pounds; sixteen pounds over the junior-lightweight limit.

For centuries, there were no clearly defined weight classes in
boxing. Combatants who were referred to as "lightweights" entertained crowds prior to some championship bouts, but fighters of
average size weren't taken seriously until the early 1800s when
English fighters weighing 154 pounds or less became known as
"middleweights." In 1853, Nat Langham became the first acknowledged champion in a weight division below heavyweight, when he
knocked out Tom Sayers in a middleweight title bout that lasted 61
rounds. Then, in 1909, the London-based National Sporting Club
established the eight weight classes that remain the backbone of
championship boxing today: heavyweight, light-heavyweight, middleweight, welterweight, lightweight, featherweight, ban-
tamweight, and flyweight.

Boxing now has seventeen weight divisions. One reason for this
proliferation is the delight of sanctioning bodies when they
increase the number of sanctioning fees they receive. Another is
the desire to give more fighters an opportunity to become a world
champion. But the primary rationale once expressed for the proliferation of "super" and "junior" weight divisions in boxing was

that fighters would no longer be forced to choose between dehydrating to make weight and facing opponents ten pounds heavier than they were. And that rationale is long gone. Despite seventeen weight divisions, the practice of "drying out" before a fight is still common. No one would suggest that jockeys in the Kentucky Derby weigh-in the day before the race and dry out during the next 24 hours to lessen their horse's load. Yet in principle, that's what boxing allows today. And a new phenomenon further aggravates the situation—the early weigh-in.

Early weigh-ins came about initially as a result of television. Traditionally, fighters weighed in on the day of a fight, and sometimes in the ring itself just before a bout started. But televising highlights from title-bout weigh-ins on the evening news is a powerful selling tool. Thus, early weigh-ins for major bouts have become routine. And fighters who are having trouble making weight understand that early weigh-ins work to their advantage.

In the old days, a fighter who dried out to make weight paid a price in terms of strength and stamina. But a fighter who dries out for a weigh-in 36 hours before a fight has time to recover. Indeed, Flip Homansky [Chairman of the Medical Advisory Board to the Nevada State Athletic Commission] acknowledges that some fighters now weigh-in the day before a fight and retire to hotel suites that are set up like hospital rooms, where they're treated by private physicians who feed four or five pounds of intravenous fluid directly into their veins.

The medical rationale for early weigh-ins is that it's dangerous for a fighter to compete in a dehydrated state where his body is deprived of fluid and essential minerals, and that a fighter needs at least 24 hours to recover from drying out. But if weighing-in a day early is okay, why not let a fighter weigh-in a week early or when the contracts are signed? Simply put, early weigh-ins are unfair to fighters who can make weight on the day of a fight. And they force fighters who might otherwise legitimately make weight to dry out and drop down a division in order to face comparably-sized opponents.

The problem has not gone unnoticed. "The first time we were aware of it," says Mark Ratner (Executive Director of the Nevada State Athletic Commission) was when Iran Barkley fought Nigel Benn. Iran looked heavy before the fight and there was a scale in his dressing room, so we weighed him. It wasn't premeditated. We were curious; that's all. And we found that Iran had gained thirteen or fourteen pounds between the weigh-in and the fight. Then, when Roy Jones fought James Toney, we weighed both fighters by design in their respective dressing rooms before the fight and discovered that Toney had put on fifteen pounds."

That led the Nevada commission to begin a study that's still underway. "We wanted to gauge the effect of weight gain between the weigh-in and the fight on the performance and health of the fighters," explains Ratner. "So for several years, we've been weighing fighters just prior to their entering the ring. The average gain between the weigh-in and the fight has been six or seven pounds, although it varies according to the division we're talking about. We believe that, by the end of 1997, we'll have enough statistical data to properly evaluate the issue. Then, if we determine that early weigh-ins pose a health danger or give a fighter an unfair advantage, we'll act accordingly."

Obviously, the health of the fighters should be at the top of any list of criteria used to make a final judgment. "That's the reason I favor early weigh-ins," says Homansky. In an ideal world, drying out wouldn't exist. And the inequity of one fighter coming into the ring ten pounds heavier than his opponent is obvious. But I can only talk in terms of what's medically right; and medically, fighters need time to recover from drying out."

Still, why not do what's safe *and* fair? Why not adopt rules that encourage fighters to move up in weight rather than dry out?

The solution is simple. Ten days before a title fight, each fighter's manager should be required to certify to the local state athletic commission precisely what his fighter weighs. Then a preliminary weigh-in should be conducted the day before the bout, so the fighters know how much weight, if any, they have to lose. The actual weigh-in should take place on the morning of the fight. Proponents of the present system argue that this plan would be "dangerous" because fighters wouldn't have enough time to recuperate from drying out. But gaining sixteen pounds in a day isn't so healthy either. And sixteen pound weight differentials are both dangerous and unfair to a fighter who legitimately makes weight.

Round 6

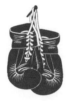

Curiosities

Most fans love round card girls. A few aficionados think they're out of place. But like them or not, the women who carry placards around the ring between rounds have become a fixture in boxing.

Round Card Girls

In recent years, the business of boxing has been bisected, dissected, and commented upon at length. Savvy fans know all about Don King's monopoly power and Sugar Ray Leonard's multimillion-dollar purses. They're familiar with Mike Tyson's managerial squabbles and the role television plays in determining who, when, and where champions fight. However, one aspect of the sport has been left unstudied—round card girls.

Round card girls weren't always with us. They first came out of the Nevada desert in the late 1950's, when Las Vegas casinos began promoting fights. And while the country as a whole has moved toward feminism, boxing has gone in the opposite direction. Today, round card girls are a fixture in fight clubs across the nation. Las Vegas and Atlantic City are reputed to have the prettiest, because they draw on casino showroom talent. But beautiful flowers bloom everywhere.

"People don't come to the fights to see the round card girls," says Steve Griffith, Director of Marketing and Public Relations for Madison Square Garden Boxing. "But there's no doubt that fans have a better time because the girls are there, and good times translate into ticket sales."

Thus, when the Michael Spinks versus Gerry Cooney promotion was going badly, promoter Butch Lewis sought to boost the event by offering Fawn Hall and Donna Rice $25,000 apiece to serve as round card girls. Neither accepted, but Lewis got what he wanted; lots of free press. Smalltown promoters frequently hype fights by holding round card girl contests several days before a bout, with local media representatives acting as judges. Back in the 1970's, a Harlem nightclub-turned-fight-club used topless round card girls to attract customers until the New York State Athletic Commission intervened.

What are the qualifications for being a round card girl?

Looks.

Looks.

Looks.

And rapport with the crowd.

Using these assets, their functions are threefold:

1. Entertain the audience, particularly during slow-moving preliminary fights when fans tend to get restless. This function, of course, is limited to male members of the crowd, although Graciella Casillas, the California women's lightweight champion, once demanded, unsuccessfully, that her promoter use round card boys during a fight.
2. Carry advertising around the ring. Round card ads are as diverse as the family of man. Once, in Akron, Ohio, a candidate for local office paid a promoter one hundred dollars to put campaign bumper stickers on the round cards.
3. Advise fans which round it is. This is fairly straightforward, since the round number is printed on each card. However, Caesars Palace complicated the matter by making the girls carry cards inscribed with Roman numerals.

The prototype of a round card girl is Pamela Sue Medeiros, who plies her trade regularly at Madison Square Garden. "The lovely Pamela Sue" (as ring announcer Ed Derrien calls her) is twenty-four-years-old, tall, blonde, and beautiful. A native of Cranston, Rhode Island, Pamela Sue came to New York six years ago to pursue a modeling career, and has appeared in such publications as *Glamour* and *Harper's Bazaar*. However, most of her printwork has been for lingerie and swimwear catalogs.

"Being a round card girl is something I always wanted to do," says Pamela Sue. "I don't know why. It just always seemed like fun. Two years ago, the Vanderveer Agency called and said, 'Pam, don't get insulted, but we have this offer for you.' I jumped at the chance."

As far as Pamela Sue is concerned, the Garden job is ideal. Her costume consists of a black leotard and white tuxedo jacket; not the more revealing lowcut dresses required by casinos. The pay is good; one hundred dollars a night. The Garden is a class operation, and she gets a good seat for the fights. "I have a boyfriend," she acknowledges, "but when I'm in the ring, he's not jealous. He figures he has what everybody else wants, so let the guys in the crowd be jealous of him."

Pamela Sue's evening begins at 6:30, when she appears in the Madison Square Garden lobby to hand out programs. Then, once the fights start, she and another round card girl ("the beautiful Sahara") work their magic. Broken down in sequence, it unfolds as follows:

1. With ten seconds left in every round, the timekeeper raps his microphone four times to warn the referee that the round is about to end. This is Pamela Sue's wake-up call.
2. The bell rings, and she walks up the ring stairs.
3. A young man designated as the "rope-splitter" parts the strands, and Pamela Sue steps into the ring.
4. Once she's in the ring, the rope-splitter hands her a round card.

5. Pamela Sue examines the card to make sure it's not upside down, raises it above her head, and moves counter-clockwise around the ring. "I don't count the seconds," she reports. "I just make a complete circle, wave to the crowd, and leave."

6. The rope-splitter parts the strands, helping Pamela Sue out of the ring and down the stairs.

Pamela Sue's closest brush with celebrity status came last year when Iran Barkley and Michael Olijade did battle at Madison Square Garden. A show called Muppet Babies was playing the Garden at the same time, and someone at NBC, which was televising the fight, got the bright idea that Miss Piggy should do a stint as a round card girl. Thus, by pre-arrangement, after the second round, Pamela Sue stepped into the ring followed by Miss Piggy, who knocked Pamela Sue on the head, grabbed the round card, and strutted around. However, Barkley had knocked Olijade down during the previous round, and NBC kept its cameras focused on the fighters' corners, not on the charade in mid-ring. Also, coming as it did at a particularly tense moment, the comedy was out of place.

Indeed, some purists feel that way about all round card girls. "I hate them," says Mickey Duff, one of Great Britain's premier managers and promoters. "Two men are fighting their hearts out, and there's no reason for some woman to be wandering around wiggling her bloomin' arse. It's an affront to the fighters and an insult to boxing."

Still, the practice goes on, and round card girls have spawned some of boxing's finest legends.

Don Elbaum began promoting fights in 1958, and has made the rounds of hundreds of arenas, including a five-year stint as promoter-matchmaker for the Tropicana in Atlantic City. Round card girls at the Tropicana are cocktail waitresses employed by the hotel and are paid fifty dollars a night. But some of Elbaum's round card girls in other locales have practiced different professions.

"I used to promote fights in Steubensville, Ohio," Elbaum remembers. "It was a wild town with some of the best-run whorehouses in the country, and the guys who ran them would give me professional hookers to use as round card girls for free. From my point of view, it was great. I didn't have to pay the girls, and I sold extra tickets to boot because the people who ran the whorehouses bought seats for their customers in order to display their wares."

Another time, Elbaum recalls, a round card girl saved one of his fighters from defeat. "I had a light-heavyweight named Tom Girardi; a prospect, a good kid. Another fighter pulled out, and Tom took the fight on short notice against some guy whose record was two-and-six. I figured it was safe, but Tom had gone to bed with his girlfriend the night before, not realizing he was going to fight, and he got tired. It was a six-rounder, and after round three, Tom came back to the corner and said he didn't think he could go six. Anyway, the referee had been staring at the round card girl all night; she was a doll. After round four, I handed the girl a card that said '6' instead of '5.' Then I started shouting, 'Last round, Tommy; you can do it.' Well, of course, the referee is staring at the girl. He thinks it's round six, makes the fighters touch gloves, and says the fight is over after what's really only round five. I cut the gloves off real quick, and Tom, who was completely out of gas, won a split decision."

Asked for more, Elbaum goes on. "In Uniontown, Pennsylvania, I had two round card girls working a show in a high school gym. Somehow, during the night, they discovered they were going out with the same guy. I gotta tell you, those two girls put on the best fight of the night; a real knock-down, drag-out, hair-pulling battle.

If I'd known in advance, I would have billed it as a co-feature. Another time, in McKeevesport, Pennsylvania, I promoted a kid named Jack Rogers; a good fighter and as handsome as a kid could be. During the middle of the fight, the round card girl sashayed by. Jack pushed his cornerman aside, and said to the girl, 'I'd like to see you after the fight.' She nodded. And you better believe, after the fight she was there."

Those who consider Elbaum a sexist will be pleased to know he got his comeuppance at Brooklyn's Rollerama Arena in 1977. "Don and I were sitting together that night," recalls fellow matchmaker Johnny Bos, "and the round card girl was particularly flirtatious. She winked; she wiggled. Halfway through the show, Don turned to me and said, 'That's a hell of a broad; I wonder who's taking her home tonight.' Then, during the last fight, the girl reached up and pulled off her wig. It was a guy!"

So, there you have it. Round card girls sell tickets, carry advertising, entertain the crowd, and, on occasion, even determine the outcome of fights.

And you thought they were just another pretty face.

The American Medical Association and boxing have been at odds for decades. In 1988, in a satirical vein, I put my two cents into the controversy.

A Modest Proposal

During 1987, boxing and the American Medical Association continued to get along about as well as Don King and the Internal Revenue Service.

Dr. Joseph Boyle (President of the AMA) has declared, "Physicians all over the country should participate in a public dialogue which would ultimately lead to persuading legislators and the public that this is a very dangerous sport and that it ought to be outlawed. Dr. George Lundberg (Editor of the *Journal of the American Medical Association*) added, "Life is very complicated. We need all the brain we can get. And to take large numbers of already-disadvantaged youths and cause them to sustain chronic brain damage which will be life-long is an obvious moral, medical, economic, and social issue."

I could respond in detail, citing boxing's better attributes, but this column is too short on space to do it properly. Thus, I'll focus instead on one particular proposal contained in the AMA's monthly journal—the suggestion that, if boxing is allowed to continue, all blows to the head be banned.

I'm not kidding! The AMA suggested it. And the idea was endorsed by a *New York Times* editorial, which declared, "Boxing can be fully rescued from barbarism by banning blows above the collarbone."

In truth, there are genuine risks attached to boxing. Over the years, thousands of young men have been injured as participants.

It is inherent in the sport that some people will take a beating, others worse; and to discount this is to deny the courage it takes for any man to step into the ring. But no blows above the collarbone? That would make boxing as worthwhile and exciting as fifteen rounds of Muhammad Ali versus Antonio Inoki.

So let me make a counter-proposal. It's not perfect. It's a compromise; one that will eliminate the danger of head injuries to fighters, yet satisfy fans the world over who clamor for excitement and valor. Let's:

1. Ban blows above the collarbone;
2. Do away with protective cups;
3. Send fighters into the ring with nothing but trunks and a jockstrap over certain parts of their anatomy; and
4. Allow punches *below* the belt.

To satisfy the AMA, boxers would wear helmets with face-guards protecting against errant high blows. Referees would be empowered to take a point away for any punch above the collarbone and give the aggrieved party up to five minutes to recover. Head injuries would become obsolete, and medical practitioners could conduct endless studies of infertility and impotence in fighters. The WBC, WBA, and IBF could operate sperm banks—just in case.

I know! You think it's crazy. But think of the excitement. Imagine the drama of Joe Louis, hopelessly behind on points, felling Billy Conn with a shot to the testicles in the thirteenth round. What could ever be more satisfying than the sight of Gerry Cooney writhing in pain on the canvas after a Larry Holmes straight right to the balls. Endless bar-room debates would evolve—"Sure, Mike Tyson is tough, but can he take a punch to the crown jewels?". . . . "Thomas Hearnes is nothing; he has a glass groin." We'd have colorful nicknames like James "Ballcrusher" Smith. And who could resist the sight of Lou Duva screaming from the corner, "Evander; keep your guard down!"

Yes, boxing increases the chance of brain damage. And cigarette smoking increases the chance of lung cancer. Of the two, cigarette smoking kills infinitely more people each year. Look at auto racing. Its underlying rationale—that you should drive a car at two hundred miles an hour—is completely antithetical to safety. I wonder how many deaths are caused each year by impressionable teenagers seeking to emulate A. J. Foyt and Mario Andretti. But General Motors and Ford are behind auto racing, and the AMA complains not at all.

So how about it?

I think boxing below the belt is a great idea, and I plan on running it up the flagpole at the next AMA convention to see if anyone salutes. Maybe they'll even take it seriously.

In recent years, with the proliferation of weight divisions and world sanctioning bodies, championship belts have been reduced to the level of costume jewelry. But they still have special meaning to the fighters who win them.

Championship Belts

James "Buster" Douglas had just knocked out Mike Tyson to score the greatest upset in boxing history. The ring was mobbed. Assorted crazies were screaming and running around. Larry Merchant of HBO was interviewing the new champion. Don King was lurking in the background. And then, in the midst of everything, someone brought Tyson's World Boxing Council championship belt into the ring.

"Here it is," said Douglas, tenderly kissing his prize. "This is truly a dream. Put the belt on me." Then, in a voice flush with emotion, he told Merchant, "I've watched you on HBO a thousand times, putting belts on guys, and I always said, 'One day, it's gonna be me.'"

Douglas was so enamored of his three championship belts that he wore the International Boxing Federation version with a conservative gray suit on the David Letterman Show. Later, he had to let the belts out several notches as his weight ballooned to Foremanesque proportions. But there was no mistaking the excitement that Douglas felt when he put on his belt for the first time.

Almost everyone enjoys trophies, and big-time athletes are no exception. Olympians treasure their gold medals. Football players long for a Super Bowl ring. Every year, the winner of the Masters proudly dons the green jacket. But boxing's world championship belts have a tradition and style all their own. One gropes for words to describe them. The image of a giant cigar band comes to mind. The belts are so garish that Don King's jewelry looks understated by comparison. Tiffany & Co. would never approve. Yet every fighter wants one.

Boxing's first championship belt belonged to the champion of England, Tom Cribb, who was given a lion-skin sash with silver claws after defeating Tom Molineaux of the United States in 1811. Seven decades later, Richard K. Fox (publisher of the *National Police Gazette*) introduced boxing belts to the United States. Fox was engaged in a bitter feud with John L. Sullivan, and when Paddy Ryan knocked out Joe Goss in 1880, the publisher presented "his" champion with a jewel-studded belt. Sullivan's followers were so outraged that they raised $10,000 to give "their" champion a gold-plated, diamond-studded prize bearing the words, "Presented to the champion of champions by the People of the United States." Legend has it that, when John L. received his bauble, he put it on and loudly proclaimed, "Fox's is like a dog collar compared to mine." In three subsequent fights, Sullivan knocked out Ryan three times.

In 1922, *Ring* magazine began publication and entered the belt trade. Jack Dempsey was the first recipient of a *Ring* belt. Now, with five world sanctioning bodies and 17 weight divisions, there are 85 world championship belts to be won at any given time.

But where do the belts come from? The answer, for the most part, is Weehawken, New Jersey. The World Boxing Association, International Boxing Federation, World Boxing Organization, and International Boxing Council all purchase their belts from a man named Phil Valentino, who lives and works in Weehawken. Valentino designs, manufactures, and sells the belts to authorized buyers for $650 each. The World Boxing Council is the lone holdout. It purchases belts from Ho Ho Arts & Crafts International Co., which has its factory in Taiwan. The WBC belt costs $500.

Taken together, the five world championship belts weigh 31 pounds. Despite the fact that they're world title prizes, Americana is a repeating theme. The IBF, WBO, and IBC belts all have a red, white, and blue color scheme, with more eagles than the United States national parks system. Taken in order of descending weight, the belts are:

IBF—Ten pounds, red leather, 73 fake rubies, 73 fake diamonds. The central ornament consists of a gold sphere, an eagle, two boxing gloves, and an enameled medallion representing the eastern and western hemispheres flanked by two more eagles perched on top of mirrors. The signature of Robert Lee (IBF President Robert W. Lee, not the Civil War general) appears both on the medallion and the belt buckle.

WBO—Eight pounds, brown leather, 56 imitation rubies and one imitation-diamond eagle's eye. The central medallion is a boxing ring with two gloves superimposed above the WBO's stunningly optimistic motto: "Dignity, democracy, honesty." This in turn rests on what looks like an upside-down bird's nest, but is probably meant to represent the rugged terrain of planet Earth. There are mirrors on either side and a Velcro fastener to hold the belt closed.

IBC—Six pounds, 23 "faux" rubies. Instead of leather, the IBC belt is fashioned from red, white and blue pleated satin. The central ornament features two eagles on a crest of pitted brass with the IBC's red, white, and blue logo below. The two mirrors (one on either side of the crest) are identical to those used on the IBF and WBO belts, which is fitting since at least one fashion expert has suggested that the entire belt looks like it was made out of spare parts.

WBA—four pounds, black leather, 114 fake rubies, eight boxing gloves, four fighters, three crowns, two mirrors, and one pewter
buckle (but no partridge in a pear tree). The central ornament is an
enameled medallion flanked by two fighters on a brass globe. The
medallion bears the WBA's somewhat authoritarian motto:
"Cooperation, conformity, control."

WBC—Three pounds, green leather. Instead of eagles and fake
precious stones, the central ornament shows a fighter with his arm
raised in victory, circled by the flags of every WBC member-
nation. Medallions of Joe Louis and Muhammad Ali are on either
side in lieu of mirrors. Some observers have suggested that medallions of WBC President Jose Sulaiman and promoter Don King
should be substituted.

Each sanctioning body pays for its own belts, recouping its cost
(and then some) through championship bout sanctioning fees.
Whenever a champion defends his title, he brings his belt to the
ring and, before the bout, symbolically hands it to a sanctioning
body official. If the fighter wins, the belt is returned to him in the
ring. If he loses, it's presented to the new champion, but then given
back to the former titleholder in his dressing room. The new champion receives his own belt by mail several days later.

Why not just bring a second belt to the fight?

"Because they're very heavy and cumbersome to lug around,"
explains Robert W. Lee. "One is enough for the supervisor to
worry about."

Of course, the presentation formula sometimes hits a snag.
When Jorge Paez won the IBF featherweight crown from Calvin
Grove, there was chaos in the ring and Paez wouldn't return the
belt. Mexicali, Mexico, being what it is, Grove had to wait until
his return to the United States for a replacement. Nigel Benn
wanted a WBO belt so badly after dethroning Doug DeWitt that he

refused to go back to England without one. Instead, he stayed in Atlantic City while Federal Express delivered the package that absolutely positively had to be there so people could see Benn "with me belt on when I get off the plane in London."

"What you must understand," explains Jose Sulaiman, "is all fighters want a belt. When they win and the belt is put around their waist, it means more to them than the money from the fight."

Well, maybe not that much. But it means a lot.

Boxing fans, more than any others, are short-changed by television coverage of their sport, as I indicated in this 1992 lament.

Televised Boxing and Aggravation

I'm a junkie. I watch all the fights I can on television. And with increasing frequency, I find myself glaring at the TV. I know life is imperfect. I never thought that televised boxing would turn into Nirvana once Howard Cosell disappeared. But as a loyal fan, I'm getting very tired of having to endure the following:

1. Did Seth Abraham and Michael Fuchs really think that Terry Norris versus Brett Lally belonged on HBO? Was Greg Haugen versus Ray Mancini worth $19.95? Fights that would have been on network television in the past, now appear on Showtime and HBO. Fights that used to be on Showtime and HBO, now reside on pay-per-view. And it's wrong.

2. At least once a week, I turn on the TV and see two preliminary fighters who look alike wearing the same color trunks. This is very stupid, since it makes it hard to tell which fighter is which. It's also an easy problem to solve. Prior to fight night, the fighters should agree on what color trunks they'll wear. Then, if one of the fighters shows up with the wrong color trunks, the promoter should give him a different pair.

3. Some boxing commentators such as Al Bernstein are spectacular. Others should stick to their day jobs. My own candidate for worst commentator on the air is George Foreman. I like George. He was a great fighter. He's a wonderful human

being, and one of the nicest men I've ever met. But if the people at TimeWarner think he comes across as a loveable combination of John Madden and William "The Refrigerator" Perry, they're wrong. George Foreman behind the microphone comes across like a 280-pound Sean O'Grady.

4. And while we're on the subject of commentators, why do so many of them never think of the obvious? For example: if a fighter is hit with a low blow, he's allowed up to five minutes to recover. So why not suggest that, if a fighter is cut by a butt, his corner can have up to five minutes to halt the flow of blood?

5. How often have you turned on the TV and heard, "Amazing! Who would have thought that old Bozo Jones would still be on his feet, two minutes into round one?" If no one expected Bozo to last a round, why televise the fight to begin with?

6. Apparently, there's a conspiracy to never show round card girls on television. Viewers hear whistles and shouts. The crowd's collective head turns as though it's on a swivel. But all we get on camera between rounds are commercials, replays, Lou Duva's handsome face, and on occasion Harold Lederman. I've asked several hundred producers, directors, and other executive personnel why the round card girls are never shown, and have yet to get a sensible answer.

7. Major problem! It seems like every time I watch a fight televised from Atlantic City, the same guy jumps out of the crowd, leaps onto the ring apron, and stops it. His name is Larry Hazzard. He appoints the referees in New Jersey, but apparently he doesn't have much faith in them because he doesn't let them do their job. Some day a fighter will be seriously hurt in New Jersey. It will happen because, instead of using his own discretion when a fighter is in trouble, the

referee will be waiting for Larry Hazzard to stop the fight.

8. I wish they'd stop putting casino hats on fighters' heads after a bout. These men are gladiators, and it's insulting to turn them into walking billboards for Trump Plaza.

9. Too often before big fights, we get thirty minutes of build-up. Joey Jablonski talking about his brother's death in a tragic bungee-jumping accident. Joey's mom saying how much this fight means to the entire Jablonski family. Joey and Papa Jablonski walking along the ravine where the bungee-jumping accident occurred. And then, after the fight, if we're lucky, we get thirty seconds with Joey. When a fight is exciting, let the fighters talk about it.

10. USA's fights are on Tuesday nights, except sometimes they're on Thursday and sometimes they're not on at all. MSG's fights seem to come from every venue except Madison Square Garden, with no apparent rhyme or reason to which hour or day of the week they're shown. Top Rank's bouts on ESPN are more constant. But as for HBO, Showtime, the three networks, and other cablecasts, who knows? How about a regular schedule!

This article ran in 1979 as a companion piece to my first article about professional boxing—the story I wrote about Mike Rossmann.

Down and Knocked Out

Knockouts are at the heart of what boxing is all about. Connoisseurs appreciate stylish exhibitions of bobbing and weaving, but the average fight fan watches a bout to see someone get hit. And when a fighter gets hit often enough and hard enough, he gets flattened.

A "technical knockout" occurs when the referee stops a bout because one of the participants is unable to defend himself or is otherwise in danger of being seriouly injured. A regular knockout takes place when a fighter is knocked down and unable to regain his feet by the count of ten. In either event, the winner hugs his entourage, and the loser retires to his dressing room to lick his wounds in silence.

But what of the loser? What does it feel like to get knocked out? Former New Jersey heavyweight Randy Neumann likens it to an injection of sodium pentothal and adds, "My first concern was getting up. My second concern was not getting knocked down again. But my reflexes were too slow to protect myself. It was strange."

Neumann's experience was not uncommon. Here are the recollections of four heavyweights regarding what it feels like to be knocked out.

Chuck Wepner

On October 30, 1974, Muhammad Ali shocked the world by knocking out George Foreman to recapture the heavyweight crown. Seven months later, on March 24, 1975, he defended his title against a journeyman fighter named Chuck Wepner. Wepner was "an opponent"—a club fighter who gave one hundred percent, but didn't have the tools to win the big one. His bout with Ali was notable on two scores. First, Ali received the then-extraordinary sum of $1 million for fighting a man regarded by many as a "stiff." And second, an out-of-work fight fan was so inspired by Wepner's courage that he sat down and wrote a screenplay based on what he had seen. The fan's name was Sylvester Stallone, and his movie was called *Rocky*.

Of his fight with Ali, which ended in a fifteenth-round knockout, Wepner recalls, "I gave it all I had, but by the fifteenth round, I was shot. Ordinarily, the punch he hit me with wouldn't have bothered me, but I was exhausted. My legs were already rubbery, and when I got hit, I felt myself losing balance. The next thing I knew, I was down against the ropes. I was more tired than anything else. Ali was the best boxer I ever fought, but Sonny Liston hit harder. I've got 390 stitches in my face, and seventy-two of them came from Sonny. Liston broke my nose and cheekbone before they stopped the fight on cuts in the tenth round. In 145 fights, I've been knocked out maybe eight times. Seven of them were technical knockouts on cuts. To be honest, when I'm in the ring, I don't feel pain. I'm so psyched up that getting hit doesn't bother me. Knockouts always hurt more psychologically than physically. What the hell! A loss is a loss, no matter how it happens."

Jimmy Ellis

When Muhammad Ali refused induction into the United States Army and was stripped of his title, his successor was a young man from Louisville, Kentucky, named Jimmy Ellis. Ellis held the heavyweight crown until February 16, 1970, when he was knocked out in the fifth round by Joe Frazier. Then, on July 26, 1971, he fought Ali in a non-title bout that was essential to the comeback efforts of both fighters.

"People were saying it would be the end of Ali's career if I won," recalls Ellis. "He had to beat me or forget about recapturing the title. I got knocked out in the twelfth round. Lots of fighters hit harder than Ali, but he hit me more often than anyone else. The shots just kept coming and, with each one, I got a little bit weaker. Finally, I lost my coordination and balance and couldn't see what was coming next. That's really what a knockout is all about. You lose your coordination and balance.

"Frazier hit harder than Ali. To this day, I don't remember what happened against Joe. We were in the middle of a round, and all of a sudden I was lying on the canvas in Madison Square Garden and the referee was counting '. . . . six. . . . seven.' They told me afterward that I'd been knocked down twice, but I only remember once. There's a blank spot on my memory. Hey, it happens."

Jimmy Young

Jimmy Young was not known as a heavy puncher. His greatest skill lay in his ability to avoid getting hit. Of fighting Muhammad Ali in particular and knockouts in general, Young says, "Ali doesn't really hurt you. He tires you out. He hits you with a lot of little punches, and if you move to avoid them, you get tired. Against a fighter like George Foreman, you only have a few punches to stay away from. Against Ali, either you use your energy by avoiding punch after punch or you get hit by them. Either way, it takes a toll.

"Most heavy-punching fighters are easy for me to beat, because they're slow. I beat George Foreman once and Ron Lyle twice. The only time I ever got knocked out was by Earnie Shavers. He hit me with something I didn't see, and I went down three or four times;

I'm not sure which. Then the referee stopped it. I can't say I was glad when the ref stepped between us, but I wasn't sad either. I think it was for the best. There isn't much more I can say about it. There's no advice I can give on how to avoid getting knocked out, except don't get hit."

Duane Bobick

Duane Bobick was a silver medalist at the 1972 Olympics. In 1977, he was unbeaten as a pro, a hard puncher, and white. All he needed to earn a title shot was to show well in a Madison Square Garden bout against Ken Norton. Norton knocked him out at fifty-two seconds of the first round.

"He hit me on the temple," Bobick recalls, "and I went down. After that, my mind was clear, but my physical world was fuzzy. I was aware of where I was and what I had to do, but my body wouldn't respond. It was weird. I staggered to my feet and wobbled like a newborn foal. Then the referee stepped between us and stopped it.

"The Norton knockout was tough, but my fight against Ron Lyle (in the amateurs) was worse. Against Lyle, I threw a jab, and, bringing it back, I told myself, 'You're making a mistake; your defense is too low.' The next thing I remember was standing alone outside the arena in minus twenty-five-degree weather. I didn't know what had happened to me. Later, I talked with my trainer about it. He told me I'd been unconscious in the ring for ten minutes. Then, apparently, when I came to, they brought me back to the dressing room, and I asked for the key to my locker, which would have been fine except it was a combination lock. Finally, I convinced everyone I was all right, so they let me shower, dress, and leave on my own. It wasn't until I got outside and the cold hit me that I really came to and told myself. 'I must have been knocked out.'

"Would I fight Lyle again? Sure, if the money was right."

Humor is an important part of boxing lore, as evidenced by the following anecdotes.

A Look at the Lighter Side

Arthur "Bugs" Baer, a noted sportswriter of the 1920's, was once asked to comment on the evolution of professional boxing. "It's different now from the 1880's," Baer responded. "If Luis Firpo had fought Jack Dempsey on a barge like fighters used to fight on, Firpo would have won."

"Why is that?"

"Simple," Baer answered. "When Firpo knocked Dempsey through the ropes, Dempsey would have drowned."

Boxing humor. It's still with us, and each generation of fighters, managers, trainers, and promoters adds to the lore. Some stories are based on the complicated nuances of boxing history. Others are strikingly simple and innocent, like the tale of an eight-year-old boy who attended a Don King press conference. Afterward, when asked what the flamboyant promotor had talked about, the child answered, "He talked about twelve hours."

Several of my favorite boxing anecdotes are retold below.

♦   ♦   ♦

Jim Jacobs was fond of recounting an incident that occurred when Cus D'Amato was 70 years old. He and Cus were walking down a street one night when two muggers, knives in hand, approached and demanded money. Jim was in the process of reaching for his wallet when Cus raised his fists, glared at the thugs and snarled, "Get out of here, you punks, or I'll tear you apart." The muggers fled. Shaken, Jim turned to D'Amato and said, "Cus, you're absolutely crazy. That's how people get badly hurt."

"There was nothing to worry about," D'Amato answered calmly. "I knew exactly what I was doing, and I had no intention of hurting either one of them."

♦   ♦   ♦

Often, managers have a predatory image, but some look after their fighters with hearts of gold. Take, for example, manager Mike Jones. After Billy Costello won the World Boxing Council super-lightweight championship from Bruce Curry and successfully defended it against Ronnie Shields, he borrowed $10,000 from Jones.

"I'm worried," Mike told a friend. "I know Billy has family obligations, but I've tried very hard to get him to save his money so he doesn't have to ask favors from anybody when his career is done. I want him to be financially independent."

"I got money," Billy said, when apprised of Mike's concern. "I got an IRA; I got a Keogh plan; I got a bank account. But I figure, if Mike Jones is willing to loan me $10,000 interest free, I'll buy a treasury bill, keep the interest, and give him back his $10,000 later on."

♦   ♦   ♦

Years ago, just before one of his fighters went into the ring to face a hard-punching opponent, Gil Clancy, who was one of the best trainers in the business, counseled, "Look, if the guy hurts you, grab him and hold on." And then, so his fighter wouldn't think there was a lack of confidence, Gil added, "And if you hurt him, don't let him grab or hold."

Clancy's man was knocked out by a barrage of heavy punches after being stunned in the second round. "Didn't you remember what I said about holding if you got hurt?" Gil asked afterward in the dressing room.

"Yeah, Gil," the fighter answered. "I remembered. But his trainer must have told him the same thing, because once he got me hurt, he wouldn't let me grab or hold on."

♦   ♦   ♦

Shaved heads are so common among athletes now that no one bothers to looks twice. George Foreman. . . . Michael Jordan. . . . The list seems near-endless. But does anyone remember the first sports superstar to shave his head? That's right. Marvin Hagler. Even before "The Marvelous One" was named Marvelous, he shaved his head. And according to legend, here's how it came about.

One day, Hagler walked into a barber shop and asked how much a haircut cost.

"Four dollars," the barber told him.

"How much is a shave?"

"Two dollars."

"All right," Hagler instructed the barber. "Shave my head."

♦   ♦   ♦

Don King is the focus of numerous anecdotes, one of them told by British promoter Mickey Duff, who managed John Mugabi.

"Early in John's career," Duff recalls, "I wanted to get him a fight in the United States, so I called King, and King matched him against Curtis Ramsey in Atlantic City. I brought Mugabi over, but then an emergency came up and I had to go home. I hated to do it, but there was no choice. All I could do was tell John's trainer, George Francis, to call with the result the minute the fight was over.

"So there I was," Duff continues, "sitting in England, biting my nails, when the phone rang and it was George telling me that

Mugabi had knocked Ramsey out in the first round. Then Don King gets on the line and says, 'Mickey, the kid's good, but we got a problem. He's begging me to take over his career. He says he wants Don King to run him, but I told him no. I said you and I are friends, Mickey, and I won't take him on unless he lets me keep you as a fifty-fifty partner.'"

"Don," Duff responded, "I didn't know you spoke Swahili."

"I don't," King answered.

"That's very interesting," said Duff, "because Mugabi doesn't speak a word of English."

♦   ♦   ♦

And speaking of the "Only in America" man, here are some ventures we might see from Don King in the future:

1. Mike Tyson versus Christy Martin—Christy Martin knows her way around the ring. At the very least, she's better than Frans Botha, who moves like Marlon Brando after the weight gain. Look for King to enliven the proceedings by hiring Robin Givens and Desiree Washington as round card girls and O. J. Simpson as a pay-per-view commentator.

2. King, it has been said, frequently wrestles with his conscience. And when they wrestle, he always wins. So why not a King-promoted bout between Gerald McClellan and Michael Watson. I can hear King now: "This is America. Disabled fighters deserve a chance too."

3. And while he's at it, King could take advantage of the sports memorabilia craze by gathering the teeth that are knocked out in fights he promotes and selling them as "Official WBC-WBA-IBF World Championship Bout Teeth." Think of the excitement! "Honest to goodness Tim Witherspoon incisors

knocked out by Bonecrusher Smith at Madison Square Garden."

♦   ♦   ♦

And then, of course, there's the incomparable Muhammad Ali. During his glory years, "The Greatest" took a shuttle flight from Washington, D.C. to New York. As the plane was readying for take-off, a stewardess instructed, "Mr. Ali, please fasten your seatbelt."

"Superman don't need no seatbelt," the champ responded.

"Mr. Ali," the stewardess said gently, "Superman don't need no plane."

After Mike Tyson was knocked out by James "Buster" Douglas in Tokyo, Don King conspired with leaders of the World Boxing Council and World Boxing Association in an effort to deny Douglas his due. Their plan was to create a phony "long count" controversy, and use it to strip Douglas of his title. But public outrage was too great, and the schemers withdrew.

Some Thoughts on the Aftermath of Tyson-Douglas

Over the past few weeks, Jose Sulaiman and Gilberto Mendoza have been subjected to an enormous amount of criticism for their actions following James "Buster" Douglas's shocking upset of Mike Tyson. However, as a true fan of boxing, I'm deeply indebted to these two men. Sure, I watched the fight, but I couldn't believe what I saw. Buster Douglas dominating Mike Tyson? Come on; who could believe that? Even Don King found it hard to swallow. In fact, after the fight, King was pleading, "Say it ain't so, Jose." And the only reason I believe Douglas won now is that, after careful investigation, those two pillars of integrity—the WBC and WBA—have told me it's so.

I wish we'd had Señors Sulaiman and Mendoza all along. If they'd been here from the start, boxing would have a far better legacy than it does today. For example, one of the most tarnished wins in ring history was Joe Louis' thirteenth round victory over Billy Conn. As any student of the game knows, Conn was ahead on points when the knockout occurred. And we also know that twelve rounds is the proper duration for a world championship fight. If Señor Sulaiman had been on the scene, Joe Louis's title could have been suspended pending thorough review, and one way or another, the matter would have been appropriately resolved.

Likewise, when Muhammad Ali regained his title by dethroning George Foreman in Zaire, there was massive confusion. Tapes of the fight show that Foreman was on the canvas for ten seconds. *But* those same tapes reveal that the closed-circuit TV announcer picked up the referee's count late and was only at nine when the bout ended. What if Foreman was listening to the closed circuit broadcast instead of the referee? Review this, please, Señor Mendoza.

> In 1990, Mike Tyson pulled out of a scheduled bout against Alex Stewart, claiming that he'd suffered a severe gash while training for the fight. But there were serious doubts regarding the source, and even the existence, of the cut. Again, satire seemed to be in order.

How Mike Tyson *Really* Got His 48 Stitches

The incredible career of Mike Tyson became a little more incredible when it was revealed that the 48-stitch gash Iron Mike suffered last month resulted from a curbside brawl with his estranged manager, Bill Cayton.

Cayton has been polishing his image as of late. Recently, he appeared on Madison Square Garden Television Network without a tie and with his shirt open at the collar. The response to his casual look was so favorable that "*GQ* Bill" decided to buy a white-leather fringed jacket with "Don't Believe The Hype" embroidered on back. With that in mind, he went to Dapper Dan's in Harlem at 2:00 A.M. As fate would have it, Tyson and Don King were also there.

Cayton and King have been at odds as of late. King made fun of Cayton's white-leather fringed jacket. Cayton threatened to cram the promoter's teeth down his throat. And that's when Tyson got involved.

"Mike stepped between them," says a source in the Tyson camp. "He told Cayton, 'To get to Don, you have to go through me.' So Cayton punched him. Mike went down like a sack of you-know-what, and King fled in terror before Cayton could get to him. I guess what happened was, Cayton got tired of being dissed."

Cayton acknowledged the incident to several confidantes, but denied a rumor that he was wearing brass knuckles. "There were no rings and no other pugilistic devices of any kind," he asserted. However, Cayton did admit to "twisting my fist at the moment of impact, the way Ali used to do."

Meanwhile, Seth Abraham of TimeWarner Sports confirmed that HBO is bidding to set up a hundred-million-dollar middleweight seniors tournament, matching Sugar Ray Leonard against Thomas Hearns and Cayton versus Roberto Duran in the opening round, with the winners to fight each other. Steve Wynn has reportedly offered Cayton and George Foreman $10 million each for a November bout at the Mirage. And when last heard from, Kevin Rooney (Mike Tyson's former trainer) was saying, "This shows that Mike needs me back. He's not moving his head side-to-side the way me and Cus taught him."

Just prior to George Foreman's 1991 bout against Evander Holyfield, I addressed the issue of George's clean-shaven head.

Why George Foreman Shaves His Head

George Foreman is different these days. He's nicer, heavier, and more religious than before. Soon he'll be more financially secure than at any other time in his life. But the most visible change in Big George is. . . . (drum roll). . . . He's completely bald.

George Foreman's head now resembles a mystical dome, and one has to wonder why. Is he a Sampson in reverse, who will lose his strength if his hair grows long? Or are there other reasons unbeknownst to us all? Recently, I launched an investigation, and learned that there are ten reasons why George Foreman shaves his head:

1. It cuts down on wind resistance when George is moving around the ring, and at 260 pounds, every little bit helps.
2. It's easier to shave his hair off than to dye all the gray.
3. George got tired of beautiful women coming up to him and running their fingers through his hair.
4. It makes him look fierce.
5. It eliminates the bald spot.
6. George has always admired Yul Brynner, Marvelous Marvin Hagler, and Telly Savalas.
7. The ring lights reflecting off George's head blind his opponents.
8. George doesn't want people to mistake him for Don King.

9. When George is eating in a hurry, he doesn't want to worry about food getting stuck in his hair.
10. George wants to be able to put on a wig and travel incognito after he fights Evander Holyfield.

And you thought that George's new look was about style.

While researching *Muhammad Ali: His Life And Times*, I traveled with Muhammad to Indonesia, where among other things, we attended a Larry Holmes singing engagement. After I wrote a concert review that appeared in *The National*, Larry telephoned and screamed at me for forty-five minutes. Part of me was honored. I told myself, "Larry Holmes, one of the greatest fighters of all time, thinks my writing is important enough to spend forty-five minutes on the phone with me." And part of me was worried: "Larry Holmes, one of the greatest fighters of all time, is really pissed."

Larry Holmes in Concert

"Super Show '90," as it was known in Indonesia, featured music, boxing, and Larry Holmes singing in the Grand Ballroom of the Sahid Jaya Hotel. "I take my music very seriously," Holmes told reporters in Jakarta. "Anytime someone comes to hear me sing, I don't want them to go away disappointed."

The evening began with Holmes lumbering on stage wearing three diamond-and-gold rings, a diamond-and-gold chain, a diamond-and-gold watch, and an outfit that resembled the uniform worn by bus driver Ralph Kramden on the "Honeymooners." Given the fact that Holmes was considerably over his fighting weight, he also looked somewhat like Kramden. Then the singing started.

Round One: The first song was about boxing, but Larry's five-man band drowned out all the lyrics except for the phrase "boxing ring."

Round Two: The second song sounded very much like the first, except the audible lyric was "she's built." Holmes suffered from apparent jock itch during this number, and tugged periodically at his crotch.

Round Three: Midway through "I Feel Good," someone in the audience threw a white dinner napkin toward the stage in a gesture of surrender.

Round Four: "Stand By Me"—"When the night have [sic] come, and the moon is clear." If it were a fight, at this point the referee would have stopped it.

Round Five: Medley—"You Really Got a Hold on Me" and "Bring It On Home." It was here that James Tillis, who was in Jakarta to box an exhibition with Holmes, opined, "I'm having fun, but Larry can't sing."

Round Six: Once again, the lyrics were unintelligible. By now, Larry was sufficiently behind on points that he needed a knockout to win.

Round Seven: "Lean on Me"—Holmes was sweating profusely, and instead of lumbering, he'd begun to lurch.

Round Eight: I don't know what song this was either, but true to his fighting spirit, Larry finished on his feet. Whereupon one onlooker declared, "Float like a butterfly, sting like a bee; Holmes can't sing as well as Ali." Or as Ali himself might say:

> If there's ever a concert in Malaysia,
> Instead of Holmes, I want Joe Frazier.

1996 ended on a positive note for boxing with Evander Holyfield's conquest of Mike Tyson. But history will record that the year began with the sorriest assemblage of "heavyweight champions" ever. Thus, with apologies to Franklin P. Adams (who penned the immortal "Tinker to Evers to Chance"), I suggested that boxing historians would look back on the start of 1996 as follows.

Bruno, Seldon & Botha

These are the saddest of possible words:
    "Bruno, Seldon, and Botha."
Where once we had champions, then we had nerds:
    "Bruno, Seldon, and Botha."
Embarrassments foisted on us by Don King,
They soiled the sport and they tarnished the ring.
Their names little known, but they said everything:
    "Bruno, Seldon, and Botha."

Round 7

Afterthought

For much of the past year, I've been traveling around the country with Muhammad Ali, speaking to students about tolerance and understanding. On February 27, 1997, our travels took us to Pensacola, Florida. The plan called for Muhammad and myself to address 7,600 students at the Pensacola Civic Center on the subject of **HEALING**. But a group of Christian fundamentalists threatened legal action to halt the event, claiming that our appearance was a plot between a Muslim and a Jew to teach heresy to their children. For several weeks, a controversy raged. Then, inexorably, the community came together in support of our visit. Florida Governor Lawton Chiles attended the assembly and praised its purpose. The event was an enormous success. My own remarks to the students of Pensacola follow.

Pensacola, Florida— February 27, 1997

As most of you know, Muhammad Ali and I have co-authored a book about bigotry and prejudice. Early in the book, there's a statement by Muhammad that has led to some controversy in Pensacola, and I'd like to discuss that quotation with you. Muhammad's words were as follows:

My mother was a Baptist. She believed Jesus was the son of God, and I don't believe that. But even though my mother had a religion different from me, I believe that on Judgment Day my mother will be in Heaven. There are Jewish people who lead good lives; and when they die, I believe they're going to heaven. If you're a good Muslim, if you're a good Christian, if you're a

good Jew; it doesn't matter what religion you are, if you're a
good person, you'll receive God's blessing.

The words I just read to you reflect Muhammad's belief that all
people serve the same God; we just serve Him in different ways.
Obviously, there are people who disagree with Muhammad's view.
They believe that the only way a person can go to Heaven is to
embrace Jesus Christ as his, or her, Savior. And that belief is their
right. But some people in this community have carried their beliefs
a step further by trying to halt this assembly.

I got a telephone call recently from one of these people. She
didn't give her name. Instead, she began by demanding, "How dare
you question the word of God?" I told her, "I'm not questioning
the word of God. I'm questioning your ability to interpret the word
of God for me, because I believe in a loving God, who bestows His
blessings upon all people." And that was the end of the conversation, because she hung up.

Now, I want to make it as clear as I possibly can that no one on
this stage today is here to challenge what any of you believe insofar as it relates to your own personal religious convictions. I hope
you like your religion and are fully satisfied with it. Muhammad
and I like our respective religions too. All we ask is that you keep
in mind that we all have the same Creator, and all of us have to
work to get along. Our message is simple. Let's understand each
other and be tolerant of our differences, whether those differences
relate to our religion, the color of our skin, the language we speak,
the country we come from, or any of the other sources of diversity
that sometimes divide us.

As you go through life, you will find that your education, your
jobs, your personal relationships, and your government, are all
dependent in varying degree upon the will of others. That's the
nature of living. No one goes through this world on their own. But

there's one area where each of you will have total control over your own destiny. Each and every one of you has complete control over your own moral fiber. That means you can be as bigoted and prejudiced and hateful—or as tolerant and understanding—as you want to be. Hate is ugly. It's ugly when it's shouted out on the street. And it's ugly—it will eat you up and destroy you—when it lies in your heart. So if you hate, let go of it.

It's unlikely that any of you will ever become as good a fighter as Muhammad Ali, or have the same impact on history as Muhammad Ali. But in your own way, each of you can become as good a person as Muhammad Ali. All you have to do is take the best qualities that people like Muhammad have to offer and make them part of your own individual personalities. But don't stop with famous people. There's a horrible misconception in our society that just because someone is famous or a big celebrity that that person is a hero or a good role model. And that's not necessarily the case. Some celebrities are lousy role models.

But if you look around, you'll find people in your everyday lives who are wonderful role models. I'm sure there are teachers in your schools who care about you and work hard to give you the best education they possibly can. Those teachers are wonderful role models. I would hope that all of you have one or more relatives who love you and provide for you and do everything they can to give you good values. Those relatives are wonderful role models. And whether you know it or not, each of you is a role model. There are kids in grade school who look up to you and want to be like you. Many of you have younger brothers and sisters who feel the same way. And as role models, you young men and women have a responsibility to be the best people you can possibly be.

Focus on what's best in yourselves. Learn to treat other people with dignity and respect. Learn how to love.

Thank you.